¡SANTO!

¡SANTO!

VARIETIES OF LATINO/A SPIRITUALITY

EDWIN DAVID APONTE

ORBIS BOOKS
Maryknoll, New York 10545

Founded in 1970, Orbis Books endeavors to publish works that enlighten the mind, nourish the spirit, and challenge the conscience. The publishing arm of the Maryknoll Fathers and Brothers, Orbis seeks to explore the global dimensions of the Christian faith and mission, to invite dialogue with diverse cultures and religious traditions, and to serve the cause of reconciliation and peace. The books published reflect the views of their authors and do not represent the official position of the Maryknoll Society. To learn more about Maryknoll and Orbis Books, please visit our website at www.maryknollsociety.org.

Library of Congress Cataloging-in-Publication Data
Aponte, Edwin David.
    ¡Santo! : varieties of Latino/a spirituality / Edwin David Aponte.
        p.   cm.
    Includes bibliographical references (p.   ) and index.
    ISBN 978-1-57075-964-2 (pbk.)
    1. United States – Religion. 2. Hispanic Americans – Religion.   I. Title.
BL2525.A66 2012
200.89′68073–dc23   2011042961

Dedicated to
Zenayda, Roberto, Carlos,
Margarita, and Patricia
and in memory of
Domingo and Reynaldo

Contents

Acknowledgments

It is fair to say that any author knows that her or his book is not the product of one person, but the result of many who helped in numerous ways. Certainly that is the case for this book. The individuals and communities that contributed to this book are far too many for me to name them, but I would be remiss if I did not publicly acknowledge at least some of them.

This book would not exist without the love, help, and support from my wife Laura Jakubowski Aponte, who in her own right is a brilliant scholar, a serious theologian who does not suffer fools gladly, and an insightful cultural critic. She made this book possible with her encouragement, theological and cultural analysis, and excellent editing skills. Our son David Stanley Aponte contributed through his ongoing creative and passionate engagement with the world and has been a constant inspiration as well as a reminder of the different expressions of Hispanic spirituality across the generations.

Past students and current friends Ana Retamal, Patricia Retamal Shepherd, and Tomas Ramirez generously shared their insights and stories, both at an early stage when this project was nothing more than a germ of an idea and at a more advanced one. I deeply appreciate our friendship over the years. They and other former students, too many to name here, who shared in the establishment of the Center of Latino Studies at North Park University in Chicago helped nurture the disparate ideas that eventually grew into this book.

Other friends and colleagues contributed greatly, especially my former colleagues at Perkins School of Theology of Southern Methodist University where the idea of this book crystallized and was first formally shared with the faculty there. Especially encouraging was Marjorie Procter-Smith who served as academic dean during the majority of my time at Perkins. Other colleagues and friends who read and commented on portions of the manuscript include Bruce G. Epperly, Katherine G. Epperly, James Siburt,

William Marshall, and Miguel A. De La Torre. Furthermore, I deeply appreciate the work of Evelyn Parker and Loida Martell-Otero who thoughtfully and publicly responded to an early version of the ideas presented here, provided helpful suggestions, and challenged me in ways that stretched my thinking. If I did not heed everything you said, it is not your fault.

I am particularly indebted to the faculty, staff, and student body of Wesley Theological Seminary who invited me to give the Archbishop Oscar Romero Lecture in March 2010. The time there provided an opportunity to share with a wider audience not only the concept of the entire book, but an earlier version of what became Chapter 7. Their overwhelming hospitality and positive engagement were most helpful and encouraging at an intensely difficult time.

I am also appreciative of the invitation extended by President Dale T. Irvin, Vice President and Dean Eleanor Moody-Shepherd, and the faculty of New York Theological Seminary to be affiliated with that great institution as a research professor. Their kindness and collegial support enabled me to finish this project during a time of professional and personal transition.

There exists in the North American academy an informal, but very real *comunidad* of Latino/a scholars of religion and theology scattered across the country and in Puerto Rico for whom I have the deepest admiration and affection. They have befriended me, supported me, and encouraged me in good times and bad. Much of their scholarship (which I hope I have not misrepresented) and wisdom have influenced my thinking and analysis. For all of that and more I am grateful beyond words.

My editor at Orbis Books, Susan Perry, has been long-suffering and saintly in dealing with this recalcitrant author often sidetracked by other responsibilities. I am grateful for her persistent support, encouragement, and keen editorial skills that not only brought this idea into reality as a book, but also made it better by her careful work.

My sisters and brothers assisted me in many ways through their interest, words of encouragement, questions, thoughtful reflections, challenges, and responses; above all, their love provided a major impetus for this book. Together as *familia* we are sorting out what it means to be brothers and sisters in a complicated family, mainland Puerto Rican (but not *nuyorican*), wrestling with the constant accusation of being *ni de aquí o allá* (neither from here or there) yet being true to who we are—Latino/a and American—in contexts of increasing diversity and complexity. While neither they nor anyone else are to be blamed for the shortcomings of this final product, I hope that my siblings particularly see something of their own encounters with *santo* and *sagrado* here. It is with deep appreciation and love that I dedicate this book to my sisters and brothers who are still on the journey with me and in memory of our two brothers who preceded us into the beyond.

INTRODUCTION

Contexts for Spirituality

SPIRITUALITY IN THE UNITED STATES

For people who repeatedly proclaim a separation between church and state, it is fascinating that spirituality continues to characterize life in the United States.[1] This fact is manifest in many ways. In the immediate aftermath of the catastrophic terrorist attacks of September 11, 2001, places of religious and sacred gathering saw a dramatic upsurge in attendance in the United States. In the midst of extensive national tragedy and grief, citizens abandoned their conventional legal concerns about a strict separation between church and state in the face of pressing spiritual and existential needs that were addressed in gatherings of mourning, prayer, and remembrance. Services were held in churches, synagogues, mosques, and temples as well as at community centers and official government buildings. Both religious leaders and government officials participated with congregations formed by circumstance. The chief example of this was the ritual at the Washington National Cathedral (officially the Cathedral Church of Saint Peter and Saint Paul) in Washington, D.C., on September 14, 2001, as part of the National Day of Prayer and Remembrance proclaimed by the president of the United States.

In this Episcopalian church sanctuary, Protestant evangelist and elder statesman the Reverend Doctor Billy Graham participated with Jewish Rabbi Joshua Haberman, and Muslim Imam Muzammil Siddiqui in the national prayer service. But President George W. Bush delivered the major address, remarks that served as a de facto sermon to a nation in the midst of shock, grief, and fear.[2] While presented as an interreligious service, the atmosphere seemed overwhelming Christian. At that time and place there was very little talk of a wall of separation between church and state or even of a privatized division of the sacred from the secular, and the moment was one of shared national and very public spirituality.

More recently in the context of a political polarization in which people's loyalty and commitment to nation are questioned, the jarring shooting in Arizona on January 8, 2011, of Congresswoman Gabrielle Giffords, the killing of Judge John Roll, and five others, and the wounding of several more, shocked the country into stepping back from divisive and undisciplined rhetoric and wondering, if perhaps only for a short time, whether political debate, accusations, and culture wars had gone too far and had somehow contributed to this tragedy. In that context of national distress on January 12, 2011, another type of memorial service was held at the University of Arizona with a Native American opening blessing offered by Professor Carlos R. Gonzales, M.D., who is a Yaqui-Mexican American, in a petition that invoked the Creator. However this entreaty did not specifically use the word "God" and received disapproval by some and praise by others. And then a different president of the United States, Barack H. Obama, addressed a nation yet again in shock and grief that yearned for words of comfort and healing.[3] Despite criticism from some quarters that the president and others imposed their personal beliefs about the divine and prayer in violation of the "wall of separation," for the vast majority, once again in a moment of national trauma, the supposedly fixed divisions between public and private, "spiritual" and "secular" came together again in a shared communal spirituality.

What occurred on the national level happens all the time with smaller groups of people and individuals. Whether as a communal public response to crisis or an everyday private quest, people in the United States pursue varieties of spirituality as they seek meaning, comfort, healing, answers, resolution, community, guidance, mystical experience, or wholeness. The widespread spiritual explorations and practices include expressions of spirituality from people of all types of religious convictions, or even those with no formal religious convictions. Leigh Eric Schmidt describes this as "the American preoccupation with spirituality."[4] Even if such a preoccupation is correct and astute observers like Robert Wuthnow have some basis to say, "Spirituality is the shorthand term we use in our society to talk about a person's relationship with God," that broad definition is too narrow to encompass the many understandings of spirituality expressed through words and actions.[5] All of this activity contributes to a context of a shifting religious pluralism that demands acknowledgment and deeper understanding.[6]

Despite being a nation where some people question the continuing relevance of any spirituality or religious conviction, different types of religion, religious practice, and spiritual beliefs and practices seem to burst from the cultural landscape in the United States. While some bemoan spirituality as useless mystical blather, there are many others who speak with certainty about spirituality, higher life, empowerment, transcendence, obtaining balance, peace, mindfulness, and deeper meaning. These discussions touch upon the diversity of spiritual and religious communities in locations where once it appeared there was only uniformity. One such community is Vallabha Sampradaya Vraj Hindu Temple, the largest Hindu temple in the United States, located in Schuylkill Haven, Pennsylvania.[7] Few in that area still dominated by the descendants of European migrants (including Germans, Irish, Lithuanians, Italians, and Poles) expected to see such variety of religious expression in suburban and rural Pennsylvania, the "Quaker State."[8] Practices that at one time seemed limited to fringe and exotic groups now find widespread acceptance in a context of increasing pluralism.[9] Men and women all over the United States of different backgrounds attend yoga classes as much for the spiritual benefit as the physical. Meditation practices with roots in Asia are readily available for beginners to experts at health clubs, community centers, churches, and synagogues. Practitioners of tai chi can be found even in commercials on mainstream network television. Individuals who do not self-identify as "born-again" Christians nevertheless talk about human lost-ness, re-birth, and a desire to understand the mysteries and meanings of life. Some describe being on a spiritual search, while others talk about trying to address a type of restlessness.[10] Moreover, many of these conversations are taking place among people outside religious institutions and insider circles where mention of spirituality would have been unheard of even one or two generations ago.

The growing popular focus on spirituality, religiosity, and spiritual and religious practices of all types can be discerned in many ways. These include more traditional settings like Bible studies and prayer meetings but also playback theater, reading groups, the chanting and contemplation of Taizé services in mainline Protestant congregations, retreats, encounter groups, liturgical renewal organizations like the Order of St. Luke, holistic exercise sessions, and a variety of religious services. A casual browse through a bookstore in any shopping mall or perusal of an online bookseller shows

the current wide-ranging interest. There are books on "traditional" religions, that is to say, the various expressions of Christianity and Judaism that seem to be in the minority on the bookshelves. Myriad books,
CDs, and DVDs address spirituality, faith, mysticism of all types, wholeness, miracles, holiness, holistic healing, enlightenment, the supernatural, inspiration, meditation, prayer and devotional disciplines, monastic
chants, psychic insight, business leadership with soul, mysticism, Eastern thought, paranormal, past lives, inspiration, angels and other spirits, metaphysical thought, dreams, astrology, divination, tarot, magical
studies, roads less traveled, the pursuit of truth, and apparently chicken
soup for everyone's soul. It even may be argued that the upsurge of the
so-called new atheism is in some fashion an expression of this cultural
current, a type of anti-spiritualism still concerned with moral behavior in
the world.[11] Some say that this reflects a spiritual poverty or vacuum that
leads to a hunt for a kind of religiosity to fill the void. When combined
with the growing literature and films on the supernatural, apocalyptic
and end-times prophecies, predictions, and interpretations, the breadth
of the interest in spirituality and things religious becomes even more
striking.

Many people in the United States rely on some type of spirituality that
makes sense in their everyday lives. Whether it is Protestant seminarians
exploring the unfamiliar ground of *lectio divina* for the first time; spiritual
formation and direction; Roman Catholic lay people attending weekend
retreats; individuals eclectically adopting the meditative practices of Won
Buddhism; cosmic seekers exploring the plethora of so-called New Age
alternatives; or persons talking around a table at a family reunion, people
are interested in spirituality however it might be defined. Indeed, the range
of definition itself is part of the interest and the search as well as an indicator that so much needs to be explored.[12] Moreover, some individuals concurrently participate in several types of spiritual and religious activities on
a regular basis and see no inherent conflict or contradiction, no matter
how disparate the philosophies or theological foundations that lie beneath.
The quest of the spiritual ranges from a turning to new traditions to a new
appreciation of received traditions in ways that may not be deemed traditionally religious.[13] Clearly, the pursuit and practice of spirituality is not
solely the concern of isolated ascetics or monks and nuns or small religious

communities on the periphery of the cultural mainstreams, but a concern of people found in all walks and stations of life.[14]

The variety and breadth of the spiritual inquiry, thought, and practice in the United States is as striking as is the assortment of the searchers, seekers, and committed adherents to alternative spiritualities. Although this tendency has always been present in the history of the United States, it is becoming more and more common for people who claim that they are "not religious" to begin a quest for spirituality or "soul." This may reveal itself in some type of connection with ultimate reality, the wider universe, or perhaps both, which will provide meaning, guidance, and a source of sustenance for everyday life. In some ways it is an old search and in others it is new. Some people in their exploration may move from a received tradition and embrace what for them is a new approach, even if the approach itself has a very long history. The spiritual explorers include new Wiccan enthusiasts disenchanted with inherited religious traditions, practitioners of contemplative psychology, businesspeople striking out on a different path to bring a "soulful" missing dimension to their highly competitive and aggressive work, or ordinary citizens trying to regain a sense of reassurance, meaning, and balance in the face of national tragedy as seen in the public congregating at places of connection with another reality, worship, prayer, reassurance, and spiritual meaning.[15] In fact, a multiplicity of approaches to spirituality can be found everywhere with no apparent end in sight.

Some analysts of culture note that the increase in personal wealth of the last half of the twentieth century seems to have been accompanied by moral and spiritual decline in the United States. But, the argument of spiritual and moral decline prevails even in the face of the so-called Great Recession of 2008–9. Drawing on many observers David G. Meyers summarizes the characteristics of what he describes as a "spiritual poverty." These include a problem of belief, a spiritual crisis, an obsession with material aspects of life, a spiritual malaise (especially among youth) an awareness of the insufficiency of individualism, an estrangement from spiritual values, a need to affirm the preciousness of human life and the call to a higher purpose, the expressions of alienation and spiritual yearnings in popular culture, and a loss of a sense of metaphysical certainties and an experience of the transcendental.[16] Meyers also argues:

> Changing values, lost community, and waning commitments to things greater than self motivate our quest for something more—for a vision of life that is both conservative and radical: conserving social wisdom accumulated over generations, while questioning the well-traveled road of individualism and materialism.[17]

While helpful and on target from one perspective, this observation simplifies a complex intersection between religion, economic opportunity, and power. Individualism indeed significantly characterizes culture in the United States as manifested across social class and racial/ethnic groups. On the other hand materialism needs to be considered by distinguishing the pervasive attitude of materialism against the possession of material prosperity for which there is a clear class differential at work. The abundance and expansion of spiritual alternatives in the last few decades attests to the fact that material prosperity has failed to provide people with the feeling of personal fulfillment, an important part of Meyer's argument. In his definition of the "American paradox" Meyer states that "we now have, as average Americans, doubled real income and double what money buys. We have espresso coffee, the World Wide Web, sport utility vehicles, and caller ID. And we have less happiness, more depression, more fragile relationships, less communal commitment, less vocational security, more crime (even after the recent decline), and more demoralized children."[18] If participation in conventional expressions of Judaism, Roman Catholicism, and "mainline" Protestant denominations (the "usual suspects" include American Baptist; Evangelical Lutheran; Presbyterian, U.S.A.; Episcopalian; the United Church of Christ; and United Methodist) is the only indicator of spirituality, then the interest in religion based on membership, has indeed crashed at the end of the twentieth century. But this restricted assessment is defied by burgeoning involvement in a variety of religious expressions outside "mainline" expressions. Pentecostal churches have flourished along with Islamic mosques, Hindu temples, and the sale of "religious" publications.

Some of the participants in this American spiritual explosion include Meyer's "average Americans," while many in pluralistic America are barely considered in discussions of the spiritual landscape of the United States. Personal material wealth certainly increased in the 1980s and 1990s, but only for specific demographic groups of the U.S. population. Ironically, many of the people experiencing prosperity are the same ones who populated the declining "mainline" congregations. But, some of these same denominations are experiencing new growth and vitality due to the influx of recent immigrant groups. So the impression that there is wholesale spiritual decline accompanied by comprehensive increase in personal wealth is based on an insular view of society and indeed may reflect only a segment of the larger society. There are many who have not participated in the material prosperity whose resources of spirituality have helped them cope with their minoritized positions within the dominant society. The intersection of personal wealth and religious interest is much more complicated than Meyers's observations would indicate. Race and ethnicity compound the connection between wealth and religion in the United States. While there may be a spiritual shortage in some groups, others may experience spiritual abundance. Responses to a need for the spiritual and the sacred are not the same across the board.

SPIRITUALITY ON THE MARGINS

As people take note of the connection between religion and popular culture manifested in everyday beliefs and practices, it is clear that the search for the sacred or holy, both old and new, permeates the United States among all groups, races, ethnicities, and classes of people, including Hispanics/Latino/as.[19] Advertisers and politicians recognize the increasing significance of the growing Latino/a population in the United States at the very least out of reasons of self-interest in terms of market consumption and votes at the ballot box. Industry, politicians, and government ignore the Latino/a population at their peril. For others the rapid growth of the Latino/a population in the United States itself is seen as the peril, especially when it is collapsed with the reality of a broken immigration system and millions of undocumented immigrants in the country. Curiously there is little public discussion of Hispanic/Latino/a spirituality. In the context of an increasing religious pluralism and burgeoning interest in religions, religiosity, and spirituality within the United States, accompanied by new understandings of religion and popular culture, it is essential to understand the varieties of Latino/a spirituality.

As noted by some observers, questions of religious and racial/ethnic diversity are part of the exchanges that sometimes come under the rubric of "culture wars" in the United States.[20] In such a context, some unabashedly advocate diversity and pluralism, while other express concern and even fear that the growing diversity of society is a mortal threat to the republic.[21] In either case, religious and racial/ethnic diversity and pluralism in the United States will remain and probably increase in the foreseeable future. As the largest racial/ethnic minority group in the United States Hispanics/Latinos are an integral part of this cultural diversity and pluralism. Therefore, a better understanding of the pluralistic Latino/a religiosity and spirituality is essential for comprehending contemporary life in the United States and possible trends for the future.

Some scholars of religion have turned their attention to U.S. Hispanic religions. Historian Philip Jenkins notes that the growing population of Hispanics/Latinos has contributed to sweeping changes in the religious life of the United States:

> By mid-century, 100 million Americans will claim Latin origin. They will then constitute one of the world's largest Latin societies, more populous than any actual Hispanic nation with the exceptions of Mexico and Brazil. By that point, 50 or 60 million Americans will claim Mexican descent. . . . The religious consequences will also be far-reaching, and in most cases, it's the Christian churches that will benefit from the change. The vast majority of Latin Americans come from Christian cultures, either Catholic or Protestant. And although not every one is equally pious—or even notionally a believer—they have all been formed in a cultural matrix that is clearly Christian.[22]

The eclectic population that is called by the collective names of "Hispanic" or "Latino/a" has steadily grown for decades with the 2010 U.S. Census showing it to be 50,477,594, which represents an increase of 15.2 million between 2000 and 2010, exceeding previous projections. This has a dramatic impact on the nation in that it reflects over half of the total population increase of 27.3 million as the Hispanic population grew between 2000 and 2010 by 43 percent, or four times the nation's 9.7 percent growth rate.[23] Officially Hispanics were determined in 2003 to be the largest minority group in the nation, although many suspected that has been the case for some time.[24] Whatever the official designation the United States is already being shaped as a country by the dynamic presence of this significant and growing population, which represents at least 16 percent of the total population. If the search for the sacred and the spiritual in the United States is on the rise, that situation cannot be fully understood without careful consideration of the varieties of spirituality among the diverse peoples known as Latinas and Latinos. Furthermore, in a context in which many are seeking to understand the changing religious pluralism in the United States, the religiosity and spirituality of Latinas and Latinos must be part of the mix of any informed analysis.

There are many different groups under the single umbrella rubric of "Hispanic" or "Latino/a" in the United States.[25] Part of the challenge for a basic understanding of Hispanics or Latino/as is to be descriptive of empirical realities while not reducing such a description to essentialist stereotypes. Philosopher Jorge J. E. Gracia summarizes the difficulties inherent in the use of pan-ethnic terms for the large and diverse population of peoples in the United States of Latin American and Iberian heritage, noting that both Latin American and Iberian are also problematical.[26] Further difficulties exist in discerning the distinctions and connections between U.S. Latino/a and Latin American identities.[27] The multifaceted multicultural Latino/a reality includes diversity and commonality in ways that are historical, contextual, social, cultural, religious, and spiritual.

Moreover, while a growing number of sociological studies focus on Latino/as as a population group, the religious and spiritual dimensions still are particularly under-explored aspects of contemporary society in the United States. Theologian Benjamín Valentín states, "Hispanic/Latino(a) theology and Latino(a) religious discourse in general have largely been overlooked in the broader spheres of religious scholarship. This neglect mirrors the lack of recognition that has more generally been tendered to the Latino(a) experience in the broader U.S. society."[28] The neglect that Valentín notes is not only of the Latino/a theology and religious discourse, but also of analysis of the lived religion and spirituality of Latino/a communities.[29] In response, this book focuses on some of the ways that Latinos and Latinas participate in the pursuit and practice of the spiritual or "holy" as part of their lived religion, formal and informal rituals, practices of self-defined piety, and devotions embraced as meaningful. If spirituality indeed is a major characteristic of life in the United States, then by exploring Latino/a religions and cultures it will be seen that all Latino/a groups have some sense of spirituality and a quality that may be considered *sagrada*, "sacred," *santo*, or "holy."

By focusing on different particular understandings and examples among various Latino/a groups and settings, this study will point to a sense of what I call *santo* or Hispanic spirituality widely conceived. If spirituality, religiosity, and religious practices of all types in the United States can be discerned in many ways, then the collective sense of the holy in Latino/a religions and cultures can be understood broadly through the avenues of particular manifestations and practices. My use of *santo* as a collective concept includes Latino and Latina perspectives on traditional religion, life interpretation and explanations (sense-making), healing, health, wholeness, understandings of existence and the future, and balancing relationships at all levels of existence.

As I shared this idea with a friend who self-identifies with what he calls the "brown/latino/hispano/mestizo/indigenous experience" in the United States he understandably asked how one explains

> the faith of a group of people that is so diverse and that cannot be defined just by race, ethnicity, cultural background, social class, or census data without creating division, yet also without clumping all of them together? How to define or make sense of the ways of the spirit without being simplistic or sounding just crazy? My answer is in that which is universal, workable, and just.[30]

I take seriously the questions and insights of this indigenous U.S. citizen from Mexico called a Latino by others and seek to discern that which is universal, workable, and just. Rather than exclusively following a small set of denominations or traditions *¡Santo!* will identify and discuss common themes that appear in everyday settings throughout the broader U.S. Hispanic experience. While on the one hand Latino/a populations in the United States are amazingly diverse, there is another sense of a growing pan-ethnic shared identity. Being Latino or Latina in the United States simultaneously is an experience of an imposed and embraced identity that is distinct from being Latin American in Latin America. The point is not that there is discontinuity between Latin American and U.S. Latino/as, but rather that there are connections and ongoing growth and development. Members of the first generation or fifth generation share roots in Latin

America that continue to evolve into something new. Certainly there is continuity, but without fossilization. Elizabeth Conde-Frazier identifies one such continuity when she notes that two aspects of Latino/a Protestant spirituality—"a profound sense of the presence and action of God in all aspects of life" and a deep appreciation for "the sufferings of Jesus"—have roots in Spanish mysticism.[31]

It is my assertion that recurring characteristics of spirituality and religiosity can be identified among the religious and spiritual particularities of specific Hispanic/Latino practices. This investigation of the varieties of Hispanic/Latino spirituality transcends the formal boundaries of Christianity and official, institutional, or establishment religions. While affirming the role and importance of formal systematic expressions and creeds, it is also necessary to affirm that the lived religiosity of Latinos and Latinas includes more than official formulations. The categories usually chosen to organize a work about religion (like Roman Catholic, Protestant, and Non-Christian) reflect the still dominant but problematic tripartite paradigm for examining American religious life popularized by Will Herberg in the 1950s, most commonly expressed in variations of the phrase that the United States is a Judeo-Christian nation.[32] My research revealed that the spiritualities present in the diverse Latino/a communities in the United States defied any such neat three-fold categorization. What might be initially labeled as Roman Catholic appears in various Protestant contexts and vice versa. Aspects of Hispanic/Latino/a spirituality and religiosity initially labeled as non-Christian beliefs and practices outside officially accepted parameters of Christianity arise inside the popular Christian religiosity of Protestants and Roman Catholics.

Some common aspects of Hispanic/Latino/a spirituality fall outside Christian orthodoxies, whether Roman Catholic or Protestant. Some Latinas and Latinos participate in traditions that are self-consciously non-Christian, while other Latino/a religious traditions have a more ambiguous relationship with an expression of Christianity. Simultaneously, many individual and familial Latino/a religious practices display an eclectic spirituality that draws on many sources without any internal sense of conflict. There is an overriding realization that Latino/as, whether they be Catholic, Baptist, Muslim, Buddhist, Pentecostal, New Age, or even atheist, are the cultural heirs of and continue to be influenced by Iberian Catholicism as mediated and developed in the many Indigenous and African-diaspora multicultural contexts of Latin America. This influence manifests itself in the form of appropriation and reworking of Latin American Catholic traditions, or in the form of conscious efforts to distance oneself from such a heritage. In either case the cultural heritage of Iberian Catholicism in the colonization and evangelization that created Latin America as it interacted in different places and different ways with Indigenous and African cultures cannot be discounted. This is part of the deep background that contributes to the creation of U.S. Latino/a identity, sometimes referred to as the presence of cultural Catholicism. Any faithful discussion of Latino/a pursuits of the holy/*santo* needs to reflect this complexity.

Therefore, this study will trace the various spiritualities wherever they lead, even as they overlap and cross official boundaries. Despite the risk of charges of misrepresentation, the various paths will be described with every effort given to a nonpartisan description.[33] In so doing a type of religious and spiritual pluralism within Latino/a communities emerges side-by-side with official forms of religion. The goal is to get a sense of the range of spiritual and theological options among Latinas and Latinos, knowing that the description of each manifestation of spirituality will not be exhaustive. Even in settings where there is animosity between certain groups, e.g., Catholic-Protestant, there exists a type of de facto Hispanic/Latino/a popular pluralism. Such a pluralism testifies that the study of Latino/a religions is exceedingly more complicated than some prevalent formulations and interpretations. Part of the concern here is to identify and to explore why multiple spiritual and religious options exist among Latino/as in the United States, especially since these options are not necessarily or obviously theological in their origin. In his study of religious groups outside dominant mainstreams R. Laurence Moore states that "the gulfs that religious Americans have invented to distinguish their various religious groups have not always, or even usually, had much to do with theology. Ecumenicists have been perfectly correct in saying that America does not need so many faiths as it has to house the range of its theological opinion."[34] There is something about religious expressions in the United States and within its Hispanic community that requires numerous avenues of spirituality, even apart from theology itself. At the same time, this does not limit the theological importance of each path toward that which is *santo*, regardless of nature and origin.

Just as the Latino/a population of the United States is much more diverse than commonly perceived, so are the many Latino/a concepts of spirituality and what is holy or *santo*. Experience shows that what may be obvious to some is new information for others. One area where I consistently meet an often naively uninformed understanding of Hispanics in the United States is among white, Anglo, European Americans seeking to do Latino/a ministry. Such persons may have experience with one group of Latino/as and apply that limited understanding to the larger U.S. Latino/a population and to the challenges of doing ministry in a particular social and cultural context. Of course, that also is a risk of the present study. The basic questions here are: Is it possible to describe a common Latino/a spirituality? If so, what are its basic characteristics? There are diverse ideas of holiness among these groups with some shared characteristics and divergent understandings. Although some concepts of *santo* have regional or ethnic roots as well as urban and rural manifestations, the growing national Latino/a cultural reality is such that these different understandings of *santo* extend beyond regional boundaries and are in contact with other traditions.

PERSONAL VOICE AND PLACE

As is increasingly common in scholarship, I do not pretend to ignore my own social and cultural location and its impact on both the gathering of information and the analysis of the same. I hold that claims to an Enlightenment type of scholarly objectivity are illusory at best. I acknowledge that my own personal experiences, interests, and commitments have an effect on understanding past and present contexts. Accordingly, in the hope of achieving some balance, any common themes that I identify in the various types of Latino/a spiritualities that can be found will then be brought into dialogue with other discussions of religion and culture as well as with other viewpoints in the fields of theology, spirituality studies, and Latino/a studies. Moreover, although I am a cultural historian of religion, this analysis crosses disciplines to discover various examples of Hispanic/Latino/a concepts and practices of spirituality and holiness.[35] In this regard, my interest goes beyond a solely historical focus on the past; it also embraces a concern for the present that is central to my understanding of the field of cultural studies. As an area of scholarly inquiry cultural studies utilizes interdisciplinary investigation of the material and symbolic manifestations of people in society—in both the grassroots population as well as societal elites who may seek to restrict the word "culture" to their own sphere. Issues of race, class, and gender are equally important as those of aesthetics in cultural studies. Culture here is more than "high culture."

While on the one hand I approach Latino/a spiritualities as a cultural historian of religion, on the other hand I myself am a practitioner, a Protestant Christian, an ordained minister of Word and Sacrament in the Presbyterian Church, U.S.A., which makes me a minority Latino in a historic mainline Protestant denomination. My path to this present location was anything but stereotypic and reflects my life journey and spiritual quest. I was born into a Puerto Rican Roman Catholic family where there was (and is) a high level of spiritual sensitivity but little attendance at formal church services. The fact that I was born and raised on the mainland and not on the *isla de encanto* (Enchanted Isle) had a profound effect on my development and religious and spiritual understandings. When we were young my mother shouldered much of the heavy spiritual work of the family. Our family connected in various ways to Christmas, Three Kings Day, devotion to the saints, rosaries, prayer books, Palm Sundays and palm fronds, meatless Good Fridays, and Easter Sundays, and for those of us who were older periodic escapes from public school to attend weekly catechism at the Catholic parochial school across the street.

I became personally active in the church when I was invited to attend a Presbyterian youth group and later an interdenominational evangelistic meeting held under a circus tent. This led to my regular attendance at Catholic mass and becoming heavily involved in the life of a local parish. I took my first communion and became confirmed as a young teen, much later than most of my Catholic peers. I was active in the religious education program of the parish and joined the weekly charismatic prayer meeting. Simultaneously I was part of the Presbyterian youth group down the street. which attracted Baptist, Catholic, Greek Orthodox, Evangelical Covenant, and charismatic young people, thereby unknowingly cultivating an eclectic and one might say ecumenical spirituality. For some time I was active concurrently in the Catholic parish and the Presbyterian youth group without any sense that there might be any type of conflict. When my theologically inquisitive nature became too disruptive in the Catholic parish, it was with deep reluctance and great sadness that I left the Roman Catholic Church and went down a more Protestant path. That path had many twists and turns including sojourns as a professor at a Wesleyan-Holiness Bible college, a university related to the Evangelical Covenant Church, a United Methodist divinity school within a research university, and as dean of a freestanding United Church of Christ seminary.

While this self-disclosure provides some limited insight to my role as an interpreter of the varieties of Hispanic/Latino spirituality, it also raises a question as to how unique are such spiritual passages among Latinas and Latinos. Certainly the details are different, but perhaps not the mixed aspect of the journey. This description of social location says nothing about my formative educational experiences, the economic situation of my family, and numerous other characteristics that would better situate me. I say this only to point out the limitations of any "self-disclosure" as essentially a type of construct in itself.[36] This limited description also gives some background for other concerns of this study: how dialogues about Christian spirituality engage Latino/a realities, as well as suggestions for how Christian theology and ministries interact in a context of ongoing transition. Since some of these perspectives and practices are trans-denominational, and sometimes interreligious, the book also will address some of the challenges that different expressions of grassroots Hispanic/Latino spiritualities bring to Christian theology and ministry. This will provide insights for Christian spirituality among Latinas and Latinos while working toward a basic definition of Latino/a spirituality. The connections between concepts of spirituality and religiosity with concepts of individual and community identity will be explored.

PLAN OF THE BOOK

This book is organized around themes rather than tracing specific denominational or traditions. As the notes and bibliography indicate, I am committed to working *en conjunto* and draw on the insights of others in addition to my own observations and conversations in Arizona, California, Connecticut, Florida, Illinois, Michigan, Nevada, New Jersey, New Mexico, New York, North Carolina, Pennsylvania, Puerto Rico, Tennessee, and Texas for my understanding of the varieties of Latino/a spirituality, or, to use my shorthand, *santo*.

Chapter 1 seeks to identify some of the diverse settings of *santo* as Latino/a spirituality but in the settings expected by conventional wisdom, namely, contexts connected to Christianity.[37] But even within those parameters it becomes clear that boundaries of the conventional wisdom are called into question. A number of different illustrations of the lived reality of Latino/a spirituality will be surveyed in a historic Roman Catholic parish, a Hispanic/Latino Pentecostal congregation, New Mexico's manifestations of *santo*, the extensive Cuban community in Florida, and evolving demonstrations of *santo*.

Chapter 2 continues the exploration of various settings of *santo*, but in contexts and expressions that illustrate the wide breadth and creativity of the varieties of Latino/a spirituality. These various understandings of *santo* in chapters 1 and 2 will be brought into dialogue with the larger societal conversations about religion, religiosity, and spirituality.

Chapter 3 provides an interpretive analysis that reviews the historical roots and the contemporary phenomenon of Latino/as in order to place U.S. Hispanic spirituality in its larger context of life in the United States. Related to this is an investigation of the creation of "Hispanic" as a population group and issues of ethnic identity as they are related to formal religions, religiosity, and spirituality followed by an exploration of the connections between the concepts of *santo* (holy), *pueblo* (people), and *comunidad* (community).

Chapter 4 describes different ways that the Latino/a search for the holy is manifested in the ordinary yet important day-to-day experiences and life passages within the Hispanic/Latino community (*comunidad*); including holidays, festivals, and special community days, both in the countries of origin and as they have been transformed in the United States. Generational perspectives are considered in the discussion of popular and formal examples of spirituality in the life cycle, particularly around the following of rubrics of birth, rites of passage, marriage/partnering, the creation and re-creation of family, and death and related beliefs and practices about the beyond.

Various expressions of Latino/a spirituality can be seen not only in attitudes toward life passages, but also in concrete daily practices, including the rhetoric that accompanies such practices. Therefore, chapter 5 focuses on the presence of Latino/a *santo* in practices and rhetoric. By rhetoric I mean to include the prayers, stories, teachings, sayings, proverbs, and greetings that are part of everyday life where there are casual echoes of a larger spiritual world and deep theological and religious reflection. The language of *santo* is expressed not only through words, but also through actions. Liturgical and ritual aspects of Latino/a spirituality, broadly understood, will be examined with a focus on formal and informal practices. Health and healing customs will provide some glimpses into what is *santos* along with relationships like friendship, *compradrazgo*, and hospitality. The connections between Latino/a spirituality, justice, and the public sphere will be considered as an expansion of these ideas.

Sacred space is the topic of chapter 6, where Latino/a spiritualities are viewed through place and location. Place and location as sacred spaces play prominent roles within the diverse forms of Hispanic/Latino spirituality. These sacred places include fixed, transitory, and temporary spaces, formal sanctuaries and temples, and other religious buildings along with homes, roadside shrines and memorials, and the moveable sacred places that are pilgrimages, as well as the other ways Latinas and Latinos sacralize their everyday spaces while on the move.

The last chapter, "Exploring Spanglish Spirituality," seeks to answer the question: Is it appropriate to speak of a pan-ethnic Hispanic/Latino identity? And if so, does this pan-ethnic Hispanic/Latino/a spirituality share a sense of *santo*. The issues of spirituality, devotion, and popular religion within the rhythms of Hispanic/Latino/a life will inform the answers to those questions. In turn, some challenges for Christian theologies and ministries interested in being in relationship with the Latino/a reality in the United States will be posed. This includes suggestions for areas that an encompassing study of Christian spirituality needs to address if it desires a dialogue with Latino/a realities as well as some suggestions for Christian theology and ministry in a context of ongoing transition, globalization, and the creation of new cultures.

ONE

Santo and Spirituality

WHAT IS *SANTO*?

Philadelphia, commonly known as the city of brotherly love, has a legacy that its citizens sometimes experience more as a challenge than a reality. Like many other urban centers in the United States, William Penn's city along the Delaware River is a place of vast contradictions. In 2010 over 37 million people visited Philadelphia to see Independence Hall, the Liberty Bell, Betsy Ross's house, and other sites associated with the birth of American democracy.[1] Philadelphia provides a home to many colleges and universities, institutions of art, such as the Pennsylvania Academy of Fine Arts with its beautiful Romanesque architecture, the Rodin Museum, and the Philadelphia Museum of Art with its fabulous collection, not to mention its rows of steps beckoning a would-be Rocky to run up to the summit. Even with its rich history Philadelphia shows extreme contrasts where gleaming contemporary skyscrapers that surround the statue of William Penn atop the Victorian splendor of City Hall symbolize wealth and commerce while abject poverty is close by in almost every direction.

Two and a half miles north of City Hall on Broad Street is Temple University, a major state-related research institution of higher education with its roots in a local congregation called the Grace Baptist (Temple) Church, a fact long forgotten by many. For many years blocks of decaying row houses inhabited mostly by impoverished African Americans sat on one side of the university campus. On the other side of Temple University, past abandoned buildings that looked like bomb-ravaged Dresden, Germany, in 1945, or portions of Iraq in 2003, stands a section of the city that the press and police in the 1980s and 1990s dubbed the Bad Lands. In a city of growing and shifting diversity, most of the increasing number of Latinas and Latinos reside in the so-called Bad Lands, where the contemporary major Latino barrio of the city begins.[2] And while many of the burnt-out blocks on both sides of Broad Street have been leveled and replaced by new construction or simply empty lots, the reputation of Philadelphia's Bad Lands persists. Here in the notorious Bad Lands, an area of town one is told to avoid, in the Latino barrio of North Philadelphia, the Christian church thrives against all odds, across the denominational spectrum and beyond, but especially within Latino/a evangelical and Pentecostal churches.

A person who might visit many congregations in North Philadelphia during a typical Latino Pentecostal service, particularly during the extended periods of song and prayer, would hear worshippers respond to their encounters with the Spirit with shouts of *¡Gloria! ¡Amén! ¡Alelúya!* (Alleluia!) and *¡Santo!* (Holy!). Despite their surroundings and the daily challenges of their lives, these Latinas and Latinos in the Bad Lands of Philadelphia declare praises to God and testify to their deep experience of God's holy presence in their lives, hence their cries of *santo. Santo* is one way they articulate their felt connection with the holy and their profound sense of the presence of God.

Upon entering a Pentecostal worship service in Latino Philadelphia one can see and hear what is common to many other Hispanic/Latino Pentecostal congregations in the United States, and indeed even in many Hispanic Protestant congregations that are not labeled Pentecostal. Liturgically many Latino/a Protestants (many of whom call themselves *evangélicos*, but usually in a sense different from the English word "evangelical"), whatever their denominational affiliation or non-affiliation share much more in common with each other than they do with many of their Anglo compatriots in the same denomination.[3] Theologian Loida Martell-Otero asserts that being an *evangélica* indicates a type of "popular Protestantism with its own distinctive expressions within the larger denominational structures present in the United States."[4] Among Latino/a *evangélicos* there seems to be a shared, creative, and somewhat flexible Protestant-*evangélico*-Pentecostal-charismatic liturgical motif at work in worship as congregants give expression to *santo*, even among those congregations that clearly state that they are not Pentecostal. Indeed, whether it is in Philadelphia, Chicago, Los Angeles, Oakland, Phoenix, Dallas, or Lancaster, Pennsylvania, one witnesses a great deal of energy, celebration, music, movement, and relational sense of community as shouts of *alelúya* and *santo* are heard in Latino Protestant worship gatherings.

Halfway across the country from Philadelphia, *santo*, the holy, is understood and experienced in a different Latino/a context. Far from the densely
populated megalopolis of the Northeast, the historic city of San Antonio
lies in the heart of Texas. Spanish expeditions in 1691 and 1709, which
encountered indigenous Coahuiltecan occupants of the area, were followed by the establishment of a Spanish military presence and the Mission
San Antonio de Valero in 1718. By 1731 four additional Franciscan missions were founded and immigrants from the Canary Islands established
the Villa de San Fernando. In that small frontier community far from the
center of an empire was laid the beginning of what became San Fernando
Cathedral. The cornerstone of the church building in San Antonio was laid
in 1738 with the walls completed by 1749, making San Fernando the first
parish in Texas.

Described by some local residents of Mexican descent as "the
northernmost city in Mexico," San Antonio exemplifies the heart of
Tejano culture, a specific contextual way of being Hispanic or Latino/a
in the United States that encompasses geographic and cultural borderlands.[5] Before the formation of a nation called the United States there was
a Spanish-speaking Roman Catholic population living in San Antonio, a
community created in the context of the expanding Spanish domain. At
the margins of that empire, with the conflicting spirits of *reconquista* and
evangelization bringing together Europeans and indigenous peoples in
the creation of first Nueva España and then modern Mexico, San Antonio
was further affected by the migration of North Americans into Tejas from
the neighboring United States.[6] San Antonio endured and developed its
unique identity through the years of Spanish colonialism, Mexican independence, as part of the Republic of Texas, part of the United States, member of the Confederacy, and once again as part of the United States. And
through all the changes and as the Mexican and Mexican American population declined and grew again, a central part of the community was and is
San Fernando Cathedral, a locus of faith and identity even in times when
the community was not fully incorporated by the larger church.[7] And it is
at San Fernando Cathedral that one can find one of the many manifestations of the holy, *santo*.

Established in 1731 San Fernando Cathedral is the oldest Roman Catholic cathedral sanctuary in the United States. A center of vibrant devotion

to Our Lady of Guadalupe, the historic building itself is both beautiful and constantly full of all kinds of intergenerational activity. Masses are held throughout the week in English, in Spanish, and in bilingual services. As part of its annual Holy Week activities and participation in the holy, San Fernando Cathedral sponsors a Via Crucis del Viernes Santo (Way of the Cross on Holy Friday) on Good Friday. The parishioners of San Fernando play the roles in this passion play based on the gospels.[8] Between Good Friday and Easter Sunday *santo* is also expressed another way in the Saturday Easter vigil in the cathedral. One year during Holy Week as my wife, Laura, and I walked the streets of San Antonio with thousands of strolling tourists, we arrived at the cathedral in the evening. The lights of that holy place blazed and people milled around outside the church. We opened the door to a cathedral packed full of people participating in a service well underway. I could say that there was standing room only, but there was barely room for that. Nevertheless, an usher promptly and personally greeted us and did not chide us for being late. He welcomed us, gave each of us a candle, and ushered us in as far as we could go so we would not be on the fringe but physically part of the congregation. There were no strangers in that place on that night. Part of what we witnessed and became participants in was joyous celebration, with music and singing, and the baptism of teenagers and adults. Each catechumen stepped into a small metal tub assisted by what I took to be their godparents, and as the words of baptism were repeated for each person, water was poured over their heads.

Not only on that special day during Christian Holy Week, but on any given weekday tourists wander through the cathedral to take in the beauty and history of the building itself, or perhaps to note the burial place of some of the defenders of the nearby Alamo. But the tourists are not the only ones there as the building is constantly in sacred use. Aside from the regular schedule of services there are persons at prayer and meditation in the pews and persons doing the Stations of the Cross. As befits a church of this history and heritage, there is a shrine of the Virgin of Guadalupe of Mexico, patroness of the Americas and closely identified with the identity and religiosity of many Mexicans and Mexican Americans.[9]

There is no doubt from what can be seen and what can be learned from conversation with devotees that that Guadalupan devotion remains central in the life of the community of San Fernando Cathedral. But, interestingly, as one enters San Fernando Cathedral one of the figures most readily visible near the entrance is not Guadalupe, but a place of great devotion and interaction that features a representation of the Black Christ of Esquipulas of Guatemala (also known as El Cristo Negro, El Señor de Esquipulas, and Milagros), an image dating back to 1594. By 1603 miracles were associated with El Cristo Negro and pilgrims have trekked to the mountains of eastern Guatemala ever since.[10] Curiously an object originally of Mesoamerican popular devotion sits in San Antonio, Texas, a city historically of Mexican American heritage where much of the Latino/a population still is of Mexican descent, in a holy building closely associated with Tejano culture and identity. This points to the fact that both the Latino/a community in San Antonio and its concepts of *santo* are much more diverse than might be supposed. Noted theologian and former rector of San Fernando Cathedral Virgilio Elizondo observed: "The Cristo Negro de Esquipulas is one of the living mysteries of San Fernando. Parishioners know very little about this representation of Christ and ask few questions, but their devotion to its miraculous powers continues to grow and spread among Catholics and Protestants alike."[11]

People recognize the Black Christ of Esquipulas in and of itself for what it symbolizes and as an exquisite work of art, but there are other objects of note besides the strikingly beautiful crucifix. There are photographs, notes, and small metal items attached to the wall around the image of the Black Christ that might overwhelm and mystify uninitiated visitors. While these may be puzzling for some, they ring true for many persons with Latin American roots, as it is clear that pilgrims arrive before this image with the definite intention of leaving a personal token. Surrounding the Black Christ are the seemingly innumerable mementos left by those who came before: photographs of babies, children, young people, and adults, rosary beads, artificial roses, and little tin items known as *milagros* hang by pins.

In Latin America and among many Hispanic/Latino Catholics in the United States it is a common devotional tradition for persons to bring a personal votive offering to the altar or statue of a saint. The little tin offerings are known as *milagros*, which literally means "miracles." *Milagros* are presented to a saint in thanksgiving for a prayer or request answered that is considered a miracle. Martha Egan writes, "The use of Milagros is most evident today at certain pilgrimage sites throughout the Americas, where the faithful gather to seek aid from the image of a favorite Virgin or saint or to pay a *promesa* (vow) in thanks for a cure or answered prayer."[12] And here at San Fernando Cathedral as elsewhere the little tin *milagros* are left as symbol of requests made or of petitions answered.

Through the Black Christ at San Fernando Cathedral, in the public ritual of the passion play of *Viernes Santo* (Holy Friday), and in the baptisms of Holy Saturday, *santo* is lived out, pursued, and practiced in the daily rituals and popular religiosity of the people of San Fernando Cathedral. They are all expressions of one way of understanding and experiencing the holy in this particular Hispanic/Latino context.

SANTO IN SOUTHWESTERN PIETY AND ART

Not far geographically from San Antonio in the neighboring state of New Mexico there is another sense of the word *santo* with its own long history. The Spanish colonization of what became New Mexico began in 1598 under the leadership of Juan de Oñate with approximately four hundred settlers following several prior European incursions in the region. As part of the colonial expansion of New Spain Christian missions were established to minister to colonists and convert the indigenous peoples to Christianity, although relations between Spaniards and *los indios* often were violent in the early years particularly with the imposition of the *encomienda* system.[13]

In the colonial context of New Mexico a cultural mix of indigenous, Spanish settlers traveling from central Mexico (Spain itself being a cultural mix developed over centuries in Iberia), and the new *mestizo* cultures was cultivated in the context of frontier life developed far from the centers of imperial power. After 1609 the province of New Mexico became increasingly disconnected from the imperial stronghold of Mexico City as well as other elements of the Spanish empire.[14] However, this relegation to the margins of empire did not mean that life, culture, religion, and spirituality stopped, but that peoples left on their own continued to work out what they needed. Spirituality and religious life found expression in many ways among the settlers and their descendents, who came to refer to themselves as Hispanos. Likewise the Hispanicized Native American peoples developed their spirituality and religiosity in ways that incorporated elements from the Spaniards and shared characteristics with their Hispano neighbors, but maintained certain amount of continuity with pre-conquest beliefs and practices.[15]

Today in New Mexico in places like Santa Fe, Albuquerque, Chimayó, and Taos there is a common understanding of *santo* that can be traced back to the colonial period. Sometimes *santo* is a carved figurine (*bulto*) or a painting (*retablo*) originally used in devotional practices. Traditionally a *bulto* is a statue of Christ, a saint, or the Virgin carved from cottonwood root or another kind of wood and painted. Occasionally the statue may have actual clothing. Contemporary *bultos* are sometimes made of bronze or other material. *Retablos* traditionally show a religious theme painted on a flat surface such as a pine board or tin.

This understanding and use of *santos* in the Western hemisphere reaches back to Spanish colonial times, drawing on centuries of Christian devotion in Iberia and the rest of Europe. In the context of New Mexico a *santo* as a carved figure (*bulto*) or painted two-dimensionally as a *retablo* are both expressions of spirituality and culture. Common New Mexican *santos* represent Nuestra Señora de Guadalupe, El Santo Niño, El Santo Niño de Atocha, San Francisco de Asís, and Doña Sebastiana, a representation of death that appears among Los Hermanos Penitentes, groups found in northern New Mexico and southern Colorado dating back to the eighteenth century and who are dedicated to acts of charity, prayer, and *el buen ejemplo* (the good example).[16]

The creators of *santo* paintings and carvings are called *santeros,* and they practice an art that was introduced in the colonial period and continues to the present day. Each *santero* has a unique, distinctive style. Most of the *santeros* were itinerant lay craftsmen who produced *santos* for use in churches, family chapels, homes, and the *moradas*, the gathering places of the Penitente Brotherhood.[17] Folk representation of *santos* as images of the saints can be found among Hispanos and Native Americans in New Mexico and continue to be crafted by contemporary *santeras* and *santeros* for devotion and as art.[18]

The Franciscan missionaries brought *santos* to New Mexico at the formation of early New Mexico when Christianity was introduced, but in time the local inhabitants began making them, some in special craft schools or *escuelitas*. As missionaries were withdrawn pious laity sought to be faithful in their spiritual and religious practices, and images of the saints (*santos*) assisted in personal, familial, and communal devotional life. "In the eyes of the people of New Mexico during the last centuries, *santos* were instruments within a network of related activities like prayer, penance, pilgrimages, processions, and the like."[19]

Because of the isolated nature of New Mexican communities during the colonial period religious and spiritual life continued and thrived under lay leadership with the use of *santos*. For the *santeros* and those who used their productions of *santos* as religious and spiritual art in northern New Mexico "religion played a large part in their daily lives [and] every home had its patron saint, an image made by the *santero*. Deeply devout, many families had an area set aside in their home where private worship could be conducted."[20]

While some *santos* seem to be the product of a single person who was moved to create one or two paintings or carvings, many of the New Mexican *santos* of the eighteenth and nineteenth centuries were crafted by *santeros* for whom it was a type of holy vocation. There is a rustic beauty to the stylized *bultos* carvings and the *retablo* paintings that represent spiritual realities for some, while others see them only as New Mexican Hispano folk art, part of the mixed heritage of Spain, Mexico, and Native American traditions in the Southwest.[21] As religious art and as folk art, *santos* are still created today, and individual pieces, both *bulto* and *retablo*, can command very high prices. And while for some collectors these are solely prized objets d'art, for the *santeros* and those who use the *santos* in their spirituality they are more than folk art; they are images as holy and sacred as a Greek or Russian icon.

This sense of *santo* as *bulto* and an artistic representation of Christ, the Virgin, or one of the saints is present not only in New Mexico, but also in many other Latino/a and Latin American cultures. In Puerto Rico *santos*, or religious figurines also continue to be carved as sacred objects and material expressions of Puerto Rican culture; their creators are known as either *santeros* or *talladores de santos*, "carvers of saints."[22] Common representations in wood, ceramics, paintings of religious figures include Santiago Apostol (St. James the Apostle), and Los Reyes Magos (the Magi Kings), referring to the Magi who visited the newborn Christchild as recorded in the Gospel of Matthew. Although in the Christian liturgical calendar January 6 is Epiphany, it is known more popularly as El Dia de los Reyes (Kings

Day) an important part of *las navidades*, or the Christmas season, even after more than a hundred years of the political and cultural presence of the United States. In Puerto Rico the Magi are held to be kings riding horses, which were brought to the island by the Spaniards.

Another prominent *santo* in both *retablos* and *bultos* is El Santo Niño de Atocha (the Holy Child of Atocha). Appearing in medieval Iberia and developing by the sixteenth century in Spain as a devotion to Our Lady of Atocha and the Holy Child, El Santo Niño de Atocha is a representation of the Christchild dressed in the blue pilgrim clothing of those journeying to Santiago de Compostela and known for healing, especially of children. During the period of the religious wars known as the Reconquista, it was believed that El Santo Niño de Atocha fed the Christian prisoners of the Moors. Like so many beliefs and practices this one made the Atlantic crossing, and the contemporary devotion to the Holy Child of Atocha developed further in colonial Mexico, especially in Zacatecas, where the Holy Child was held to be the protector of silver miners, and later among many Mexican Americans.

Beginning in the mid-1800s the strong devotion to El Santo Niño spread widely from Zacatecas to northern New Mexico to the shrine of the Black Christ of Esquipulas in Chimayó (the same object of devotion as found in Guatemala and San Antonio, Texas).[23] Beyond the devotion's growth in colonial Mexico, El Santo Niño de Atocha is found in Latino/a communities throughout the United States, in Latin America, and in Spain. Thus, a Spanish image associated with the reconquest of Moorish lands in Iberia was brought to Mexico and initially revered by Spanish colonists and *criollo* (Creole) elites as a symbol of Spain's hegemony. It then underwent a transformation to become a major object of devotion for the common people.[24] From San Juan, Puerto Rico, to Santa Fe, New Mexico, and places beyond, *santos* and *santeros* can be found.[25] But the exact sense and meaning of *santo* and *santero* is not the same in all places and all times.

OTHER FORMS OF *SANTOS*

In South Florida other people share a common understanding of *santero* or *santera* that differs from that of an artisan carving a devotional statue. This concept draws on the extensive multicultural Cuban heritage in Florida, a context in which a *santero/a* mediates between humans and the *santos* (saints), also known as the *orishas*. In this eclectic tradition the African spirits, or *orishas* (Spanish: *orichas*; Portuguese: *orixas*) also traveled across the Atlantic with the captured enslaved Africans to the Americas. In the context of the horrific persecution and death that defined colonial slavery throughout the Americas, transported African-based belief systems interacted with the Christianity presented to the slaves, as well as with indigenous beliefs and practices. These enslaved societies of the African diaspora in the Americas formed and fashioned new ways of knowing and being connected to the past that have contextual relevance to the present time. The transplanted African traditions developed in many ways in the Americas. One way this blended and contextualized sense of the holy developed was in the tradition that developed in Cuba, commonly known as Santería, "the way of the saints," but also by the name Lucumí (also spelled Lukumi), La Regla de Ocha (the way of the Ocha), or as Ifa/Orisha worship.[26]

Santos and Spirits

Like in the work of the New Mexican or Puerto Rican *santeros*, beauty and artistry infuse the material expressions of Santería/Lucumí, and research points to an aesthetic that bonds with the ideas and ritual practices of the tradition.[27] But, unlike a *santero* in New Mexico, a *santero* or *santera* in Santería is a specialized, consecrated intercessor between humans and the *orishas*, sometimes considered a priest or priestess who also acts as the representative of a specific *orisha*. In the Cuban context the identity, characteristics, and representations of the transplanted *orishas* were re-worked with that of certain Catholic saints. Thus, the Virgin of Caridad de Cobré is indeed a representation of the Virgin Mary and the patron saint of Cuba, but she is also perceived by some as a representation of Ochún (Oshún), the *orisha* of rivers and fresh water associated with love, health, and money.[28]

Santería, or Lukumi, is an African-based religion that developed in the cultural context of Cuba, in which the African spirits/*orishas* figure prominently. It is practiced by many Cuban Americans, as well as other Hispanics and non-Hispanics.[29] Theologian Miguel De La Torre provides help in beginning to understand this complex and evolving understanding of the holy through a pithy description of Santería as made up of "an Iberian Christianity shaped by the Counterreformation and Spanish folk Catholicism, blended together with African orisha worship as it was practiced by the Yoruba of Nigeria and later modified by nineteenth century Kardecan spiritualism."[30] The spiritualism to which De La Torre refers gained popularity in the nineteenth century in Latin America as a result of the teachings of Allan Kardec (H. L. Rivail, 1804–69).[31] In everyday folk or popular religiosity and spirituality, the terms *espiritismo* (spiritism) and *espiritualismo* (spiritualism) are used interchangeably both as they influence other traditions and in their own right. Other scholars expand on De La Torre's definition by identifying other non-Yoruban African influences and in the ongoing development of Santería from the colonial period.

African religious-cultural metaphysical traditions emphasize maintaining good and balanced relationships with all of life, especially between human beings and "spirits," or *orishas*. A common belief in a supreme being that exists over and above all of life saturates these faith systems. Some perceive this supreme being as removed from the everyday, whereas it is the multiple intermediary spirits, or *orisha,* who are the active beings with whom humans have the most daily contact. Within this Africa-based perspective devotees honor the spirits of their ancestors and recognize their continuing influence in everyday life. The resulting African–Latin American, and then U.S. Latino/a synthesis, of which Santería is one example, continues to be a sacred way of life that sees all of existence infused with the spiritual and connected to the supernatural—not one that adheres to a strict sacred/secular modernist division of life.

Maintaining balance and keeping good relationships between the different realms of existence ensure that the resources needed to negotiate life are provided daily. Various forms of divination establish balance, provide guidance, address spiritual problems, dispense knowledge, and allow communion with the ancestors and *orishas* who remain central to this way of life. Often a type of sacrifice can result in a deeper relationship with the *orishas*. Drums and dances figure prominently as divination and sacrifice and are combined in an experience of *orisha* consciousness.

Santería

Santería represents both a re-creation of and continuity with African worldviews in the midst of destructive and oppressive contexts. One such path that emerged is Santería. During the period of slavery, Africans exerted a major influence in shaping the developing Cuban culture in its entirety through attitudes, music, dance, spirituality, and religion. As it developed, Santería spread beyond its original slave adherents and was embraced by others; it also proved to be extremely adaptive through all phases of Cuban history from colonial times, through the fight for independence, dominance by the United States, dictatorship, revolution, and the creation of a Cuban diaspora.[32] The African *orisha/oricha*, paired with European Roman Catholic *santos* (saints), were perceived as sharing particular characteristics. Examples of connections between the saints and the *orishas* include Changó with St. Barbara, Yemaya with Our Lady of Regla, and Oshun with the Virgin of Caridad de Cobre.[33]

Since 1959 and with each successive wave of Cuban migration the beliefs and practices of Santería spread further, and aspects of Santería can be found in Latino/a communities throughout the United States. In Charlotte, Orlando, Dallas, Nashville, Lancaster, Pennsylvania, and Bridgeport, Connecticut, there are small shops named Botanica La Madrina, Botanica Kalifa, Botanica Yemaya, Botanica Sacaempeño, or Botanica Santa Barbara. Whether it is the Chango Botánica in the Oak Cliff section of Dallas, the Botanica Chango in Philadelphia, or the Botanica Chango in San Diego, shops like them are scattered throughout the United States.

While these shops are certainly places of business, they also serve as spaces for alternative spirituality and medicine, with an ongoing mixture of Santería and other streams of spiritism. A combination of spiritual resource center, folk pharmacy, and bookstore, *botánicas* serve physical, psychological, and spiritual needs and provide information, tools, supplies, and other services. Displayed on the shelves of the *botánicas*, supermarkets, discount stores, and other shops are tall, glass-enclosed votive prayer candles with pictures of Roman Catholic saints. On the reverse side of most candles printed in Spanish and/or English is a prayer to recite with a particular focus. Specialized books and pamphlets in Spanish and English are available.[34] The reciprocal influence on the *botánicas* and supermarket shelves is seen in the presence of candles with the image of El Santo Niño de Atocha, prominent in Mexican American spirituality. Interestingly, in *Santeria* the Santo Niño de Atocha also has become recognized by some as a representation of Eleggua, who is the guardian of the crossroads, the overseer of pathways, and one of the Siete Potencias Africanas (the Seven African Powers).[35] In the context of Afro-Caribbean spiritual traditions *santero/as*, *curanderos*, and *curanderas* ask the Santo Niño de Atocha to intervene on behalf of those in need.

Partly through the influence and impact of Cuban exiles, Santería is increasingly known in the United States, gaining adherents from other Latino groups and among non-Hispanics, especially African Americans. Santería and other religious-cultural systems like it emerged as a means of maintaining continuity with the African past in the colonial present, while accessing elements of Spanish Christianity (especially folk or popular religion) with aspects of the indigenous cosmovisions.

While Santería as religion, a religious system and practiced religiosity, has its more immediate origins in Cuba, in addition to roots in Africa and Europe, its presence and influence in the United States extend far beyond the Cuban American communities of south Florida. Santería is also a living and vibrant tradition of the African diaspora. In Santería, borders are crossed, expectations are smashed, and we are challenged to expand our understandings of how people construct their spirituality and how they define *santo*.

Jewish Latino/as

Latinas and Latinos are not all a variety of Christian; some are also Jewish, which surprises some and defies popular perceptions. This path of the holy, or *santo,* is followed by Latinos and Latinas whose families have been Jewish as long as anyone can remember. For others Judaism is a path pursued by those who turn to or in some instances feel that they are returning to Judaism, an experience of conversion for some and recovery for others.

Some of these Jewish Latinos and Latinas trace their Jewish heritage through the U.S. Southwest and back to Iberia, where there was a major Jewish population through the Middle Ages until the 1490s. During the period of Islam in Iberia, called Al-Andalus, there was a large and at times thriving Jewish community in the areas that later became Spain and Portugal; it was called *Serafad* in Hebrew, from which the Sephardic branch of modern Judaism takes its name.

The medieval Jews of the Iberian Peninsula, known as the Sephardim, spoke Ladino, which was written in Hebrew script. Ladino is also known as Sefardi, Judezmo, and Judeo-Spanish (*judeoespañol*), although more precisely it is linguistically a mixture of Hebrew, Old Castilian, and Portuguese.

When the Sephardi population was forced out of Spain in 1492 and some of the exiles resettled in the eastern Mediterranean, elements of Greek and Turkish were incorporated into Ladino. Over time Cuba became a major resettlement location of Sephardic Jews (called *turcos* in Cuba) with Havana becoming a center of Ladino publishing.

As the Iberian Christian kingdoms pursued their policy of *reconquista,* that is, the reconquest of Muslim-controlled territories, many Sephardic Jews were forced to convert to Christianity during the years between 1391 and 1497. Even with such conversions the *conversos,* or so-called New Christians, were often suspected of continuing the practice of Judaism behind closed doors. Some of the *conversos* did in fact continue to practice Judaism covertly in attempts to avoid coming to the attention of the Spanish Inquisition. With the expulsion of Jews from Spain in 1492, many Sephardim, later joined by additional Jewish refugees from Portugal, relocated to the Turkish Empire, including the Balkans, as well as Syria, Palestine, Egypt, North Africa, and Italy. Still later Sephardic diaspora communities developed in the Netherlands, the West Indies, and the Americas. At an early stage many crypto-Jews left Spain and Portugal to settle in the Caribbean and Mexico in the hope of being beyond the reach of the Inquisition.[36]

Interestingly, there is still a persistent survival of hidden Jewish family identities, practices, and traditions in New Mexico and the bordering areas. Those Hispanos who also identify with the "hidden" Sephardic Jewish legacy in the U.S. Southwest are also known as *conversos,* secret Jews, crypto-Jews, *anusim* (Hebrew for forced converts), and "Southwestern Jews." Although historically the word *marrano* also was used for *conversos,* this term is generally avoided because it usually taken to mean pig or swine.[37]

People with ancestry in the U.S. Southwest are discovering and exploring their Jewish or crypto-Jewish heritage. Historically some exilic Sephardic crypto-Jews always practiced Judaism secretly, whereas others reverted to Judaism or continued for generations as adoptive Christians. But even in those situations, there are many examples of families practicing traditions that are unambiguously of Jewish derivation.[38]

Examples in New Mexico include "family traditions" such as the lighting of candles on Friday nights, abstention from pork, eating a type of unleavened flatbread called *pan de semita* (Semitic bread) for Easter, and the circumcision of newborn boys. There are many instances of tomb-stones with a Star of David or menorah etched in them or small stones left at the graves by visitors honoring the memory of the departed.[39] Stories also exist of New Mexican men who gather for weekly prayer in neigh-borhood *moradas* wearing *tallits*, as well as the persistence and practice of other Jewish traditions. For some, this buried family history reveals an interesting past, while other Latinas and Latinos have seen clues in these family practices concerning the inexorable power of aspects of their Jew-ish heritage. Such vestiges have prompted reappraisals, leading some to embark on a journey of exploration, in some cases a recovery of Sephardic ancestry and a contemporary embrace of Judaism.[40] Even for those who do not embrace Judaism, "The persistence of crypto-Jewish rituals has there-fore affected the development of the descendants' spiritual consciousness, informing their religious choices as they find themselves at the intersection of crypto-Judaism and Christianity, each of which has influenced their cul-tural and religious upbringing."[41]

Some Latino/a Jews in the United States represent a more recent migra-tion of people than the sixteenth-century migration to New Mexico. In Florida a growing population of Cuban Jews has its origins in the migration of an estimated ten to twelve thousand people going into exile in 1959 with the victory of Cuban Revolution and the rise of the Fidel Castro regime.[42] Spain approved official Jewish migration to its colony Cuba in 1881, and some of the first Cuban Jews ironically were Sephardim, the descendants of those expelled in 1492, with the majority arriving in the period of 1902 to 1920. Others were of Eastern European Ashkenazic origin, with an esti-mated eighteen thousand migrating to Cuba between 1921 and 1930.[43] In Cuba these Jews were called *polacos* and *turcos* in a colloquial reference to their major points of origin. An additional influx of European Jews began in the mid-1930s as they sought to escape Nazi persecution. Some of the Jews saw Cuba as a way station to gaining admittance into the United States while others put down roots. A wave of anti-Semitism contributed to the SS *St. Louis* incident in which a boatload of refugees were refused admittance to the United States and returned to Europe. Thus in the Cuban context there was a significant mixing of Sephardim and Ashkenazim before 1959.

After fleeing to Florida many of these early Cuban-Jewish immi-grants found themselves ignored or the targets of ethnic and linguistic discrimination from south Florida's Jewish population.[44] Nevertheless by 1961 the newly exiled established themselves in a community called El Cír-culo, out of which emerged Temple Beth Shmuel, also known as the Cuban Hebrew Congregation of Miami; it is mostly Ashkenazi in its heritage. In 1980 Sephardic Cuban Jews established a synagogue of its own, Temple Moses, also in Miami.[45] In a manifestation of the diversity and ongoing change in self-identification, some Cuban Jews in south Florida refer to themselves as Jewban or Jewbano. The term is an obvious conflation of Jewish and Cuban, but it also embraces all the parts—Jewish, Cuban, American—of a multicultural religious and racial-ethnic identity.

MORE TO THE STORY

While this brief geographic and spiritual survey gives some sense of the diversity of beliefs and practices among Latinas and Latinos, it only begins to tell the story of the incredible variety that exists. To be sure, in offi-cial numbers the majority of religious adherents fall within the categories identified in this chapter, but there are other religious and spiritual paths that Hispanics in the United States follow. Moreover, some follow multiple paths concurrently without any sense that there might be a conflict. The next chapter explores more examples of *santo*, religiosity, and spirituality that go beyond "the usual suspects."

TWO

Santo:
Beyond the Usual Expectations

EXPECTATION AND ACTUALITY

In the previous chapter we reviewed different expressions of *santo* and *sagrado*, holy and sacred, in traditions that meet most usual expectations. After all, if the usual assumption is that "all Hispanics are Catholics," it is to be expected that manifestations of *santo* will be described in Catholic settings, whether it is the popular piety in San Antonio or Santa Fe. However, as chapter 1 demonstrates, *santo* can be described in a variety of settings, some Christian and some non-Christian. In an elastic way the basic assumptions and expectations still hold that Hispanic religion and spirituality form basically a Christian story.

Of course, the presence of African diasporic traditions such as Santería/Lucumí challenges any assertion of an uncomplicated Christian story for Hispanic religion and spirituality. The response to that challenge by some is to see beliefs and practices solely as an extension of Catholic popular piety. More difficult to explain away is the presence of Hispanic Jews, but here again defenders of the usual expectations adopt the language of the shared roots of Christianity and Judaism and allow for a further caveat that Hispanic religion and spirituality are part of a Judeo-Christian story.

However, the actuality of the diversity among Latinas and Latinos goes beyond the Judeo-Christian rhetorical construct that still has power in the United States. Indeed, the examples provided in chapter 1, it showed that simplistic tagging into predetermined categories does not represent the reality of Hispanic/Latino spirituality. The deficiency of succumbing to easy-to-use categories was pressed home to me when a friend shared a bit of his own story in response to my request asking him to define *santo*:

To make sense of it I guess I'll start by explaining part of my own hectic, yet beautiful experiences and observations in the realm of the sagrado, which of course transits through the road of purpose and identity. Let me define myself, I am not Latino or Hispanic. I identify a lot with Chicanos, Boricua-Taínos, first nations and immigrants worldwide. I am also a member of the Chichimeca nation, Huarave and Jonáz are my clans through my parents, I am a member of the confederacy of Mexica groups of Cemanahuac (Meso-America), a Mexican national, a former undocumented-documented migrant and U.S. resident, now also a U.S. citizen, a former Chicagoan and a new New Mexican. I am also a voice carrier for a few groups that work with youth, people struggling with addiction, and I facilitate ceremonies for the Native American church.[1]

His story captures not only his understanding of the *sagrado* aspects that overlap with the stories of chapter 1, it also clearly describes dimensions that go beyond those boundaries. This present chapter continues the exploration of *santo* that goes beyond the "usual suspects" by considering beliefs and practices that are clearly beyond the boundaries of Christianity and Judaism, but also along the path that my friend so aptly described as "the road of purpose and identity."

LATINO/A MUSLIMS

Many Latino/a Muslims also pursue the holy in a multicultural way with deep purpose but in a context of sporadic hostility. Regrettably, the only information some people have heard about Latino/a Muslims may be restricted to knowledge from the media's coverage of José Padilla, a Brooklyn-born Puerto Rican, also known as Abdullah al-Muhajir, who converted to Islam in the early 1990s. In a post-9/11 world Padilla/al-Muhajir was arrested, held for a number of years as an enemy combatant, and later tried in a civilian court that convicted him of terrorism conspiracy charges.

Before Padilla's arrest in 2002 in a context where the popular assumption still was that all Latino/as are Catholic, probably few Americans knew that there were any Hispanics in the United States who were Muslim. In fact the Latino/a Muslim population is one of the most rapidly increasing communities in the nation.[2] A small but growing number of Latino/as embraced Islam perhaps as early as the 1920s with some estimates placing their number between about forty thousand in the mid-1990s to at least two hundred thousand nationwide at the present.[3]

While Martínez-Vázquez correctly observes that it is difficult to construct a linear history of Latino/a Muslims, it was in the 1960s and 1970s that the initial significant conversions of Latinas and Latinos to Islam took place.[4] In some cases these conversions were related to the growth of the primarily African American Muslim groups, including the Nation of Islam (known also as the Black Muslims and American Muslim Mission). This group is not to be confused with the group led by Louis Farrakhan, which since 1981 is also known as the Nation of Islam.[5] Martínez-Vázquez also notes that the Latino/a Muslim community grew in the 1990s concurrent with the growth of the Internet, which "allowed for U.S. Latino/as to make contact with Muslim groups and [has] allowed U.S. Latino/a Muslims to actually create their own groups and establish *da'wah* [invitation to Islam through education] to other U.S. Latino/as, especially those of the younger generations."[6]

Significantly there has been a growing number of Latino/a Muslims since 1997, when the Latino American Dawah Organization (LADO) was founded, even with the events of September 11, 2001, and its aftermath, which included waves of anti-Islamic prejudice.[7] Latino/as can be found in mosques across the United States in cities like Chicago, Dallas, Houston, Los Angeles, New York, Miami, and many other cities. People of Puerto Rican and Dominican descent make up the majority of Latino/a Muslims in the East, whereas in California and Texas a majority is of Mexican and Mexican American or Central American heritage.[8] Spanish-language–oriented Islamic centers have been established in New York City and in southern California. Spanish translations of Islamic texts and study guides also give testimony to this growing community.

By far the largest group of Latino/a Muslims in the United States enters the faith by conversion. Some Latino/a converts to Islam are ex-Roman Catholics or Protestants disenchanted with ecclesiastical teachings and practices.[9] Some convert when they marry a Muslim, others encounter Islam through a friend, and many relate that different aspects of Islamic faith and practice were appealing and nurturing for their lives. Some of these converts were persuaded by interactions and invitations from other

Muslims encountered in everyday life as coworkers, acquaintances, friends, classmates, and partners.

At the time she became a Muslim Elizabeth Chawki was a student at Pasadena City College with a spiritual and religious background that included Roman Catholic roots and born-again Protestantism.[10] Chawki's brother, Benny Garcia, also became a Muslim. They attended the ILM Foundation, an Islamic center in Los Angeles. Both describe the spiritual and intellectual appeal of Islam for them. Chawki and Garcia adhere to Islamic religious practices, such as prayer five times a day, and think that Islam has much to offer Latino/as, including unity across national and ethnic divisions and an answer to spiritual searching. However they may have been introduced to Islam and with acknowledgment of each person's unique spiritual story, Martínez-Vázquez identifies a process that many experience that includes context, crisis, encounter, quest, and consequences.[11] The conversion and ongoing observance of U.S. Latino/a Muslims entails a reconstruction of their own U.S. Latino/a identities.

Some Latinos and Latinas who leave another religious tradition to become Muslim describe their spiritual experience of connection with Islam not as a conversion, but as a "reversion," a recovery of their Muslim heritage repressed and forgotten by the Reconquista. The website *Hispanic Muslim* describes this belief that all "people are born Muslims. Our parents and society are what make us choose other religions. We believe people are born in a state of fitrah. Fitrah is our natural tendency to believe in one God. Consequently, by embracing Islam, you return to your natural disposition."[12]

For some this represents not only a return to the created state, but also a recovery of Muslim roots that date back to Iberia and the time of Al-Andalus, the period of over seven hundred years of Muslim (Moorish) presence in western Europe.[13] Al-Andalus was the Arabic name for the areas of Iberia under Moorish rule starting in 711 C.E. through the completion of the Christian Reconquista or "Reconquest" of 1492 with the defeat of Moorish Granada by the armies of the "Catholic monarchs" Ferdinand of Aragon and Isabella of Castile.[14] By the end of the century Moors were forced to choose between death, conversion to Christianity, or exile from Iberia. Many who chose conversion (called *Moriscos* by the "old Christians" of Spain) maintained a hidden Muslim identity and practice.[15] Evidence shows that some of the exiled Moors from Iberia found their way to the Americas despite the work of the Spanish Inquisition to keep them out.[16] The Moorish and Arabic heritage is experienced daily in unperceived ways through the thousands of Spanish words of Arabic origin.

There are some Latina and Latino Muslims who would argue that the influence of Al-Andalus is felt in more profound ways and who describe their conversion to Islam as a "reversion," claiming that in some sense their ancestors in Iberia were Muslim. A first-generation Dominican American from New York City described his experience on "the straight path" after he took his Shahadah at age eighteen:

> I still remember the first time I entered a mosque. Coming from a Catholic background and attending church services where everyone was either Puerto Rican or Dominican, and to now attend Friday congregational prayers at a mosque where no one is from the same country is quite a change. In my opinion, the best feeling is to walk into a mosque and not know where everyone is from. I have yet to find a place more diverse than a mosque. Only there will one find brothers from the Philippines, Senegal, Bangladesh, Brazil, and Palestine, all praying side-by-side to the One God, in the same language, with the same beliefs. The fact that I could pray alongside a person who doesn't even speak the same language as I do moves me. It shows me that Islam truly transcends culture, language, class, race, and any other artificial divisions that humans tend to set up amongst themselves.[17]

Although the number of Latinas and Latinos is steadily increasing, such conversion/reversion is not an easy matter since in many cases there is not initial acceptance from non-Muslim family and friends. Nevertheless, for some Latino/as the spiritual value is worth the cost, and for some it also means a strengthening of their Latino/a identity. Martínez-Vázquez relates how one Latina named María gained a deeper sense of identity as a result of her reversion: "Actually, I feel it has reinforced my identity because in my perspective I am actually going back to my roots. I think people who are Christian, who are Catholic, have gone away from their Latino roots because we have our roots in Spain. We have our roots in the Moors."[18]

While it appears that the majority of Latino/a Muslims embraced Islam through conversion/reversion, other Latino/a Muslims in the United States are of Arab descent mediated through the prior migration of parents, grandparents, and great-grandparents to Latin America. This represents a transnational movement of peoples over generations that in some cases was tied to the collapse of the Ottoman Empire, as well as to origins in other parts of the Middle East.[19] Estimates place the Muslim population of Latin America at approximately 6 million (both immigrants and converts) with 1.5 million in Brazil and 700,000 in Argentina. Latino/a Muslims ought not be so easily dismissed as a group of odd, potentially hostile people who are allied with foreign terrorists.

LATINO/A BUDDHISTS

It may be another surprise to many people that there is a small but increasing number of Latino/as who follow some tradition of Buddhism. Hispanic Buddhists are widespread in geographic presence and diverse in their backgrounds. Alex Castro from the Latino/a majority town of Oxnard, California, follows a path of Buddhism based on the teachings of Nichiren Daishonin (1222–82), a Buddhist monk from thirteenth-century Japan. Nichiren Buddhism, a branch of Mahayana Buddhism, asserts that persons can discover within themselves the power to bring happiness, inner peace, and harmony to themselves and to others. In his faith Castro holds that part of the human condition is that "People are unhappy in their own life and they don't know how to help it."[20] Castro found happiness and help in Buddhism introduced to him by his mother, Rosalva Castro, who had been a non-practicing Roman Catholic on a spiritual quest of her own when she embraced Buddhism in 1984. Now as an adult Castro continues his life as a Buddhist, active as the National Brass Band Leader of the Youth Division of Soka Gakkai International–USA, the Buddhist Association of Peace, Culture, and Education.[21]

World-renowned Chicana poet and fiction writer Sandra Cisneros was born in Chicago, one of seven children of a Mexican father and a Mexican American mother. She is the author of *House on Mango Street* (1991), *Woman Hollering Creek* (1992), and *Caramelo* (2003), among other works. Cisneros also identifies herself as a Buddhist, stating that she has found the work of Vietnamese Buddhist poet Thich Nhat Hanh, to be "illuminating and life changing" for her.[22] In addition to being a poet and author, Thich Nhat Hanh (b. 1926) is a Buddhist monk, teacher, and peace activist whose writings, especially his teachings on living mindfully in the present, are highly influential throughout the world.[23] Thich Nhat Hanh's book *Being Peace* appears as a recommended book on Cisneros' website.[24] But it is also clear that Cisneros is as creative in her Buddhist spirituality as in her literary work. In an interview with journalist Ray Suarez of PBS Cisneros discussed how Buddhism is related to her writing, particularly in her second novel *Caramelo*:

RAY SUAREZ: These stories, whether true and based on your own family, or whether invention, are done from the point of view of the young Lala without judgment, with a tremendous amount of affection even when people are not at their best—the way that we love to see our family.

SANDRA CISNEROS: Yeah, you know, I wish I could be . . . say that was me, but I'm very judgmental and I make all kinds of quick assessments. And the nice thing about writing a novel is you take your time, you sit with the character sometimes nine years, you look very deeply at a situation, unlike in real life when we just kind of snap something out. And it allowed me to be more generous than me the person. The author is always much more compassionate than Sandra Cisneros the human being.

RAY SUAREZ: But also done from the point of view that these events, whether we like them or not, happened and made us who we are today.

SANDRA CISNEROS: That's right. Well, I'm Buddhist, Ray, and so part of my Buddhism has allowed me to look a little more deeply at people and the events in my life that created me. And I think a lot of that Buddhism comes out in the worldview in this novel.

RAY SUAREZ: (Laughing) Even with its heavy devotion to the Virgin of Guadalupe?

SANDRA CISNEROS: Ray, you can be Buddhalupist, as I am, you see, where you're a devotee of Guadalupe and Buddhism, and that's the nice thing about Buddhism, it allows you to look at the jewels of your own culture and incorporate that into your Buddhism.[25]

In an earlier interview Cisneros had expanded on her concept of Buddhism and a being a Buddalupist. "For me, who had walked away from the Catholic Church, it just brought me back to parts of myself. . . . The amazing parts about Buddhism is that it is taking me back to my culture and my family spirituality. Buddhism for me is a way of helping to guide my life work. It focuses on serving humanity."[26] Cisneros's practice of Buddhism informs her spirituality and helps her create her own sense of cultural identity as a Latina.

In an online blog Chicago Latina Jennie Arteaga writes about her life as a Buddhist in a Roman Catholic family.[27] Arteaga became a Buddhist and vegetarian at the age of twelve, news that was not well received in her Mexican Catholic family, and yet it is a dual commitment she has maintained for the past ten years, despite the fact she has not met many other Latino/Latina Buddhists. Reflecting on aspects of the challenge of her commitment for her and her family, Arteaga wrote, "You're simply born into the religion and to ask questions about other spiritualities is a personal attack on your family's decency, pride and culture." Yet, despite challenges and opposition, this Latina continues on her Buddhist path, finding guidance for self-examination and examination of the world. "The first thing I learned in Buddhism is that before you can understand the heart of others you must first understand your own. This means sitting down with yourself and taking a good look in the mirror, then digging deeper, through the reflection into the skin and underneath."[28]

José Ignacio Cabezón, an internationally recognized scholar of Tibetan religion and culture, is the first professor to hold the XIV Dalai Lama Chair in Tibetan Buddhism and Cultural Studies at the University of California, Santa Barbara.[29] Growing up in Boston as the son of Cuban immigrants, Cabezón is a self-avowed Buddhist who was a monk at the Tibetan exile Sera Monastery in south India, and he describes himself as an academic Buddhist theologian and scholar.[30] Because of his fluency in languages, he has served as a translator/interpreter from Tibetan to Spanish and to English for the Dalai Lama.[31] Cabezón has reflected on his multiple identities and the consternation it causes for some as it confounds predetermined categories:

> I frequently confront the oddity—the unnaturalness—of my being
> a Caribbean Latino who studies Buddhism, and I often ponder the

extent to which I myself have internalized this unnaturalness, learning to laugh at my "unusual" predicament: that my scholarship should be "so at odds" with my ethnic identity. Of course my teaching and scholarly work is no more at odds with my ethnicity than is the scholarship of a white European who studies Buddhism, but no one find it strange or humorous that white Americans or Europeans study Buddhism.[32]

Cabezón's reflection highlights not only issues that arise when one understands only predetermined categories, but also the ways that race and religion are used for scripted social constructions of identity.

For many Latinas and Latinos who embrace a form of Buddhism, a common theme in their stories is a sense of delight in what they encountered. Some have found in one of the paths of Buddhism what they had been seeking and needed. Others embraced Buddhism as part of a more eclectic spirituality that they are still constructing. And yet some others, while appreciative of their encounter with Buddhism, were not compelled to be Buddhist but rather confirmed that there was some important knowledge to be gained from exploring the world beyond received traditions.

ALTERNATIVE CHRISTIANS

Religious studies scholar Gastón Espinosa in his study on faith-based political action among Latino/a clergy identified a cohort that does not quite fit usual categories. Espinosa described the members of this group as "alternative Christian," which helpfully lifts up the principle of self-identification by religious groups themselves.[33] There are religious communities that Latino/a Catholics and Protestants might consider beyond the pale of what is Christian (ironically there are those in these two large camps who would not consider the other Christian). Nevertheless they self-identify as Christian. Sometimes referred to by researchers as "Protestant sects," these groups have seen a greater than anticipated growth in the years 1990 to 2008.[34] Two of the numerically largest groups still showing rapid growth are Mormons and Jehovah's Witnesses.

Seeing two young Euro-American males, usually wearing white shirts with ties and carrying knapsacks, is quite common throughout Latin America and in Latino/a neighborhoods. Usually they are Mormon missionaries

seeking new adherents for the Church of Jesus Christ of Latter-day Saints
(LDS). Based on popular perceptions of Latinas/os, the idea of Mormons
in the barrios may seem incongruous, but they have made considerable
inroads since 1978. Established in 1830 the Mormon Church is sometimes
described as one of the homegrown American religions. It emerged in
upstate New York through the experiences and teachings of Joseph Smith,
and Mormonism has since grown to be a worldwide phenomenon. Some
of the most significant global growth among Mormons has been among its
Spanish-speaking membership in Latin America (over five million members) and the increase of Spanish-speaking U.S. congregations. In addition
to the outreach efforts of the LDS based in Salt Lake City, the Community of Christ, formerly known as the Reorganized Church of Latter-day
Saints based in Independence, Missouri, is also evangelizing in Latino/a
communities.

The Pew Forum on Religion and Public Life reported that in 2009 about
7 percent of all U.S. Mormons were Latinas/os.[35] The growth of Latino/a
Mormons is all the more amazing given the history of racial exclusion of
the Utah branch of the LDS. It was only through a new revelation in 1978
that the LDS reversed its longstanding ban by granting the lay priesthood
to all men, regardless of race.[36] Some observers say that part of the appeal
of the LDS to Latino/as is its emphasis on family and the church's teaching
that after death people are reunited with their ancestors. The LDS website
includes a response to the question "Why I am a Mormon?" that seems
directed to Latino/as. Marcelo, described as a young married businessman,
originally from Ecuador and now residing in Arizona, answers:

> Me bautice en el verano del 2011, es el mejor pasa que e podido dar
> en la vida, de conocer el evangelio; Actualmente imparto clases sobre
> principios del evangelio, que si bien en cierto conforme aprendo tam-
> bién enseño, esta es una de las mejores muestras del amor que tiene
> Jesus para mi.

> [I was baptized in the summer of 2011, it was the best thing to be
> given in life, to know the gospel; presently I give classes on the prin-
> ciples of the gospel, but it is certainly true that I learn as well as teach,
> this is one of the best demonstrations of Jesus' love for me.][37]

Another group with a growing presence in Hispanic communities is the Jehovah's Witnesses. As of June 2011 the city of Yuma, Arizona, had a dozen Jehovah's Witnesses congregations with an estimated total membership of thirteen hundred. While that may not seem dramatic, the perspective of an elderly Latina is helpful in putting this in context. With tears in her eyes seventy-seven-year-old Maria Luisa Garcia reflected on the change since the 1950s when she and four other women in Yuma started to share their faith: "From five people, look at the growth. There are now many congregations. I cry at conventions when I see so much growth."[38] The Jehovah's Witnesses now have more than one million members in Latin America, compared to a little over one million members in the United States, and a growing number of the latter group are Latino/as.

Although Jehovah's Witnesses reject being called a Protestant religion, the roots of the group are in nineteenth-century Protestantism, and specifically through the teachings of Charles Taze Russell, who in turn was influenced by Adventist teachings. The Watch Tower Bible and Tract Society, which is the core institution of the Jehovah's Witnesses, was founded in 1881. The Witnesses (as they call themselves) claim a biblical basis for their teachings, and their beliefs include a radical separation from other groups and a distinctive millennial view that includes a belief that Jesus Christ has been ruling in heaven since 1914.[39] Each gathering meets in buildings called Kingdom Hall (*Salón del Reino*). Their main publications for dissemination are *Watchtower* and *Awake!*, as well as a variety of tracts. The Witnesses are known for their house-to-house visits to share their faith, which is a major means of literature distribution.

Regarding these and other alternative groups, again Gastón Espinosa provides excellent insight when he notes:

> The impact of alternative Christian traditions is evident not only in the growth of Latino Jehovah's Witnesses and Mormons, but also in other alternative Christian traditions such as the Seventh-day Adventists and the Oneness Pentecostals—the latter of which reject the doctrine of the Trinity and insist that true Christians must be baptized in Jesus' name only for salvation.[40]

These rapidly growing groups are part of the theological and multicultural diversity of Latino/a religions and spiritualities.

"A DIFFERENT KIND OF HUG"

The preceding discussion has indicated a few examples of the different ways in which Latinas and Latinos have pursued the holy. There are many and diverse ways that *santo* is understood in various U.S. Latino contexts. These searches for *santo* include both older and newer options. They may have to do with a particular culture, or a search for roots, or a quest for the answer to an unspecified but deeply felt spiritual longing. Some have found traditional expressions of religion, especially within the institutional church, restrictive, negative, and unsatisfying. Nevertheless, they have not abandoned altogether a sense of a greater reality and desire to be connected to that greater reality.

Some well-educated second- and third-generation Latinos and Latinas in, for example, New York, Chicago, Dallas, Santa Fe, Los Angeles, Austin, and San Francisco have also connected with the larger societal trends that come under the generic umbrella of "New Age" spirituality, but for some even that term New Age is problematic as an inappropriate, limiting, and misleading label. One person described it this way, "Augh! Another label! The last thing I wanted to have happen was to have another label placed on me where people would again pre-judge me, make assumptions based on the biases they had toward the label and in many cases have their thoughts and feelings about me set, before we even had a conversation."[41]

Some Latinas and Latinos have embarked on a pilgrimage to explore and study what other cultures have to offer, especially in terms of life and what they consider holy. In this Latino/a multigenerational, multicultural context, *santo*, the search for and practice of the holy, is eclectic and flexible as it seeks different but meaningful ways of spirituality. Searches for the holy are not forsaken; rather new paths are explored. And they draw on whatever assistance the past can offer as they gather new aids along the way.

Certainly these alternate expressions of Latino/a spirituality are discrete in their foci and the beliefs and practices with which they interact, but they do share some characteristics in the pursuit of the holy, even in their definition of the holy. While they touch many of the traditions discussed so far, they do not neatly fit into those categories. Notwithstanding the inherent danger of labels, we can say that there are some shared characteristics of this approach to *santo*. This cluster is simultaneously a quest and an eclectic approach to life and spirituality that is comfortable with a fusion of paths, methodologies, practices, and teachings. There is often some overlap with other paths to *santo* where "traditional" and "nontraditional" religions are accessed. They may draw on many sources with no particular pattern or method in mind, other than a shared affirmation that there *is* no one dominant pattern or method.

Adherents of the ways of *santo* as cosmic spirituality often are members of the 1.5-generation, second, third, or later generations of Latinas and Latinos. This search for a type of spirituality beyond labels seems to represent a desire for a cultural home as well as a spiritual one by exploring any and all expressions of the human experience. Moreover, new generations find a greater inter-ethnic Latino/a mix, for example, a Chicana partnering with a Puerto Rican, a Guatemalan–Puerto Rican marrying a Salvadoran, Latinas marrying non-Latinos, all of which seem to foster not only new cultural identities, but also religious eclecticism and spiritual creativity. In essence new religious/spiritual cultures develop through a type of pragmatic fusion.

Practitioners often articulate a common desire and challenge for humanity to recognize an intrinsic beauty in all human beings and indeed in all of life the creator bestowed. These seekers commonly embrace the challenge to work for the end of strife and violence resulting from human behavior and to work for healing and balance in the whole world. Latinos and Latinas on the many paths of this open tradition have found resources for living that they did not find elsewhere. For some, "the church" distanced them from "the source" from which beauty and peace emanate, whereas communing with nature brings them closer to things of deepest meaning. Communion with nature marks many of these spiritual journeys, while for others drawing on Eastern traditions isfulfilling; yet others seek ways to draw it all together into a type of cosmic spirituality that gives direction, purpose, and fulfillment for life.

An example of such a searcher lies in the life of musical entertainer and activist Carlos Santana, whose worldwide audience transcends national, cultural, social, racial, and ethnic categories. In response to an interviewer's question about the source of his spirituality Santana said,

> I guess I knew, even before my mom and dad told me, that there was a divine purpose. When they took me to church and I was a kid, a

child, a lot of that stuff didn't make any sense to me, although I knew that God wasn't Santa Claus. It wasn't fictitious or it wasn't Peter Pan, there was some kind of connection with a Supreme Being. It's almost like when you hear a song before you actually play it. So, I started searching. Especially after the first wave of the Woodstock and the *Abraxas* [album], and you know, we hit really hard. For some reason I found myself craving a hug from God. So, I started playing John Coltrane's music and listened to Martin Luther King's speeches and Mahalia Jackson, and what everybody else was doing. You know, we all did it together, the stuff you get into when you get your first royalty checks. Then you go crazy buying motorcycles or drugs or chicks or whatever, you know? And I was feeling that I needed a different kind of hug than a physical hug. That's for me where it began, where I knew that God was very intangible but at the same time very present.[42]

In his search for "a different kind of hug" Santana seems to embody a view of life that is concerned with transcendence in ways that are simultaneously both traditional and nontraditional. Santana's website summarizes part of Santana's outlook in the statement, "God created a circle of Light and Love so vast no one can stand outside of it."[43] Born in Jalisco, Mexico, and raised in San Francisco, "Santana, began to develop a style that blended the acid-rock of the Haight-Asbury era with blues and New York salsa."[44] The band Santana is characterized by a fusion of jazz, blues, rock, Cuban, and Puerto Rican rhythms mediated through the matrix of New York City, combined with a reworking of Mexican melodies from the San Francisco Bay area. Santana is a worldwide musical phenomenon with concerts in Europe, Mexico, and the United States.

Santana's spirituality and approach to *santo* are present in his music and his performances. "Sacred Fire: Live in Mexico," concerts in Mexico City performed in May of 1993 provide an example. Thousands attended the two performances. At the start of the concert Santana addressed the audience in Spanish saying,

We are all enchanted and inspired to be in your presence. Before we begin with the vibration of music, remember that in this moment if you take the time to see with your heart and the mind we shall see that we are surrounded completely by angels. We see the ancient ones (literally, *"los antiguos"*) and feel them dancing, always dancing in the flesh.[45]

Later, halfway through the concert and as an introduction to the song "Make Somebody Happy," Santana paused again to speak to the audience. As the music of the organ, guitars, and percussion played softly, not just in the background, but also in dialogue with what he was saying, Santana spoke these words in Spanish to his Mexican audience:

> We want you to know that we are very grateful to return to the heart of this country, which is this city, to be here with you and to let you know that you are very blessed. You are centered in the heart of Mexico, which is the Virgin of Guadalupe. Her vision is the same vision as in all our hearts. That the day will come when there will be no more flags, no more borders, and no wallets, so that the only thing that will exist will be the same thing that exists in Heaven, which is compassion, light, and harmony . . . compassion, compassion, compassion.[46]

Santana is a Latino who makes his home in the United States. He embraces and celebrates his Mexican roots, but also incorporates so much more that his appeal crosses many boundaries. In the concert the audience receives both a type of benediction and a charge to take responsibility, as Santana sends forth the audience from this spiritual encounter to do good to each other and to the wider world beyond the confines of the shared experience. Santana continues this pattern in his concerts, for example, in the more recent Shaman tour in which the concert attendees are invited to move beyond being spectators and in some sense to be cosmic participants; the audience receives a charge by Santana, who ended the concert with the song "Make Somebody Happy" and go forth with compassion.

Many Latinas and Latinos engaged in alternative spiritualities describe life as a spiritual journey. They explore something different from "traditional" religions, although not all see themselves as breaking from received religious traditions (whether they be Catholic or Protestant) as much as augmenting and completing what was lacking. One second-generation-Puerto Rican, born and raised in the United States and living in California described it this way:

I felt compelled to leave behind the Roman Catholic roots by which we were raised. It's funny . . . in making this choice I turned away from religious dogma and actually began having a truer relationship with God. In walking away from the church I started walking down the spiritual path. I intuitively believed that that we came from one source, the word "God" wasn't even important in those early years. . . . I also felt that the purpose of our lives was to deepen our connection, understanding, and expression of this source. It also made sense that if we were all from one source that we are united by this heritage in much deeper ways than the color of our skin, the location on the earth we were born and raised and the racial, social, cultural groups that we belonged to.[47]

Some Latinas and Latinos on this spiritual path describe moving from the Christian background of their families to explore varied traditions such as the Essenes, the mystical and esoteric traditions of Christianity and Judaism, the Gnostics, the Kabbalah, different types of Buddhism, Confucianism, Taoism, Hinduism, creation spirituality, the writings of Charles Fillmore (one of the founders of Unity Church), Ernest Holmes (the founder of the Church of Religious Science), the writings of Helena Petrovna Blavatsky (also known as Madame Blavatsky), one of the founders of the Theosophical Society, to name a few.

While many describe their spirituality as a journey, there is also a general recognition that people may follow different paths in life. Although there may be similarities, each is perceived to be unique. One such Latino explorer described the start of his journey this way:

I learned early that my travels down the spiritual path were not all about studying different religious traditions. I included yoga and meditation into my regular practice (I have been doing both since I was sixteen or seventeen years old). I certainly learned about the roots of these practices from the religions of the Far East, but they really became a part of my life because I initially recognized them as a way to maintain sound physical, mental, and emotional health. I found maintaining spiritual health was easier to do with these being tended to (I was thinking holistically before I even knew the term existed). I developed a spiritual credo. Whenever people reacted in surprise to learn that as a spiritual person I didn't attend a specific church, I told them I followed the old saying that the body is the temple and through staying conscious and aware of my body constantly, that I was in church every day. My wide net also included exploring psychic and astrological studies as well as other paranormal phenomena. Soon, anything that was considered metaphysical interested me.

This informant emphasized what he perceived to be the practical aspects of his path, which for him and others coincided with the appearance of the so-called New Age movement in the twentieth century. Some on their spiritual trek saw that if everything in the physical world, whether we can see it or not, is made of the same basic atomic matter, then all of life is truly from the same source. For Latinas and Latinos on these paths with many names, this one source is obviously intelligent beyond human comprehension and in some way connects to the feeling that some call love and others call God, the source that binds us all together. From the perspective of this particular understanding of *santo* all human beings have the opportunity and the challenge to love selves and others enough to create heaven here on earth.

TOWARD DEFINITIONS OF *SANTO*

With so many different concepts and expressions of the holy in many types of Latino/a contexts, is it possible to identify any common characteristics? Is there such a thing as one definition of *santo*? Standard Spanish dictionary definitions of *santo/santa* include the idea of something or someone who is "holy, saintly, blessed," and *santo* can be a designation for a saint or the image of a saint. But, as we have seen through the preceding brief stories and vignettes, *santo* can indicate many things. Before suggesting a working or wide-ranging definition of Latino/a spirituality, we need to consider what is meant by the term "spirituality."

As we have seen, the pursuit of spirituality is not solely the concern of cloistered monks or nuns or small religious communities on the periphery of cultural mainstreams. Sandra Schneiders describes spirituality as an existential phenomenon that is "a conscious and deliberate way of living."[48] Like many others, theologian Michael Downey recognizes there are many understandings of the nature of spirituality. Nevertheless, Downey sees two common understandings in the various contemporary definitions.

First, there is more to existence than the visible and the material, that is to say, that there is more to life than what can be apprehended physically; and second, people see spirituality as "a quest for a personal integration in the face of forces of fragmentation and depersonalization."[49] Elsewhere Downey characterizes many approaches to spirituality as being concerned withidentity, the basic question of "Who am I?"[50]

From a different perspective sociologist of religion Wade Clark Roof notes that respondents in the last part of the twentieth century defined spirituality as contrasted with being religious. "To be religious conveys an institutional connotation: to attend worship services, to say Mass, to light Hanukkah candles. To be spiritual, in contrast, is more personal and empowering and has to do with the deepest motivations of life."[51] Likewise, scholar of religion Robert Orsi observes that in popular culture in the United States the distinction made between being "spiritual" and being"religious" really points toward a value judgment being made between "good religion" and "bad religion" in which that which is perceived as good or true is called spirituality.[52] Pressing a difficult task of nomenclature further, sociologist Peter Holmes says that "hazarding a definition of spirituality, one can treat it (very inadequately) as the human search for meaning, particularly relationally, and that for many today this incorporates a supernatural/corporeal dimension that suggests many of us have discovered we are more than our physical biology."[53]

Even with a growing interest in the practice and definition of spirituality as different from institutionalized religion, sociologist Robert Wuthnow notes a shift in the United States from a "dwelling" spirituality to a "seeking" spirituality:

> There is profound confusion about how best to practice spirituality, especially because information now besieges people from all parts of the world, making particular religious traditions seem increasingly local and historically contingent. Thus, Americans are not simply people of faith who need to get religion back into the public life of their country; they are often confused individuals who are interested in spirituality but are unable to let organized religion solve all their problems and who therefore must work hard to figure out their own lives.[54]

Even in this brief survey we see that Latinas and Latinos also participate in this effort to practice spirituality, drawing upon multiple sources to
make sense of their daily lives.

There are generational differences in both dwelling and seeking types of
spirituality, and there are also various racial and ethnic realities, perspectives often overlooked in studies of spirituality. In a different context theologian Flora Wilson Bridges makes a very helpful observation regarding
African Americans and their religious expressions: "The African American
community, with its cultural tendency toward a unified worldview, does
not confine spirituality to religion, a building, or an institution. African
American religion and African American spirituality are not identical,
though the latter includes the former; African-American spirituality permeates all of black culture."[55] This reminds us that whatever Latino/a spirituality may be, it ought to be understood on its own terms.

Ronald Rolheiser describes spirituality as fundamentally human, an
internal unquenchable fire, an unrelenting desire at the core of human
experience, no matter what one's religious commitments or non-commit-
ments. Rolheiser expands on his claim:

> Long before we do anything explicitly religious at all, we have to do
> something about the fire that burns within us. What we do with that
> fire, how we channel it, is our spirituality. Thus, we all have a spiri-
> tuality, whether we want one or not, whether we are religious or not.
> Spirituality is more about whether or not we can sleep at night than
> about whether or not we go to church. It is about being integrated or
> falling apart, about being in harmony with Mother Earth or being
> alienated from her. Irrespective of whether or not we let ourselves
> be consciously shaped by an explicit religious idea, we act in ways
> that leave us healthy or unhealthy, loving or bitter. What shapes our
> actions is our spirituality.[56]

If Rolheiser asserts correctly that actions are shaped by spirituality,
that is all the more reason to emphasize the *lived* religion/spirituality of
lo cotidiano as Hispanic people seek to interact with the divine or the
transcendent, whatever they may call it, in their daily lives. Spirituality is
the relationship that exists, is experienced, reflected upon, and cultivated
for self-knowledge. It includes identity formation, insights about others,

creation of community, wisdom for living in the world, and answers to the big questions in life.[57] And it is at the level of popular religion or popular religiosity and spirituality that we have the greatest access to the varieties of *santo* in Latino/a spirituality.

It is now time to address a question that has been lurking in the background: Is it even appropriate to speak of a common, shared Latino/a spirituality when there are so many different definitions of spirituality? Moreover, is it legitimate to speak of a single Latino/a population? Even the U.S. Census Bureau with the imperfections of its system recognizes the variety that exists among U.S. Hispanics. And when greater attention is given to ethnic and regional differences, generational differences, and the importance of culture and context, is it fair to ask how one can speak of a common Latino/a spirituality without falling into some sort of essentialism?

The goal of this study is to focus on the impact of spirituality on real life, to explore the practical, and in turn to provide insight into the philosophical, theological, and lived aspects of spirituality. I maintain that the key to understanding the existence of a common, shared Latino/a spirituality lies in the connection between the many expressions of popular religion and the notions of Latino/a spirituality. The concept of popular religion has been widely explored, and it usually refers to lived religion at an everyday grassroots level and the location for doing theological reflection.[58] Popular religion also is seen as part of a "dynamic process of creating and maintaining personal worlds of meaning and the interconnectedness of the religiosity of a people within a given society."[59] Anthropologist and theologian Harold Recinos describes popular as "a defining characteristic of a social class which has common identity, based upon a situation of inequality."[60]

Theologian Orlando Espín, among others, has done extensive work in the area of popular religion. Speaking about popular Christianity in general and specifically about popular Catholicism and its connection to the relational networks of *lo cotidiano*, daily life, Espín observes that it "embodies and epistemologically organizes these daily relationships and symbolically expresses their connections to/with the broader social networks—including the 'sacred' networks—through the rites, beliefs, objects, and experiences of the people's religion."[61]

What Espín says about popular Christian religion is also true of forms of Latino/a religiosity and spirituality beyond the boundaries of Christianity. It is that daily mix of practices, beliefs, and rituals small and large in diverse contexts, that point to an abiding and overarching sense of compelling impulse and desire. Hence, this book is organized around themes. By addressing themes from different traditions, similarities and differences among the variety of traditions can be noted, with the assumption that in the context of life in the United States some overlapping elements of spirituality will emerge.

Whether or not the many manifestations of spirituality are called "Hispanic" or "Latino" is a separate issue from the cultural and social realities of daily life of people with Latin American roots who live in the United States. All of these different groups come under the rubric of "Hispanic" or "Latino/a." All of these individuals and groups have some sense of spirituality and call something *santo*, which represents a mutual human search for relational meaning that encompasses an aspect beyond the physical. There are many senses of holiness, some sharing things in common, some in opposition, sometimes both operating together in daily life of Latinas and Latinos. And although certain concepts of *santo* have regional or ethnic roots, the present growing national Latino/a reality is that these different understandings of *santo* are no longer exclusively regional characteristics or curiosities, but also are in contact with other traditions as they transform present understandings and actions. Just as the Latino/a population of the United States is more diverse than commonly perceived, so are the many Latino/a concepts of spirituality and what is holy, of what is *santo*.

THREE

Latino/a Peoples and the "Holy"

WHAT'S IN A NAME?

William Shakespeare's famous play about the ill-fated young lovers Romeo and Juliet contains a well-known line spoken by Juliet of the house of Capulet. It is delivered as she ponders on a moonlit balcony her beloved Romeo and his being a member of the enemy Montague clan: "What's in a name? that which we call a rose / By any other name would smell as sweet (*Romeo and Juliet* Act II, Scene II).

Does a name really matter? Does it make any difference what we call someone? Does it matter what someone calls us? For Shakespeare's teenage Juliet yearning for her lover, Romeo's name did not matter, but for the rest of her world it did, as we know from the tragic tale of the star-crossed pair. Moving from fiction to reality we can say that—certainly in the context of the United States, with estimates projecting that by the year 2050 at least a full quarter of the population will be of Latino/a origin—naming clearly does matter, especially in the area of racial and ethnic identity. In a very true sense the peoples called Hispanic, Latina, and Latino can be considered a "rose by any other name," with their rich identities, cultures, stories, systems, and indeed their own names. But in the racialized environment of the United States not only are certain peoples designated Hispanic and Latino/a but they also are given other names, identities, and groupings, some in an attempt to be descriptive, others in an unrelenting attitude of prejudice, discrimination, and hate.

Who are the peoples called "Hispanic"? This chapter will briefly review the historical roots and the contemporary phenomenon called by the name Hispanic and Latino/as in order to get a sense of what they are called by others, and by whom. This chapter will also consider how these people name themselves as well as chart those identities in the larger context of life in the United States. In so doing, an important matter will be addressed, namely, whether or not we have seen the creation of a "Hispanic" identity in the United States. This in turn has an impact on understanding the religions, spiritualities, metaphysical understandings, and ritual practices of those named Hispanics or Latino/as. We will consider ethnic identities as they are related to religion and the various concepts of *santo* (holy) in the various communities. We will also consider the concept of a *pueblo* (people) with a common *latinidad* and the possibility of a shared pan-Latino/a spirituality.

TRANSNATIONAL AND HISTORICAL PERSPECTIVES

Naming Hispanics and Latino/as in the United States has roots in history that precede the creation of the nation and extend beyond its present national borders, calling therefore for both historical and transnational approaches. Perhaps more often than not, when people encounter the word "transnational," the term evokes the large-scale economic operations of international corporations, globalization, and the international movement of resources and capital; and they would be correct. But transnational also can refer to social formation across borders. Transnationalism may include a consciousness of being connected simultaneously to two places, a type of cultural production that encompasses notions of hybridity of social institutions and everyday practices; it may also encompass the transference and reconstruction of particular social spaces.[1]

Jorge Duany offers his definition of transnationalism as the creation of "dense social fields through the circulation of people, ideas, practices, money, goods, and information across nations. This circulation includes, but is not limited to, physical movement of human bodies as well as other types of exchanges, which may or may not be recurrent, such as travel, communication, and remittances."[2] A transnational perspective is one that recognizes the multiple and complex connections and interactions that link people or institutions across the boundaries of modern nation-states.

Although not always recognized, in world history there have always been significant migrations of people. Many of the people who became known as Hispanic are the results of individual and group migrations, with the notable exception of those Spanish-speaking peoples who became part of the United States through the territorial expansion of the nineteenth century, most notably the incorporation of what became the U.S. Southwest. Since the mid-twentieth century until the present, there has been an unprecedented global movement of peoples increasingly characterized by what some refer to as "grassroots transnationalism":

> Immigrants have not only moved across national borders in increasing numbers, but now use technological advances ranging from the Internet and cellular phones to inexpensive air travel in order to tap strategically into the resources and networks available to them in their countries of origin. Yet, even as they manage to keep in close contact with their societies of origin, immigrants become integrated into their countries of settlement.[3]

These immigrants draw upon grassroots social capital in several locations as they carve out new lives for themselves in the United States. At the same time transnational migrations are not the same and that attention should be given to these different forms.

With the growth of concurrent local and global everyday experience of transnational lives, there is no clean, clear, and final break with the home country. Indeed, in some cases in prior generations there never was such a break either, in that some bond may have been retained, either real or imagined. Exploring the concept of globalization and some of the challenges it presents, Manuel Vásquez and Marie Marquardt advocate a concept of globalization seen as:

> a complex, historically contingent cluster of processes involving multiple actors, scales, and realms of human activity. These processes have contradictory effects for local life and for religious organizations, discourses, and practices. Globalization is not just about domination and homogenization. It also involves resistance, heterogeneity, and the active negotiation of space, time, and identity at the grassroots.[4]

In an increasingly globalized society, migrants and their children retain links with the sending country in terms of practices and relationships, identities and social structures, contributing to a situation in which individuals and groups acquire and live with multiple and concurrent names and identities.[5] Therefore, a fuller understanding of who Hispanics and Latino/as are can be obtained only when those people are considered through the lenses of globalization and transnationalism and how they impact transnational identities.

Within the context of globalization and transnational movements, simply stated the peoples called Hispanics, Latinos, and Latinas in the United States are those who have roots in Latin America. But as is the case for much of life, what seems simple may be quite complex. Some of these people are recent arrivals to the United States as transnational migrants (indeed the popular image is of swarthy "illegal" immigrants in the shadows of society). In fact most are U.S. citizens with families who have been in the United States for generations. Many persons in this group are English-dominant and have less of a directly felt connection with ancestral homes than do their parents, grandparents, and great-grandparents; at the same time, however, they may fervently claim an identity as Dominicana, Salvadoreña, Cubana, Puertorriqueño, Chicana, Mexicano, and for many in some sense simultaneously Latino and Latina.[6]

When it is realized that certain recent Latin American immigrants are indigenous people who do not speak Spanish or speak it as a second language, the issue of using language as a common criterion for a shared identity is further complicated. Moreover, sometimes people from Brazil have been included in this collective U.S. group even though the common language of that nation is not Spanish but Portuguese, reflecting its colonial history and the broader history of Europe and the Atlantic world.[7] Curiously, while Brazilians may or may not be included in the Hispanic/Latino grouping, people with direct roots in Portugal usually are not included in the Hispanic or Latino/a category.

Origins in Mexico

There have been people of Spanish, Portuguese, and Latin American descent in the United States since the founding of the nation, including Spanish-speaking residents of Louisiana when that territory was acquired from France in 1803. The first major influx of people, however, who became known as Hispanics-Latino/Latinas was not due to immigration. Approximately 55 percent of the territory of Mexico was acquired as victor spoils in the U.S.-Mexican War of 1846–48 (also known as the Mexican-American

War).[8] Spanish-speaking people of European, indigenous, African, *mestizo*, and other "mixed" descents experienced the international border crossing as the lands where they lived became part of the United States. The provisions of the Treaty of Guadalupe Hidalgo gave these former Mexicans only minimal citizenship and property rights, rights that in the decades that followed were abused and ignored.[9] The new border had an imagined aspect to it that could be seen in the second half of the nineteenth century and in the early part of the twentieth, and movement across the new international frontier was relatively open as Mexicans and Mexican Americans moved freely back and forth in response to personal, familial, economic, and political concerns.

The Mexican Revolution that began in 1910 and the Cristero War of 1926–29 were upheavals that provided one catalyst for the movement of people from Mexico to the United States in the early twentieth century. Another was the economic demand in the United States for cheap labor from Mexico. During World War I the U.S. federal government actively recruited workers from Mexico. After the war, many of those Mexican workers stayed in the Southwest, but others showed up in other parts of the country, for example, laborers for the Pennsylvania Railroad and in the mushroom houses of Chester County, Pennsylvania, or as manufacturing and agricultural workers in the upper Midwest.[10] Some of these people remained even after hostilities ended in Mexico.

With the advent of the international Great Depression in 1929, Mexicans and Mexican Americans were seen as competitors for the decreasing number of jobs and declining wages, becoming scapegoats for the economic crisis. In the period between 1929 and 1939 this perception prompted the U.S. government to forcibly deport, in most cases without due process, between five hundred thousand and one million people to Mexico, many of who were U.S. citizens.

The areas targeted were those that had large populations of people of Mexican descent, including California, Texas, Colorado, Illinois, and Michigan.[11] Ironically the deportation policy was reversed when with the entry of the United States into World War II in 1941, there was a new need for manual labor, especially agricultural labor, and the United States and Mexico negotiated the Bracero Program. This was an arrangement that intentionally recruited Mexican guest workers from 1942 to 1964 and at its peak drew up to four hundred thousand Mexican workers a year.[12] Even long after the end of the Bracero Program economic factors continue to draw Mexican workers to the United States. Many of these workers were seasonal, but some remained, and their children born in the United States were of course U.S. citizens.

Origins in Cuba

Elsewhere international interventions by the United States contributed to an early transnational flow of people from Cuba, Puerto Rico, and the Dominican Republic. In the Spanish-speaking Caribbean, the United States had a long-time interest in Cuba, which came to a head when the Cuban war for independence from Spain got wrapped up with the Spanish-American War of 1898. Through that conflict the United States openly claimed its role as a global empire, acquiring Puerto Rico, the Philippines, and Guam from Spain, establishing a military occupation of the technically independent Cuba (1899–1902), and creating to all intents and purposes a protectorate over the new Cuban republic under the Platt Amendment (1901) until 1934.[13]

Within this context initially the majority of early Cuban immigrants went to New York City as the ideal entry point to the United States. It was a familiar location, for since the early nineteenth century Cuban businessmen, political activists, and artists had been traveling there. The Cuban community in Florida, and particularly in Miami, grew more slowly, starting only in the 1920s, with some modest growth after World War II and spiking after 1959 in response to the Cuban Revolution. Other waves of Cuban immigration took place, including in 1961, 1965, and 1980 with the Mariel boatlift.

Origins in Puerto Rico

Another result of the war of 1898 was that in 1917 Puerto Ricans were granted U.S. citizenship, but not all of the constitutional rights of that citizenship. In 1952 the Estado Libre Asociado de Puerto Rico (Associated Free State of Puerto Rico) was established, giving the island limited self-government as a U.S. Commonwealth, though what that exactly means is still hotly debated. Although since 1898 there had been a small but growing migration of Puerto Ricans to the mainland and Hawaii, it was the

Commonwealth government and its predecessor that drove the major migrations of Puerto Ricans in the late 1940s through the 1960s, particularly through its Farm Labor Program, with the majority of the agricultural workers going to the Northeast. The majority of these *tomateros* ("tomato pickers") worked in New Jersey, Connecticut, Delaware, Massachusetts, New York, and Pennsylvania.[14] After World War II and the advent of regular and subsidized air service, waves of Puerto Ricans migrated to the mainland. Their status as U.S. citizens allows Puerto Ricans to travel back and forth, with generations growing up outside the island, creating separate diaspora identities.[15]

Other Origins in the Caribbean

Major Dominican migration and the growing community in the United States also are tied to the actions of the United States on the island of Hispaniola.[16] The United States intervened militarily in the Dominican Republic in the years 1916 to 1924 because of internal instability and foreign debt, and again in 1961 in the wake of political unrest following the assassination of the dictator Rafael Trujillo in 1961.[17] Immigration aided by migration networks continued through the late 1970s due to ongoing political repression and growing unemployment. Another major wave of Dominican migration to the United States began in the 1980s.

To an astonishing degree Dominicans have cultivated an active transnational consciousness, practice, and identity as part of their lives in the United States, particularly since the Dominican government allows Dominicans to retain their citizenship even after becoming U.S. citizens.[18] Since 1961 the Dominican population has continued to increase. Moreover, a significant Dominican migration to Puerto Rico has added to the diversity of Hispanic/Latino peoples while also challenging racial categories in the United States.[19]

Origins in Central America

Historically U.S. foreign policy in Central America and South America has reflected the attitude that intervention was acceptable because this was the "backyard" of the United States. In Central America, of course, it is well known that during his presidency Theodore Roosevelt was instrumental in the creation of the nation of Panama and the construction of the Panama

Canal, which then allowed the United States to be involved in Panamanian affairs for decades.

Elsewhere in Central America the United States intervened directly in Nicaragua (from 1912 to 1933, and again in the 1980s); in El Salvador (1980 to 1992); and in Guatemala (1960 to 1996). Guatemala experienced a U.S.-backed dictatorship beginning in 1954. The related political upheavals during the period 1974 to 1996 contributed directly to up to as many as three million persons seeking refuge in other countries, including Mexico, Canada, and the United States.[20] Massive human rights violations and the threat of death caused people to flee for their lives, many arriving in the United States, ultimately resulting in the present communities of Nicaraguans, Salvadorans, and Guatemalans. The 2010 U.S. Census showed that Central Americans represented 8.1 percent of U.S. Hispanics with Salvadorans as the largest group at 1.6 million, followed by Guatemalans (1.0 million) and over 633,000 Hondurans.[21]

Origins in South America

In response to the overthrow of the elected government of Salvador Allende and the establishment of a repressive dictatorship under Augusto Pinochet in 1973, during which thousands of people were imprisoned and others disappeared, many Chileans arrived in the United States as political refugees. Since the 1980s, due in part to economic and political turmoil, there has been increased migration to the United States from Brazil, Peru, Ecuador, and Colombia. Many of the rural migrants are indigenous peoples of South America, for example, the Quechua and Aymara.[22**] Again, people sought political refuge in many cases with the hope that it would be for only a short while, only to see such exiles transformed into something longer lasting.

The preceding is simply a synopsis of the international actions and movements that resulted in the presence of the peoples named Hispanic and Latino/a. Much is made of comparisons with earlier migrations to the United States, particularly of those peoples from northern Europe. Lest one succumb to romanticized revisionist history, Timothy Henderson's observation is extremely helpful:

> In a letter dated 1753, no less a figure than Benjamin Franklin vented
> against German immigrants to Pennsylvania calling them "ignorant,"

"stupid," "swarthy," and a threat to American culture and freedom. Similar scorn has, throughout American history, been heaped upon the Irish, Italians, Spaniards, Jews, Catholics, Slavs, Asians, Africans, Muslims—that is, virtually every group of people that has alighted on these shores in numbers large enough to get themselves noticed. American history is punctuated with "nativist" movements, that is, movements that seek to privilege the interests of the native born over those of immigrants. A great irony of American life is that each generation of nativists are themselves likely the descendants of immigrants, who may have been reviled by unwelcoming citizens in an earlier day.[23]

A significant difference from earlier immigration waves from Europe is the ongoing migration from Latin America and continuing transnational connections with the nations of origin, including the flow of capital, correspondence, news, and information, which has an ongoing impact on the creation of communal and individual identity in the United States. There are not only financial remittances, but also "cultural remittances" that are transforming both the home communities and those in the United States, which for some is the new home. Juan Flores states that "cultural remittances—eminently transnational as a consequence of circular migration and the ubiquity of contemporary communications technology—implode in the national territory as something foreign, and yet in their local relevance not so foreign after all."[24]

Other Origins

In some cases the issue of U.S. Hispanic identity is not restricted to persons with roots in Latin America. Aviva Ben-Ur explores the subject of Sephardic Jews who immigrated to the United States from Europe, the Mediterranean region, and the Middle East, and how they fit into U.S. racial and ethnic categories. The ambiguity of Hispanic identity comes into play when the Iberian element of Sephardic heritage interacts with U.S. concepts of race and racial minority status. In 1992 a U.S. federal court of appeals ruled that Sephardim are entitled to the protection offered Hispanics under the U.S. Civil Rights Act of 1964. Ben-Ur observes that in this context "ethnic identity—and its more recent intensification into implicit racial identity—is shaped by numerous internal and external factors, some imported from the 'old country,' others forged on American soil, testifying to shifting group identity."[25] An additional layer is added to the identity of those Jews, whether Sephardic or Ashkenazi, who came to the United States after some individual or family sojourn in Latin America; they are classified as Hispanic.

While agreeing with other scholars that there is historical support for the view that some Sephardic Jews preserved their Jewish identity and practices in colonial New Spain (Mexico), Ben-Ur questions whether there is evidence that supports the claims of contemporary Southwest Hispanos of crypto-Jewish heritage.[26] The contention arises because some Southwest Hispanics who claim crypto-Jewish heritage also say that they are Christian, either Catholic or Protestant, and some also acknowledge Native American and other European aspects of their heritage. All of this brings into question what constitutes Jewish identity and what represents a continuity of self-identity and praxis from the early modern period to the early twenty-first century. Are selected family stories, interpretations of contemporary practices and their history, and suppositions about genetic characteristics enough to confirm crypto-Jewish identity? And how does Jewish identity interact with U.S. Hispanic identity?

Origins in the United States

As mentioned previously, a significant part of the U.S. Hispanic population has never immigrated. Over 62 percent of Latino/as were born in the United States, and the majority of those so born are English-dominant, while a number are bilingual, and a very small percentage Spanish-dominant. Of those surveyed, the overwhelming majority of the adult children of Hispanic immigrants speak English.[27] For many of the people called Hispanic or Latino/a, especially since 1965, their lives and identity are influenced by the experience of migration, which may also be understood as exile or diaspora, whereas those born and raised in the United States may be treated as unwanted strangers in the land of their birth. Another illustration of the complexity that constantly defies preconceived categories is the testimony of self-identification. For example, "I am the United States born daughter of an African American man and a Mexican woman. I grew up in a Black neighborhood in Los Angeles, but I spent my first eighteen summers in Mexico City where my mother's family lives."[28]

The multiplicity of individual and group histories and experiences contribute to the creation of such complex identities. Moreover, as Manuel Vásquez writes, the increasing demographic diversification of Latino/as also contributes to increased religious diversification that includes "the rapid growth of 'pneumatic' Christianity, the revitalization of traditional popular Catholicism, the proliferation of African-based and mediumship-based religions, and the reaffirmation of traditions (*costumbres*) connected with indigenous identity."[29]

THE POWER OF NAMING

The peoples in the United States named Hispanics-Latino/as are part of a long, complex transnational movement of peoples from Latin America to the north. For various historical, political, social, and economic reasons, there is a desire in the United Sates to have a collective designation for these diverse peoples with their varied history. On the one hand, Latinas and Latinos are connected with their varied roots whether they are recent arrivals from Latin America or trace their family's presence in North America over several generations, or even a few centuries. On the other hand, Hispanics do not come from one country nor are they of one race in the usual sense of race.

For some people the use of "Hispanic" or "Latino/a" to refer to the same group is confusing and frustrating. There does not seem to be an established way to predict who will use which term when and for what purpose. There might be localized preferences for one term or the other and even a reaction of deep offense when a certain collective term is used. Others use the terms interchangeably. At one time the federal government seemed to favor "Hispanic," whereas recently the term "Latino/a" is being used more often.

Among some people of Latin American heritage, the gender-sensitive term "Latino/a" is the preferred self-designation because it is perceived as better able to describe the Latin American roots of the various communities, deemphasizing any connection to Spain. Strictly speaking, according to advocates of the designation "Latino/a," not all Latinas and Latinos are Hispanic, in the sense that they are of Latin American or Caribbean heritage and not of European descent and for whom Spanish may be a second language. Such is the case among indigenous groups in Central and South

America. Hence it is argued by many within the community that "Latino/a" is a more appropriate designation.

But an appeal to Latin America for a common designation is problematic in that the concept of Latin America has its origin in a nineteenth-century attempt to connect the Romance language areas of the Americas with the Romance language–speaking regions of Europe; the reasoning was that "Latin America" together with "Latin Europe" were component parts of a "Latin race" that was engaged in a struggle with the "Anglo-Saxon race." With adherents in the Americas, this concept of Latin America was particularly appealing to the French under Emperor Napoleon III, who sought to expand France's influence and presence in the Americas, especially through intervention in Mexico.[30] Thus, the geographic and cultural designation "Latin America" (from which Latino/a derives) appeared in the nineteenth century as a way to connect those areas of the Americas that spoke Spanish, Portuguese, and French with the wider linguistic and cultural heritage of ancient Rome as manifested in Europe. At its inception the concept of Latin America was a Eurocentric hegemonic effort connected to the neo-colonial/imperial project of modernity, even if that fact generally is now long forgotten.[31]

While "Spanish" and "Spanish-speaking" (as well as numerous pejorative expressions) were used as early collective labels, the term "Hispanic" gained wide usage starting in the 1970s. But from the start there were those who pointed to "Hispanic" as a politically incorrect reference that reeked of European hegemony. So, while the critique of the term "Hispanic" as a designation of the dominant society is compelling for some, the use of the term "Latino/a" also is problematic, at least historically, as it evokes the European, Spanish-Latin heritage at the expense of Native American, African, Asian, and non-Spanish European heritages of Latin American or Caribbean peoples.

To complicate matters further, there are many in the United States who reject "Latino/a" as too closely linked with radical left-wing politics in both the United States and Latin America. Then there is the case of those in New Mexico who wish to affirm their Spanish heritage and call themselves Hispanos. The compounded irony is that both terms used as self-identifiers and descriptions mask the complexity of a diverse cultural heritage of the very people they seek to describe.

The power of naming disguises the ethnic, linguistic, cultural, and class distinctiveness and differences that are present in U.S. society. Depending upon the nature and origin of a name, a false consciousness can be fostered, both externally about a group and internally among the people being named. In other words, naming may be interpreted as a concerted effort to tell people that they are something other than what they perceive themselves to be. This imposition can be made through ignorance, coercion, deceit, or a combination of factors. When it happens, individuals and groups are then expected to subscribe to a classification constructed by others, and they often fall into the trap of domination, sometimes unawares.

A people's cultural past is often ignored or reinterpreted to accommodate the dominant cultural constructions and myths. For example in Morris County, New Jersey, Fairfield County, Connecticut, and Lancaster County, Pennsylvania, it is still very common to hear Latin American cuisine referred to as "Spanish food." But the food usually originates with people of Latin American descent; while these dishes have their origins in, for example, Ecuador, Puerto Rico, the Dominican Republic, or Cuba, none of it is made by Spaniards.

During this present period filled with rhetoric about multiculturalism and pluralism in the United States, a powerful cultural concept of the melting pot works against pluralism. The melting pot is defined as the process of assimilation of disparate groups into a larger uniform entity in which all are equal and all are treated impartially. Versions of the metaphor have been in use since early in the life of the United States, but the concept was popularized by the 1908 staging of the play "The Melting Pot" by Israel Zangwill, which was enthusiastically endorsed by President Theodore Roosevelt.[32]

Contrary to the account of this influential social myth, the melting pot does not function in this fashion. In the United States there is not and never has been a single homogenized unit, "the melting pot," but rather the constrained fabrication of two homogenized groups: one "white" and the other "black," essentially two races divided by a purportedly objective "color-line."[33] W. E. B. Du Bois identified this problem of the color-line in the United States as the great problem of the twentieth century, and there is every indication that it will continue into this twenty-first century. As theologian Michelle Gonzalez succinctly puts it, "The rhetoric of race in the United States allows for two possibilities: one is either black or white."[34]

In the debate regarding use of either "Hispanic" or "Latino" there is a sense that Latin Americans and people of Latin American descent are forced into the fixed categories of "white" and "non-white," with the latter defined in terms of blackness, whether or not African heritage actually is involved. Individuals and groups are socially positioned as members within the dominant white society or they are assigned to the category of the "colored" other.

Of course this analysis of the existence of a twofold racial division is not unique, although it is not always widely accepted. In a series of public lectures the French philosopher Michel Foucault explained that "the war that is going on beneath order and peace, the war that undermines our society and divides it in a binary mode is basically, a race war . . . [one in which the] social body is articulated around two races."[35] At a time of increasing population diversity and a growing declaration of multiracial identity, the concepts of race and ethnicity in the United States continue to be dominated by those two specific predetermined racial categories.[36] Any deviation from these categories results in the renaming of a group and often an attempt to impose a new consciousness.

The rich diversity of peoples in the United States is reinterpreted by the dominant society through the rubric of the color-line. There have always been some designated "unmeltable" ethnic groups in the United States applying to those of non-Anglo-Saxon European descent, and today this group includes the peoples called Latino/as.[37] Moreover, racial and ethnic homogenization into a common category is often accompanied by a historical and political amnesia that seeks to brush aside the history of conquest and colonization that resulted in immigration. The imposition of racial identities in the United States in which Hispanics are forced to one side of the color-line belongs to the context that impacts the maintenance, creation, nurture, development, and re-creation of Latino/a practices and expressions of religiosity and spirituality.

In the case of Latinas and Latinos this is a problem of both a homogenized category and a problem of nomenclature. The racial/ethnic-based labels in the United States are problematic in that they are neither truly descriptive nor do they positively add to a description of peoples who are already cross-cultural, multiracial, and multicultural. Reducing people to preconceived stereotypic traits and interchangeable generic categories erases their unique characteristics while perpetuating prejudiced perceptions and actions of the dominant society. The use of socioeconomic class, internal concepts of ethnic identity and national origin, and racial and ethnic stereotyping masks distinctive cultural heritages and various types of oppression.

Both the ongoing power of the myth of the melting pot and the difficulties that arise in sustaining it can be seen in the decennial counting of the population of the United States. That this is a social construction of race rather than a description of self-evident universal types can be readily seen in the categories used by the U.S. Census Bureau in 2010 for Hispanics or Latinos. The recent census form first asked each respondent if they were "of Hispanic, Latino, or Spanish origin." If the answer was yes, the respondent was then asked to check one of the following categories "Mexican, Mexican Am., Chicano," "Puerto Rican," "Cuban," "another Hispanic, Latino or Spanish origin" (with the option to write in that identification) "for example Argentinean, Colombian, Dominican, Nicaraguan, Salvadoran, Spanish, and so on."

The next census question then asked the respondent to identify her/his race using the following categories: White; Black, African Am., or Negro; American Indian or Alaska Native (print name of enrolled or principal tribe); Asian Indian; Chinese; Filipino; Other Asian (print race, for example, Hmong, Laotian, Thai, Pakistani, Cambodian, and so on); Japanese; Korean; Vietnamese; Native Hawaiian; Guamanian or Chamorro; Samoan; Other Pacific Islander (print race, for example, Fijian, Tongan, and so on); Some other race (print race).

While from one perspective this recent listing of categories represents an improvement over previous census designations, especially in allowances made for people who identify with more than one race, peoples of Latin American ancestry still have difficulties with these categories. In the United States, race and ethnicity are falsely seen as descriptive and immutable conceptual terms, objectively available for all to see and appropriate. One example that defies common racial understanding can be found in the complexity of Dominican identity in the United States.[38] In such a context "Hispanic" is not descriptive of a homogeneous people but a designation of the dominant society's preconceived notions of what is Hispanic. This can readily be seen in the concerted efforts of marketers, media, occasionally politicians, and even religious communities to reach out to "Hispanics."

The arbitrariness of the categories is also seen in another of the racial options, "American Indian or Alaska Native," which then allowed a respondent to indicate a specific "Tribe." According to the Census Bureau, "American Indian or Alaska Native" refers to "people having origins in any of the original peoples of North and South America (including Central America), and who maintain tribal affiliation or community attachment. It includes people who indicated their race or races by marking this category or writing in their principal enrolled tribe, for example, Rosebud Sioux, Chippewa, or Navajo." The 2000 Census showed a significant growth in the number of people who self-identified as "American Indian" *but also* in the number of people who identified themselves as both Hispanic and American Indian. In other words, self-identified Latin American indigenous migrants could "identify both ethnically as Latinos and racially as American Indians."[39] Indigenous peoples from Latin America who find themselves in the United States are placed in categories that do not reflect their historical realities where the tribal definitions of the United States are not applicable.

THE SOCIAL CONSTRUCTION OF RACE

The preceding brief historical sketch of historical roots in Latin America indicates that the grouping of Latinos and Latinas in the United States is not a self-evident or natural categorization, but rather the result of dominant understandings of race and ethnicity and the social construction of race in the United States. One aspect of the challenge is determining exactly what we mean by race. Michael Omi and Howard Winant effectively articulate the social construction of race in the United States. In actuality there are no essential racial characteristics, but rather a history of race in which there always has been a certain flexibility in racial categories. For Omi and Winant, racial formation is "the sociohistorical process by which racial categories are created, inhabited, transformed, and destroyed."[40] Howard Winant writes elsewhere:

Race is a concept that signifies and symbolizes sociopolitical conflicts and interests in reference to different types of human bodies.

Although the concept of race appeals to biologically based human characteristics (so-called phenotypes), selection of these particular human features for purposes of racial signification is always and necessarily a social and historical process.[41]

Rather than being objectively descriptive labels, "Hispanic" and "Latino/a" are expressions of the dominant social construction of race. In the social, cultural, and ideological naming process "Hispanic" and "Latino/a" are interpretative codes and racial descriptors with meanings in the everyday experiences of people in the United States that can shape "the presentation of self, distinctions of status, and appropriate modes of conduct."[42] There is no place on the globe where we can point and say, "That is where all the Hispanics, Latinas, and Latinos come from." A person with Latin American roots is designated as a Latino or Latina in the context of the United States.

Race-based labels are problematic in that they are not truly descriptive nor do they positively add to the discussion. They do violence to the people they purport to describe, and they support members of the dominant society in their prejudiced perceptions and actions. This is done by reducing people to preconceived stereotypes and interchangeable categories, emphasizing contingent identities of race rather than dealing forthrightly with issues of socioeconomic class, national origin, and religious identities.[43]

Prior to coming to the United States (or the United States coming to them in the case of Chicano/as and Puerto Ricans), Latin Americans understood themselves in ways different from the common Eurocentric understanding of the dominant society. Self-identification was often made in terms of national or distinct subgroups found within particular nations of origins. Additionally people of Latin American heritage living in the United States carried with them their concepts of class divisions as experienced in their nations of origin, as well as alternative concepts of race existing in those contexts. Upon arrival in the United States they perceived another class arrangement at work, one couched in different terms. Although for many Latin Americans the division between "white" and "black" is not anything new, nevertheless it is inadequate for incorporating racial, ethnic, and cultural distinctions found in their countries of origin. At the same time there is a recognition of "the way things work," which compels them to deal with the power of the U.S. color-line.

The difficulty is that these types group together U.S.-born people, recent arrivals, Spanish-dominant, English-dominant, those whose everyday language is neither English nor Spanish, bilingual, and bicultural peoples of European, indigenous, African, and mixed ancestry all under one homogenized label that masks the differences of culture, history, religion, gender, and class. While employing a homogenized term may be beneficial to government and to those involved in politics and advertising or ecclesial and other religious groups, the creation of a core identity around one characteristic, that of the Spanish language, masks the diversity of the many Latin American and U.S. elements of the group while advancing the notion "that there are indeed some essential and intrinsic characteristics that all 'Hispanics' share."[44]

LATINIDAD, MULTIPLE CONSCIOUSNESS, AND SPIRITUALITY

While there are problems with the designations Hispanic and Latino/a, nevertheless, there is still a need for a common term to cover these diverse populations collectively, because within the context of the United States there is an ongoing sense of a collective pan-ethnic and pan-racial identity that paradoxically maintains much of the diversity of the component parts. This in turn impacts the understanding of the religions, spiritualities, folk metaphysical understandings, and ritual practices of those called Hispanics or Latino/as. There are connections between ethnic identities as they are related to religion and the various concepts of *santo* in the various communities and the shared concept of *pueblo* (people) with a common *latinidad.* This in turn impacts the entire religious and cultural landscape of the United States.[45]

As we seek to name this pan-ethnic, pan-racial reality Michelle Gonzalez appropriately challenges theologians (and others) on issues of unity and diversity as a feature of Latino/a theology: "Latino/a theologians must become more nuanced in their elaboration of Latino/a identity. We cannot afford to erase or marginalize portions of our population in favor of a more generalized description of our identity. To do so is to do violence to the communities we ignore and forget. An emphasis on particularity within community is both theological and ethical."[46] So the challenge is to describe the shared identity without falling into an essentialized fantasy or obliterating the particular components.

Part of the response to this challenge lies in recognizing the complexity of a shared *latinidad*, a type of "Latino-ness." Juana María Rodríguez helpfully and succinctly poses the issue before us in defining what is meant by *latinidad*:

> Here different discourses of history, geography, and language practices collide. *Latinidad* serves to define a particular geopolitical experience, but it also contains within it the complexities and contradictions of immigration, (post)(neo)colonialism, race, color, legal status, class, nation, language, and the politics of location. So what constitutes *latinidad*? Who is Latina? Is *latinidad* in the blood, in a certain geographic space? Is it about language, history, and culture, or is it a certain set of experiences?[47]

My answer to the questions posed by Rodríguez is "yes" to all of the above. I think that the key to recognizing a shared Latino/a identity, a collective *latinidad*, is a willingness to recognize that it is fluid, shifting, and adaptive in nature. Race, ethnicity, class, language, location, and religion compound whatever hybridity is brought to the changing conditions of the U.S. context, but they are not wiped away in a mythological melting pot nor confined to a racial black/white binary. Marta Caminero-Santangelo helpfully explains the nature of the shared *latinidad* at work":

> If we can imagine not a single, monolithic *Latinidad* which must continually make a case for overarching commonalities among all groups—a case which inevitably fails—but rather, multiple *latinidades*, which reach across national-origin lines but need not account in some comprehensive way for *all*, then the notion of panethnicity does indeed begin to make more sense, as one form of identity— among several—with which we can engage.[48]

Such a shared, shifting, and creative *latinidad* occurs every day and is recognizable, but is not reducible to any one characteristic.

Latinidad is distinct from notions of race and ethnicity, signifying that Latinas and Latinos have coexisting multiple identities. In a sense *latinidad* interacts with the social construction of race in the United States and the various notions of race that have roots in Latin America. Simultaneously *latinidad* becomes an expression of multiple consciousnesses. Multiple consciousness seems to be an especially prevalent reality for second and later generations of Latinas and Latinos, complicated further by parental couplings that go beyond traditional boundaries, for example, parents who are Ecuadorian and African American, Puerto Rican and Anglo, Guatemalan and Salvadoran, Mexican and Puerto Rican, Cuban and Syrian, Afro-Puerto Rican and White Jew, Chilean and Mexican, Argentine and Spaniard, and so on.

Certainly one aspect of multiple consciousness, whatever one's heritage, is intermingled identities in a social context that likes to view things in black and white and in which the affirmation of one thing means the denial of another. This poses challenges for the dominant society in the United States, according to Henry Goldschmidt, who says, "The first commandment, so to speak, of American multiculturalism [is]: Thou shalt define thyself in terms we understand."[49] Robert Atkinson, who participated in a study about Latino/as in Maine, makes an observation about identity construction that is applicable here: "The first is: the world will tell you who you are until you tell the world. The second is: The story we tell about ourselves is who we are."[50]

After all the previous discussion, is it still appropriate and legitimate to discuss such a thing as Latino/a spirituality? The answer is yes with the proviso that there are different definitions of spirituality just as there is in a variety of Hispanics who have ethnic and regional differences and generational distinctiveness. Shared characteristics across groups include the *importance of community and family* and the *shared experience of assigned identity* in the United States.[51]

In all of this the importance of culture and context is visible. There are many constructions and meanings given to *latinidad*, and spirituality is one of the paths on which that construction happens. As theologian Dwight Hopkins observes, "Culture is where the sacred reveals itself. As a result, one only knows what she or he is created to be and called to do through the human realm of culture."[52]

Despite all the difficulties and caveats, in a very real day-to-day sense there is a pan-Latino/a reality, a *latinidad* in the United States that has emerged. Whether this cultural reality is called Hispanic or Latino or goes by the name *mestizaje* is a separate issue from the social reality of this developing, collective, pan-ethnic identity of people with Latin American roots living in the United States.[53] The conditions of life in the United States, including imposed racial identities, compel this growing sense of group identity. In this context of the U.S. color-line, "what is in a name" can best be seen through consideration of the sacred, spiritual, and religious practices, life passages, rhetoric, traditions, and sacred spaces of the peoples called Hispanic and Latino/a.

FOUR

Rituals in the Passages of Life

It is commonly agreed that all persons experience different stages or cycles of their life. The challenge is not to project one's own life passage as normative for everyone else. In considering major theories regarding the stages of the life cycle, the late scholar of social work, public health, and psychiatry Sonia G. Austrian, showed that developmental theories about the human life cycle are not new and appear in the Talmud, Confucius, and Solon, all of whom identified in their own ways different phases of life, and interestingly all focusing on adulthood.[1] This chapter explores different ways the search for the holy and the practice of the sacred are manifested in the ordinary, yet important experiences of life passages within the diverse Hispanic /Latino community.

Because of ongoing transnational connections and identifications with the countries of origin in Latin America, consideration of this aspect of *santo* includes how life passages and milestones are noted in places of *raíces* (roots) as well as how they are transformed in the United States. In addition, the transnational migration and movements of people reconstruct understandings and practices within the life cycle and contribute to the formation of global cultures.[2] Life cycle rituals in the community include both popular and formal examples of spirituality.

MARKING COMMUNITY THROUGH RITUAL

Within Latino/a communities special days are remembered and celebrated, some widely, with others marked only by smaller groups. These distinctive days of celebration and commemoration are landmarks in the life of the community, its families, and individuals. For some persons, these days are the most important markers of the passage of time.

Some of these specially designated passages are connected to the Christian liturgical year, but many Latinas and Latinos celebrate them regardless of their profession of Christianity (or lack thereof). Indeed, some

Latinas and Latinos express discomfort praying and partaking in the rituals of Christian life, but participate because of their connections to family. Others embrace new ritual or ceremonial markers for life by creating a new type of ceremony, for example, be a naming ceremony for a boy that does not include circumcision if the boy is the child of a Jewish and Latino couple. Others who practice different traditions, such as the teachings of the Buddha, have also embraced a path beyond their received traditions.[3] There often is an embodied aspect to these rituals, commemorations, special days, and events that may have greater impact on the participants than any formal teaching associated with them. In any case, there do appear to be expressions of Latino/a spirituality connected with these passages.

What exactly is ritual? A ritual can be understood as the repeated performance of specific rites, usually with a fixed set of prescribed and recognized words and actions at particular moments of life, all of which are not exclusively determined by the participants. Rituals may involve both tradition and innovation, but in such a way that there is a general recognition that something extraordinary is occurring with something other than individual need or preference being a determining factor.

In addition to specific words and actions the performance of a ritual may involve the use of dedicated objects, all with a special purpose in mind. On this point theologian Jeanette Rodríguez asserts that "all human beings are symbol-creating creatures who use ritual behavior to organize socially meaningful ways to express values and traditions. . . . Ritual is not just an activity with no purpose, but rather it is the way in which human beings construct their worlds."[4] Examples of rituals include prayers, testimonies, dances, and specific ceremonies.

As cultures have developed, there is a transmission of specific traditions at certain key moments of life involving content and procedures that have been determined appropriate and in some cases necessary for individuals and communities to practice. Anthropologist Roy Rappaport wrote that the distinctiveness of rituals is such that they are "not simply an alternative way to express any manner of thing, but that certain meanings and effects can best, or even *only*, be expressed or achieved in ritual (original emphasis)."[5] Certain passages in life demand to be articulated and recognized in distinctive ways.

While all humans pass through different stages of life, some also participate in certain formal rites that have been learned and transmitted. Tom

Driver refers to this as ritualization, which involves constructing "a pathway through what would otherwise be uncharted territory. . . . As a particular act of ritualizing becomes more and more familiar, as it is repeated so often that it seems to circle upon itself, it comes to seem less like a pathway and more like a shelter."[6] The way we mark important moments and stages in our lives, including rites of passage, can provide those safe havens.

Ritual studies scholar Catherine Bell identifies six categories of ritual action: (1) rites of passage; (2) calendrical and commemorative rites; (3) rites of exchange and communion; (4) rites of affliction; (5) rites of feasting, fasting, and festivals; (6) and political rituals.[7] Bell further claims, "In most cultures, social life is a series of major and minor ritual events. While predominately secular cultures may have just a few rites to mark birth, marriage, and death, more traditional or religious societies may envelop one in a nearly endless sequence of ritual obligations."[8] All of these categories are present in Latino/a religion and spirituality. In order to better understand rituals and their connection to life passages in U.S. Hispanic contexts, I draw on Bell's classifications and provide some examples of rites of passage and calendar and commemorative rites that function as both pathways and havens.

STAGES OF SPIRITUAL DEVELOPMENT

In the hope of better understanding Hispanic/Latino spirituality as it is played out in the life cycle, it is helpful to consider what some have called the stages of faith or spiritual development. Frequently when the topic of spiritual passages comes up, the work of James Fowler is mentioned. As a theologian and researcher in human development, Fowler proposes a six-stage theory of faith development that is commonly accepted.[9] Fowler asserts that there is connection between one's faith (and we can say more broadly one's religion or spirituality) and one's life and actions.

Briefly, the six distinct stages of faith development that Fowler identifies are: (1) "intuitive-projective faith" characterized by initial self-awareness, growing awareness of reality, and apprehension of basic cultural norms; (2) "mythic-literal" faith, in which symbol and ritual start to be integrated and literal interpretations of myth and symbol can occur; and (3) "synthetic-conventional faith" characterized by conformity, socialization, and integration. Fowler asserts that the majority of people reside at this stage. The remaining stages include (4) "individuative-reflective," a stage of angst and struggle; (5) "conjunctive faith," in which a person after having moved through angst and struggle arrives at a point of acknowledgment of paradox and transcendence; and (6) "universalizing faith," which may be experienced as enlightening for the person threatening by others at an earlier stage.

Fowler and others recognize that the various stages of faith are not measures of individual accomplishment, but rather levels that one's faith goes through as it develops. While seemingly no research has been undertaken to determine if these stages are fully appropriate and descriptive of the faith, religious, and spiritual experiences of the varied Latino/a peoples, Fowler's theory may provide insight in examining Latino/a passages of the sacred.

Latino/a life-cycle rituals may be the vehicles of traditions and their transmission, but they might also serve as areas of contestation and cultural experimentation. Nancy Pineda-Madrid maintains:

> Ritual practices reflect the historical contexts out of which they emerge; they attempt to convince partakers of a particular way of viewing the world; they reflect a purpose inherent in the world view they embody; and finally, they may generate in partakers a mixed reaction. They demand of their partakers an evaluation or judgment, one that is unique to each person and consists of a combination of both consent and resistance.[10]

Rituals that mark the social stages of life and calendrical and commemorative events give meaning to the passage of time. Examples of such commemorative events may be overtly religious while others less so, for example, Carnaval; Ash Wednesday and Lent; the festival of Calle Ocho in Miami; Santa Semana (Holy Week), including Palm Sunday and Good Friday; Corpus Christi; Easter; Cinco de Mayo and Puerto Rican Day (or week); El Grito of September 16; Día de la Raza; the feast celebrations of various national Virgens, for example, in Cuba, Mexico, and Peru; Hispanic Heritage Month; Día de los Muertos; Advent, the celebration of the Virgin of Guadalupe, Christmas, and El Día de los Reyes. There are also the events of the Muslim religious calendar, based on the lunar year, that move through the seasons and provide a context for marking the social stages of life with commemorative rites.

Ritual life may also include a daily routine of faithfully following the pattern of "prayer, worship, testimony, song, and witness" at the Pentecostal Latin American Bible Institute in California.[11] And there are special days connected to devotions to unofficial saints and unconventional healers of the U.S.-Mexico borderlands that have spread far from the border, including the *curandera* (healer), mystic, and political activist Teresa Urrea (1873–1906); *curandero* (healer); El Niño Fidencio (José de Jesús Fidencio Constantino Síntora, d. 1938); Jesús Malverde (the ambiguous Robin Hood–like character who has become the unofficial patron of narcotic traffickers); Don Pedrito Jaramillo (known as the healer of Los Olmos, d. 1907); Juan Castillo Morales (known as Juan Soldado, d. 1938); and La Santísima Muerte (Most Holy Death or Saint Death).[12] In different ways all these remembrances can mark the religious, spiritual, and cultural organization of life.

FAMILIA AND LIFE PASSAGES

Much of what occurs in Hispanic religious and spiritual passages happens in the context of family and personal relationships. There is no single idealized model of what a Hispanic family is because there is so much diversity along the lines of national and ethnic origin, regional contexts, language, and socioeconomic class.[13] Nevertheless, in nearly all Hispanic contexts *familia* is important in the passages of life, whether marked by the presence of good and healthy actual and fictive familial and spiritual kinship, or in far too many cases by deficient or even absent relationships.

In many Latino/a milieus the familial kinship system goes beyond actual blood relations and includes fictive but very true relationships that are established and maintained over generations. One notable example is the practice of a *hija/o de crianza* in which "families take in children, often through informal networks, not because they are blood relations but simply because they need a home."[14] This kinship system also includes godparents who become *comadres* and *compadres* (literally, co-mothers, co-fathers). The *compadrazgo* (co-parenthood) system is still very important in many U.S. Hispanic settings where being a godparent is much more than a one-day fulfillment of an honorary role. Godparents as *comadre* or *compadre* are part of the child's family and members of an extended social network *compadrazgo* can also designate close relationships made in a solemn commitment to be a second parent to the child. Godparents very naturally blend into an extensive spiritual kinship system.

BIRTH OF A CHILD

A fundamental life passage is welcoming a newborn into *la familia* and *la comunidad*. Latino/a Christians have various ways of acknowledging and formally and publicly incorporating a newborn child into a community. The majority of Hispanic Protestants, especially those who call themselves *evangélico/as*, view the baptism of an infant as nonbiblical. However many do formally and publicly present the baby to God, which is typically done in the midst of a church service. It is hoped that at some point later in life the child will make a public declaration of faith and be baptized at that time. There is also a difference regarding believer baptism among those Latino/a Pentecostals who are Trinitarian in theology and baptismal practice, and those who are adherents of Oneness Pentecostalism, who baptize only in the name of Jesus.[15] Latinas and Latinos who belong to different branches of Mormonism also practice vicarious baptism for the deceased.[16] But probably the vast majority of Latinas and Latinos who participate in this Christian rite practice infant baptism, which includes the presentation and baptism of the child in a worship service in which the Christian community welcomes the new baby. Through baptism the child is formally incorporated into the community. As James Empereur and Eduardo Fernández note, the role of baptism in Hispanic popular religion is "not only as entrance into the church but also as affirmation of a family and a culture is a very important solidifying event."[17]

The baptism of an infant may be an occasion for the participation of the entire family network, parents, godparents (*padrinos*), grandparents, and other *ancianos* (elderly), *comadre* or *compadre*, literally, co-mother, co-father, and family members. In many contexts the closeness of the *compadrazgo* relationship includes not only spiritual and emotional support and reciprocity, but also financial assistance when needed, and, as Eugenio Matibag relates, assistance with immigration and maintaining family links.[18] "After baptism, the parents and godparents will address each other as *compadre* or *comadre*—a term that implies a close and sacred relationship."[19]

Some Mexican American families practice the tradition of *el bolo*, in which after the baptism the godparents throw a small package of coins outside the church door to the children and adults assembled. Another ancient tradition from Iberia is that after the baptism the godparents (often the *madrina*/godmother), returning the baby to the parents, say "*Me lo entregaste moro, y te lo devuelvo cristiano*" ("You delivered to me a Moor [Muslim], and I give back to you a Christian"), a remnant of centuries-old hostility between Christian and Muslim in the Spanish-speaking world.[20]

Another sacred practice of incorporating a child into the community is seen in the Muslim ceremony for a newborn called the *aqiqah* (also spelled *akika*). The *aqiqah* incorporates a naming and blessing ceremony for a new baby that includes a sacrifice and charitable gifts to the poor and needy.[21] Traditional Islamic law calls for an *aqiqah* to be offered at any point after a child's birth, but typically within the first week (and ideally on the seventh day). In keeping with the fact that Muslims worldwide practice this ritual, Shinoa Matos, a Latina Muslim who with her husband, Julio, describe themselves as "reverts" to Islam, relates what transpired during her daughter's *aqiqah*:

> I met Imam Muhammad Shamsi Ali at the Islamic Cultural Center of New York where I first started attending his classes on Islam. I recall being drawn to his amiable personality and his affection for converts. Always sympathetic to the difficulties we reverts face, he did his best to transition us into Muslim life as easily as possible. He's an outstanding leader and it was only fitting that he should perform my daughter's Aqiqah, introducing her to the Muslim community as well as to our non-Muslim family and friends. . . . As soon as everyone arrived, Imam Shamsi gathered everyone around me, Julio, and the baby to begin. He did a wonderful job of demystifying the Aqiqah for my non-Muslim family—clearly explaining the Sunnah, its obligation and its beauty—I saw them smile and sincerely nod their heads in affirmation to everything he was referring too. Insha'allah may Allah guide them to Islam. . . . Julio and I have been entrusted by Allah to raise a righteous Muslimah, the first generation Muslim to be born within the Ortiz-Padilla family. It was both frightening and humbling. We stood at the very same point that the Prophet and his Companions faced in the beginning of the revelation. They too had just come to Islam; they too were Muslims in the mist of non-Muslim family and friends—facing ridicule, loneliness, and feelings

of outcast. They too were creating new families and bringing forth Muslims into the world.[22]

This rite of passage is yet another example of formally welcoming a new child into several communities, that of her parents, their non-Muslim family of blood, and the wider Muslim community. It is clear from what Matos writes that this passage for her infant daughter might be the first step of a spiritual pathway for the rest of her non-Muslim Hispanic family, even as she and her husband create a new family.

QUINCEAÑERA AS RITE OF PASSAGE

One of the most distinctive rites of passage in the United States is an explicit female initiation rite that goes by the name of *quinceañera*. This passage transcends denominational, generational, ethnic, and national boundaries. For the majority of the dominant "white" European American culture, except for the occasional "sweet sixteen" party or the debutante balls of a bygone era, nothing quite equals the *quinceañera*. Its ongoing and indeed increasing popularity can be seen in the cable television program *Quiero mi quince* and the film *Quinceañera*.[23]

The cultural roots of a *quinceañera* in Latin America are in a ceremony to mark that a fifteen-year-old female was ready to be married. Obviously that cultural impulse is no longer the major reason for the continuance of the custom, but as Empereur and Fernández indicate, "one traditional understanding of the rite is still quite functional today. Her childhood is over."[24] Thus a *quinceañera* as a coming-of-age ceremony and celebration marks the cultural, social, and religious passage from childhood to womanhood, similar to what occurs in a bat mitzvah.

The *quinceañera* tradition normally includes a religious ceremony at church, followed by a reception party held in the home, at a church hall, or a banquet hall with dinner and the cutting of a multitiered cake. Even families of modest means may host lavish celebrations on this unique day. The girl/young woman wears an extravagant white or pastel ball gown, perhaps similar in style to a wedding gown. The reception party can include food and music. Traditionally the *quinceañera* chooses persons to make up her Court of Honor; these are usually her closest friends, siblings, and cousins. During the celebration males take turns dancing with the girl/young woman, but customarily, the first dance is a waltz with her father. Another common feature is that the father or a favored male relative ceremoniously changes the girl/young woman's flat shoes to high heels and gives her a "Last Doll," symbolizing a childhood being left behind.

On a trip to southern California I had the opportunity to observe a *quinceañera* mass. It was held under a permanent tent in the beautiful central courtyard garden of a hotel, with the same space used later in the day for a wedding. Indeed, much of the service/ceremony was reminiscent of a wedding. The young woman, flanked by her parents and others, was radiant in her white gown. Her court of *damas* (ladies) were in matching white dresses, while the young men called *chambelánes* (chamberlains) stood in complementary outfits that were a stylish mix of tuxedos and military uniforms trimmed in gold. The *quinceañera* mass was followed by a celebration in one of the ballrooms with dinner and a live band.

Interestingly, many families today are merging their Hispanic and American heritages by choosing to combine a *quinceañera* with a sweet-sixteen party. I observed such a celebration at a Presbyterian church in Dallas, where a working-class Mexican American/Tejano family went all out to host the combined party in the church hall to which family, friends, and the entire congregation were invited. This is one example of re-crafting a traditional celebration in a way that made sense in their context.

MARRIAGE AND PARTNERSHIP

Entering into marriage and other types of relational partnerships is one of the most significant social stage and life passages a person experiences. Marriage, partnership, and similar unions involving two persons in a committed relationship in a Latino/a context, with the great importance given to family, are so important the relationship encompasses more than just two people. Timothy Matovina describes the important and life-long role of godparents (*padrinos*) in a Mexican American Catholic context, noting that they "are chosen not just for baptism and confirmation but also for First Communion, the maturing to adulthood of a young woman (*quinceañera*), and marriage."[25]

While entering into solemn relational partnership may still be held up as the ideal, this is not the reality of many Latinas and Latinos today. Instead, many young Latinas and Latinos become parents outside the boundaries of formalized partnership, either through marriage or some other means. Some men and women are partners in common marriage or *unión libre*. Single persons who do not enter monastic life or become clergy are in an ambiguous social location that goes against the mainstream Hispanic cultural current. There is also the issue of those who do partner and/or marry and unfortunately experience a troubled marriage and family life. Further, there are men who marry but have children with other partners while married.

For Latinas these challenges are compounded by the power of the pervasive stereotype of *Marianismo*, which Michelle Gonzalez describes as placing "women on a pedestal, arguing that in their chasteness and purity they are superior to men. Any woman who falls short of this ideal is quickly disregarded as a fallen and tainted woman."[26] A second stereotype works in tandem: the pervasive sexism in Hispanic cultures that goes by the name of *machismo*, an exaggerated sense of maleness that often expresses itself in abusive behavior to women and other men. Ada María Isasi-Díaz calls attention to another stereotype as she names this multilayered challenge.

> An important example of the way the dominant group—men and women—mix ethnic prejudice and sexism is seen in the use of the word *machismo* by English-speaking persons nowadays despite the fact there is a perfectly comparable term, "male chauvinism," in the English language. Use of *machismo* implies that Hispanic men are more sexist than Anglo men. Using *machismo* absolves somewhat the sexism of Anglo men and sets Anglo men and culture above Hispanic men and culture. Hispanic women do not deny the sexism of our culture or of most Hispanic men. But it is not greater than the sexism of the U.S.A. society in general and of Anglo men in particular.[27]

This observation by Isasi-Díaz highlights that there are also cross-cultural challenges for Latinas and Latinos. In addition, the still contentious issue of same-sex relationships and marriage for same-sex partners has people divided across all lines including social, theologically, and familial. Orlando Espín issued a clarion call to Christian theologians that if they "intend to address real-life situations and issues" then "we cannot ignore LGBT blacks and Latino/as in our theologies, because sexual orientation is an unavoidable real contextualization—as real and unavoidable as race, gender, ethnicity, or culture."[28]

Yet, despite all the challenges, struggles, difficulties, misunderstandings, and oppression, there is still the human allure of finding a mate, for either a lifetime or a season, as people seek intense, committed, mutual, loving relationships. Finding a suitable and faithful partner is one of the challenges described by a young Latina Muslim woman:

> As a Latina convert, I have a whole other worry that some Muslim women don't have: *my ethnicity*. As I've mentioned before, there is no room for racism or ethnocentrism in Islam. But sometimes people seem to forget. From articles and from hearing actual stories from others, it is still present not only in Muslim communities, but just in the whole world in general. The story of the Cuban convert (referenced in another story) trying to win over his Algerian in laws is heartbreaking and since the author is blunt, I will be too in saying that this is *racism*. It is scary that this fear that a convert who is not of the same culture is not good enough exists to this day. However, I know I am not completely innocent in this either. I know I have sometimes thought, "I just want to marry a good Latino man" or "I think I want to marry a Latino because this would make life so much easier." This is something that I, and we, as an Ummah, need to work on. And I know in my heart that it is *Islamically* wrong if someone does some day discriminate based on my cultural identity. But for us convert girls who don't belong to a traditionally Muslim culture, there is that fear, what if my in-laws don't think I'm "Muslim enough" because I'm not Arab, Persian, etc.[29]

This short reflection by this anonymous Latina Muslim names issues of race, religion, spirituality, culture, compatibility, multiple identities, hope, and desire.

The New Life Covenant Church in Chicago articulates its congregational vision "to bring unbelievers to Jesus, to bring them into Membership, to encourage spiritual Maturity through the Word, to support their call through Ministry, to ignite a passion for worldwide Missions, All for the glory of God."[30] New Life Covenant Church has five worship services in Spanish and English every weekend at the Roberto Clemente High School.

A congregation of the Assemblies of God, New Life Covenant's ministries include Gangs to Grace, an outreach to gang members, and the Chicago Dream Center (CDC), which provides a residential/recovery program for homeless women with food, shelter, spiritual guidance, and a program to overcome addiction and/or prostitution. The Reverend Wilfredo De Jesús is the senior pastor of this growing Pentecostal congregation, where his wife, Elizabeth De Jesús, also serves as a pastor, along with a staff of six other pastors and ministers.

In fulfilling its mission, New Life Covenant Church has committed itself to providing assistance to those going through the life passage of marriage by offering "The One in Him Marriage Ministry." The goal of this congregational ministry is "to divorce-proof marriages" through inspiring, encouraging, and equipping "those who are married and those who are preparing for marriage through practical/biblical resources and teachings." The ministry is also guided by two verses from scripture: "Therefore a man shall leave his father and mother, and shall be joined to his wife, and the two shall become one" (Gen. 2:24) and "Unless the Lord builds the house, they labor in vain those who build it" (Ps. 127:1). New Covenant's One in Him Marriage Ministry has a rigorous intentional program that includes small group Bible studies, premarital workshops of five weeks in length offered three times a year, "biblically based" marriage counseling, and regular marriage retreats and conferences.

This Pentecostal congregation also recognizes the reality of contemporary life often called the blended family, and offers "Blended in Him: Remarried Couples Ministry." This program seeks to be "a resource of help, education, and comfort for married couples as they face issues concerning families. To glorify God by giving remarried couples and their children the opportunity to prosper as they develop into loving and peace-filled families." The church recognizes that in a blended marriage one or both partners were married previously and suffered the loss of a spouse through divorce or death. Moreover, one or both partners of the blended marriage may have children from a previous marriage resulting in a new, blended family. Using the verse from Jeremiah 29:11 as a mission guide, "'For I know the plans I have for you,' declares the LORD, 'plans to prosper you and not to harm you, plans to give you hope and a future,'" this program combines relational, social, cultural, and spiritual elements with commemorative ritual acts.

PASSAGES OF DEATH

Two accounts of death within a family illuminate the importance of this passage.

A group of sisters and brothers were scattered across the United States while their parents had retired back in Puerto Rico. As in many extended Puerto Rican families, the desire for a better life for the younger generation, convoluted circumstances, and the distance of the miles across the sea had separated those who lived *afuera* from those who lived on the island. However, the illness of a family member would bring them together in a way that bridged the miles, languages, and cultural differences. In the heat of August the eldest child, a woman, made the telephone call to the others, "Mamí is sick and in the hospital. I'm going to PR to see what's going on." This is expected of the eldest and the siblings wished her well, asking to be kept informed. Things were as dire as feared so subsequent calls were made and those who could manage it quickly flew to Puerto Rico.

Days were spent in the small waiting room of the hospital outside the intensive care unit in a facility that did not begin to approach what the siblings were used to in the States. Finally one doctor was willing to have an honest talk with the three-member delegation of the siblings, the eldest sister and two brothers. Speaking in Spanish in a kindly but straightforward manner, the doctor explained the grave situation in which there were no options. The younger of the brothers, shifting from Spanish to English, said, "I don't understand." His sister replied softly and slowly, "Mamí is dying." And before those spoken words could sink in, an alarm sounded and a nurse rushed to get the doctor. The doctor quickly returned and informed the siblings that their mother was in distress, that their parents had signed a do-not-resuscitate order, and asked if they wished to honor that. The three quietly said yes, and were left alone. Together they sat silently, knowing that at that very moment their mother was leaving.

In a few minutes their worst fear was confirmed, and they had to inform the others in the waiting room. One brother wailed upon receipt of the news, someone called the father to return to the hospital, and someone else made the call to other family members outside Puerto Rico. The three brothers, grown men, but in a certain sense boys again, gathered around the body in the hospital bed and said a prayer for their mother and for themselves.

The following days were a blur with much to do, including preparing for the *velorio* (wake) and the burial. There were cultural clashes between the mainland and *isla* sides of the family as ways to deal with death on the island conflicted with ways it was done *afuera* (outside). An open-casket viewing was held, but not for as long as the island *tías* (aunts) wanted. After a memorial service in the *capilla* of the funeral home, all traveled to the cemetery where other mourners met them. At the gate of the cemetery under the hot sun, around the casket of the deceased, even though some of the relatives did feel like outsiders, the different branches of the family, along with friends and strangers, were woven together.

A lay Catholic deacon read from the Gospel of John and then invited others to speak. An aunt who lived *allá* before returning to Puerto Rico spoke as the grown children of the deceased were either too grief stricken and unfamiliar with the culture and language to be able to say anything. As they moved from the cemetery gate to the gravesite, unbidden by any person, the older sister of the deceased, Tía to many there, began to sing, and others joined in the words of the refrain:

Señor, me has mirado a los ojos	O Lord, with your eyes you have searched me,
y sonriendo has dicho mi nombre;	and while smiling have spoken my name;
en la arena he dejado mi barca;	now my boat's left on the shoreline behind me;
junto a ti buscaré otro mar.	by your side I will seek other seas.[31]

Together the entire group slowly moved forward as one, carried by the song known by some, but comforting to all, reminded that the beloved departed was known by name. In those moments—when sons, nephews, and friends lowered the casket into the ground, as daughters, sisters, brothers, nephews and nieces, *comadres* and *compadres*, and a host of others encircled the grave—the few yards from the cemetery gate to the gravesite became a sacred space, an expression of living religion and spirituality in the face of the passage of death.

In Arizona, in the borderlands of Mexico and the United States, a scholar of Mexican American studies, Yolanda Broyles-González, relates her understanding of the spirituality and story of her grandmother, Polita Gastelum Rodríguez, when she "went into spirit."[32] Confounding imposed categories of race, ethnicity, and nationality, Broyles-González's grandmother Abuelita Polita was a Yaqui/Yoeme woman from the tribal borderlands of Sonora and Arizona who did not leave much in formal written records, but whose three-day funeral choked the *colonia* with all the people who showed up. Polita was a widely known *curandera* (healer) who helped countless people over the years; loved and respected by many, she served as the spiritual center of a large extended family and an equally large spiritual kinship network that included numerous *comadres* and *compadres*.

Broyles-González reflects that her grandmother's "spiritual practices were marked by the particulars of her native region, economic class, gender, and race. In her life—as in the lives of many—those practices were at the heart of *lo imprescindible*, the indispensable acknowledgement of the sacred life-cycle and our place within it."[33] Polita embodied that cycle in her life and in her death in a context of incredible cultural and political change. Her lifetime ran from the Porfirio Díaz dictatorship of the 1880s in Mexico through the appearance of NAFTA in the 1990s. It was in that context that Polita's Yaqui identity, worship, and celebration were camouflaged under the rubrics of "Mexicanness" or "Hispanic," and Catholic.

Broyles-González tells how her grandmother and others merged Yaqui beliefs and ceremonies with Catholic terms, concepts, and symbols, observing, "The adoption of this or that Catholic feature (ironically) provides protection and fortifies the overall Native American cultural matrix."[34] Examples include the observance during Lent of Yaqui Waehma, a springtime celebration; the deer dancers and Pascola ("Old Man of the Ceremony") dancers that are part of the celebrations of Fiesta de la Santísima Trinidad; the feasts of an array of saints (San José, San Ignacio de Loyola, Santa Cruz, Virgen de Guadalupe, San Juan, San Miguel Arcángel), and Semana Santa (Holy Week). But while Polita was a keeper and transmitter of Yaqui beliefs and practices, she also was a member of the pan-Mexican Guadalupana Society with a deep devotion to the Virgen de Guadalupe. Her spirituality also made space for devotion to unofficial saints, for example, Santa Teresa de Cabora (Teresa Urrea), the Yaqui/Mayo *curandera* and revolutionary, and Jesús Malverde.

Hundreds of people made the pilgrimage to visit Polita during her last weeks before death. But, according to Broyles-González, she had other visitors as well.

Among those who visited her in her last weeks and days were the *ánimas benditas* (blessed spirits) of some already gone. Abuelita easily moved between the two sides of existence; her attention shifted seamlessly between the spirits and the visitors sitting in a circle around her bed. In mid-conversation with us, her eyes would suddenly gaze upon this or that deceased relative. As she acknowledged each one's presence by name, she also acknowledged their importance as guides into the spirit world. Virtually immobilized in her last weeks, my Abuela Polita tended almost exclusively to the spiritual preparation for a good death. "En esta vida no hay nada mas difícil que una buena muerte" (nothing is harder in this life than a good death).[35]

Polita's family had been instructed and trained to prepare for her final passage to the other side. Particular individuals were given specific tasks: one aunt was to maintain the home altar, seeing that there would be fresh roses from the garden; others were assigned to fulfill particular *mandas* or *promesas*, remaining spiritual debts. Broyles-González herself was assigned to visit the shrine of Jesús Malverde with a *milagro* foot as a token of thanksgiving for the healing of Polita's foot sores after she prayed to Malverde. Polita Gastelum Rodríguez's good death in a certain sense was a passage in which her entire biological and spiritual kinship network participated.

The ritualization of death includes formal rites as well as what emerges during the period of mourning. The two different stories related above are both expressions of a spirituality involved transmitted rituals as well as practices particular for that passage. These stories of two different deaths involve multigenerational families and highlight the complexity of identity and the multilayered dimensions of spiritual beliefs and practices.

In most Latino/a cultures, understandings of the death of a family member go beyond a passage for the person who dies. Some believe persons go to their eternal reward and others to punishment and damnation. Some followers of the paths of Santería/Lucumí hold that the human soul in death may transform into an ancestral spirit, an *egun*. Others do not believe that life continues after death. However, death is also a passage for the survivors, a path into a life in this world where the departed one is no longer physically present with those who remain. Homiletics professor Thomas Long muses:

> Which came first, the ritual rhythms of death or religious awe? Perhaps the knowledge that we cannot finally untangle the knot points to

the fact that death and the sacred are inextricably entwined. In both, human beings stand on the edge of mystery and peer into depths beyond our knowing. What we do when the shadow of death falls across our life—the acts we perform and the ritual patterns we follow—etches in the dust of material life a portrait of our sense of the sacred.[36]

DAYS OF THE DEAD

In some Latino/a communities one way of dealing with the passage of death and the presence or non-presence of the departed is through the Mexican Day of the Dead. Increasingly every year around the U.S. holiday of Halloween there is a growing number of celebrations of what is usually referred to as the *Día de los Muertos*, "Day of the Dead," but also known as *Días de los Muertos*, "Days of the Dead," and as *el Día de los Difuntos* (Day of the Deceased). In popular culture, the Day of the Dead is associated with family visits to a cemetery (*camposanto*, literally "holy field"), small candied sugar skulls, and the skeleton prints of José Guadalupe Posada. While casually referred to as "Mexican Halloween," these celebrations are much more than that. Chicana/o studies scholar Lara Medina observes:

> Publicly communing with the dead contests mainstream fears embedded in Euro-American Western cultural practices. As a ritual that honors and interacts with the dead in a familial and joyful manner, the tradition challenges a society that silences the dead shortly after a funeral. Western cultures enclose death in gated cemeteries void of color and merrymaking. Días de los Muertos does not replicate patterns of exclusion. The rite, with its color, humor, and friendly spirit, invites all people to approach death and the "other" without fear. The silence of death and the pain exclusion are challenged in the festivity of this public mourning ritual.[37]

Typically what happens during the Days of the Dead involves distinct but overlapping events in the home, the wider community, and at the burial place. Preparations include the construction of intricate home memorial altars called *ofrendas* (offerings) with candles, flowers, photographs of the deceased and other religious pictures, and offerings of fruits, vegetables, favorite foods enjoyed in life by the deceased. *Calaveras,* or skeletons, are made along with sugar-candied skulls that are placed on the altar to be eaten by children after the holiday. Intricately designed *papel picado*, or cut colored tissue paper is used for decorations. *Pan de muerto*, "bread of the dead," a special anise- or orange-flavored bread, is baked. Family members decorate gravesites with flowers and candles where all-night vigils are held. In some communities parades are staged to welcome the dead. The commemoration begins on October 31 when it said that deceased children, called *angelitos*, begin to arrive for All Saints' Day on November 1. It also is believed that the departed adults arrive on November 2, which is All Souls' Day.

Days of the Dead commemorations draw upon Mesoamerican and Catholic customs, beliefs, and rituals with roots in Mexico and they are practiced by Mexicans, Mexican Americans, and Chicano/as.[38] While rooted in traditions in Mexico, the observance of Day of the Dead was spread in conjunction with the rise of the Chicano/a movement and given additional impetus by more recent waves of immigration from Mexico. As practiced in the United States, such observations are also leading to greater awareness of the Christian All Saints' Day and All Souls' Day. And while Mexican Day of the Dead celebrations are finding greater cultural acceptance, it should be noted that *Día de los Muertos* is also remembered throughout Latin America, including in Guatemala, Bolivia, and Peru, where the phrases *Todos Santos* (All Saints) and *el Día de los Difuntos* are considered more appropriate names.[39]

The impact of Day of the Dead celebrations is not limited to those who are Catholics. Hannah Gill describes the cultural tensions felt by a North Carolina Mexican Baptist woman with this aspect of her Mexican heritage, "My mom became Southern Baptist, so we didn't celebrate the Day of the Dead. I grew up Southern Baptist. . . . In Mexico, everyone was Catholic, but my religion was different."[40] This Latina had an awareness of the cultural importance of *Días de los Muertos*; although she was not allowed to participate, she still maintained her Mexican identity as a Baptist.

Day of the Dead rituals have now gone beyond being solely Mexican celebrations. Other Latino/as resonate with its themes of formation and maintenance of identity, and a tangible and accessible means for dealing with a universal human experience.[41] In some ways the pan-Latino/a celebration of the Day of the Dead illustrates beliefs and practices about what occurs beyond death for the living and the dead. Not all who participate believe in life after death, but they do find meaning in remembering those who have died. While there is no uniformity regarding beliefs about the nature of death and about the afterlife, the fact that many Latinas and Latinos hold some kind of belief in existence beyond death is quite common. In essence, the Days of the Dead celebrations are one avenue for the living to deal with the powerful forces of life and death, as well as provide opportunities to continue to commune with their beloved dead. By affirming both life and continued communion with those who have died, *Días de los Muertos* declares that death is not the final passage of life.

CONCLUSION

The presence and practice of the passage rites just described contribute to contextualizing the sense of community and connection among Latinas and Latinos. In some instances they simultaneously serve as a vehicle for traditioning, address human needs at different development stages, and address sociocultural expectations. Some rites of passage connect with initiation into a family, such as infant baptism, infant blessings and dedications, circumcision, and naming ceremonies. Other rites recognize important moments of transition and movement to a new stage, such as confirmation, bar and bat mitzvah, and *quinceañera* celebrations.

In addition, major moments of covenant and dedication are ritualized in marriage and commitment ceremonies, ordination, and religious profession, whether in giving a *testimonio* at the time of adult baptism in a Pentecostal church or declaring *Shahada*, the Muslim profession of faith at a mosque. The rituals and practices used in responding to death illustrate in a poignant way Latino/a attitudes regarding what is sacred. And through it all, in the midst of social, economic, cultural, and religious changes and developments, while the particulars about some rituals may undergo change, there still remains a need to mark the passages of life.

FIVE

Rhetoric and Traditions

LO COTIDIANO AND SACRED RHETORIC

Exploring the connection between *santo* and sacred rhetoric means considering the ways that Latino/as use language to express their religiosity and spirituality in their communities and society. Different aspects of Latino/a spirituality can be seen not only in the attitudes toward life passages considered in the previous chapter but also concretely in specific daily practices and the language or rhetoric that accompanies such practices. In this chapter I set out to identify and analyze verbal expressions of *santo* (holy) and *sagrado* (sacred) to better understand them. The analysis focuses on naming and understanding the everyday religious and spiritual rhetoric of Latino/a peoples, and not to summarily dismiss or disdain such discourse or pass theological judgments of orthodoxy or heterodoxy. While such activity is important within the context of specific communities, that is not my main task here. However, discussion about what is "in" or "out," that is, what is within acceptable boundaries of any given Latino/a community, is helpful to note as part of the rhetoric that is employed.

By rhetoric, I include the authorized language of prescribed prayers, sermons, homilies, and other formal liturgical, ecclesiastical, and specialized religious language in a variety of settings. I also include in this category of sacred rhetoric unsanctioned expressions and practices, including private and familial prayers, stories, teachings, sayings, proverbs, greetings, and *testimonios* that are part of everyday life; they are often echoes of larger spiritual worlds as well as deep theological and religious reflections that happens in *lo cotidiano* (the regular daily routine).

Practices include both formal and informal words and actions involving health and healing. Rhetoric and practices are also expressed in formal and informal relationships, including those of friendship, *compadrazgo*, and hospitality. And I will consider on the connections between Latino/a spirituality, justice, and the public sphere.

Many definitions of sacred rhetoric can be advanced. Susan Harding recognizes discourse as rhetorical when a formal argument is being advanced and a method of implementation accompanies the argument; in other words, there is an associated practice.[1] Argumentation certainly is one form of rhetoric, but in this context I am thinking of it more broadly. Just because something is not formal or official does not mean that it is not rhetorical. The helpful insight from Harding connects rhetoric and practice. Thus, given this understanding, rhetoric happens all the time when what is said impacts action in the world.

The spiritual and religious discourse of Latino/as takes many forms. For those involved in recognizable religious communities, aspects of rhetoric and discourse are readily available, including the words of the mass, the prayers of Passover, the confession in union at a Presbyterian service, or Friday prayers at a mosque.

The commonly held public and private division that is at least rhetorically prominent in U.S. American life is not the dominant perspective within Latino communities. It is a perspective, instead, that is learned, and one that Latinas and Latinos in their bicultural existence become adept in practicing. However, Latino/a spirituality approaches everyday life in ways that confound the public/private division. The Latin American and U.S. Latino/a approach to everyday life is often summed up in the concept of *lo cotidiano*. *Lo cotidiano*, the everyday, is described by Justo González as "an emphasis developed first of all by feminist critical theory, mostly because in most societies women are put in charge of *lo cotidiano*—cooking, cleaning, nurturing—while men claim for themselves the extraordinary, *lo histórico*.[2]

Latina feminist theologian María Pilar Aquino was an early and strong advocate for giving importance to the concept of *lo cotidiano*, especially for understanding the perspectives and agency of Latinas. Aquino asserts,

> The methodological importance of daily life is grounded on its being the privileged locus for an intercultural theology, since the cultures and religious experiences of our communities converge in it. Theologically, daily life has salvific value because the people themselves, in lo cotidiano of their existence, let us experience the salvific presence

of God here and now in their daily struggles for humanization, for a better quality of life, and for greater social justice.[3]

Paying attention to *lo cotidiano* is to be open to the presence of God or the divine in the spaces and happenings of everyday life.

THE SACRED RHETORIC OF PRAYER IN SONG

For Latino/a Pentecostals, the most common forms of public prayer in congregational worship occur in two ways, either through a prayer in the moment and not for repeated use, which might be formulaic, to express praise or a petition. The second is the singing of *coritos,* which are constantly utilized in a wide variety of settings. In terms of Latino Protestant sacred rhetoric, this includes *coritos* that are succinct choruses that are simultaneously worship songs and localized and inter-communal theological affirmations.[4] They are often scriptural citations or allusions put to music, and they often play multiple roles. One of the most common choruses appearing in all kinds of Latino/a Protestant settings, including Pentecostal, Charismatic, Evangelical, *evangélico*, and historic mainline, is *Alabaré* (I will praise). A quick Internet search reveals the tune and what appear to be standard words:

Alabaré, alabaré, alabaré a mi Señor	I will praise, I will praise, I will praise my Lord
Alabaré, alabaré, alabaré a mi Señor	I will praise, I will praise, I will praise my Lord
Juan vio el número de los redimidos	John saw the number of the redeemed
Y todos alababan al Señor	And all praised the Lord
Unos cantaban, otros oraban	Some sang, some prayed
Pero todos alababan al Señor.	But all praised the Lord.
Alabaré, alabaré, alabaré a mi Señor	I will praise, I will praise, I will praise my Lord.
Alabaré, alabaré, alabaré a mi Señor	I will praise, I will praise, I will praise my Lord

Exploring what he describes as the Jesus of Hispanic Pentecostal spirituality, theologian and pastor Sammy Alfaro cites the words of a popular *corito,* "Pass through Here Lord."

> Pass through here Lord
> Pass through here.
> Oh, Oh, Lord, pass through here,
> Holy Spirit, fill me with you.
> Oh, Oh, Lord fill me with you.[5]

Alfaro explains that although the words may seem simply the juxtaposition of Jesus and the Spirit demonstrates a theological understanding that the presence of Jesus is revealed through the Spirit. These and other *coritos* may be sung as a type of bidding prayer, in a manner very similar to a Taizé service, or during moments of petition. And even though there is a new wave of worship songs in Latino/a Protestant, including Pentecostal, for congregations influenced by English-language worship music, the old choruses have staying power and are still sung. Even a luminary such as Marcos Witt often will include a *coritos* segment in his performances.

Historian Daniel Ramírez notes that the popularity and extent of these Pentecostal choruses extends far beyond Latino/a Pentecostalism. In his analysis Ramírez insightfully observes:

> The difficulty in precisely tracing the origin and dissemination of most Latino Pentecostal hymns and choruses suggests that these ride in the luggage and in the hearts of a very mobile religious proletariat that often does not bother to check in with civil (immigration), ecclesiastical, and academic authorities. How for example, did "Alabaré a mi Señor" ("I Will Praise My Lord"), "No Hay Dios tan grande como Tú" ("There Is No God Greater Than You"), and "Mas allá del sol" ("Beyond the Sun") travel from Pentecostal to mainline Protestant and popular Catholic hymnody?[6]

This use has implications for understanding Latino/a sacred rhetoric in multiple settings since these manifestations can be identified widely, certainly among Latino/a Protestants, but, as Ramírez observes, in other contexts as well.

A story told by a Latina Protestant illustrates the overlapping of multiple Protestant traditions. An adult Chilean American whose parents had been refugees during the dictatorship of Augusto Pinochet and had become a devout Christian, she recalled worship services she had attended as a child of seven or eight years of age. She remembers an *hermano* (brother) who would volunteer for special music. "He would always sing the same hymn. I even remember the name of the hymn, 'Amarte Solo a Ti Senor' and it feels like yesterday, sitting in church on a Sunday morning and listening to him sing. He did not have the best voice in the world and there was often no one playing accompaniment, but what he did have was a conviction about what he was singing."[7] The words of the hymn mentioned above, "I Love Only You, Lord," provide another example of this type of sacred rhetoric:

Amarte sólo a ti, Señor,	I love only you, Lord,
Amarte solo a ti, Señor,	I love only you, Lord,
Amarte sólo a ti, Señor,	I love only you, Lord,
Y no mirar atrás	and I don't look back.
Seguir tu caminar, Señor,	Continuing in your path, Lord,
Seguir sin desmayar, Señor,	Continuing without losing heart, Lord,
Postrado ante tu altar, Señor,	Prostrated before your altar, Lord,
Y no mirar atrás,	And I don't look back.
Seguir tu caminar, Señor,	Continuing in your path, Lord,
Seguir sin desmayar, Señor,	Continuing without losing heart, Lord,
Postrado ante tu altar, Señor,	Prostrated before your altar, Lord,
Y no mirar atrás	And I don't look back.[8]

Even in a setting of a free-church tradition influenced by Pentecostalism, Methodism, and North American Evangelicalism, where there was an authorized structure for the worship service, there is still space for grassroots articulation. This song, like others, articulates a personal connection with God in Christ. The insight of Carlos Cardoza-Orlandi from his study of other songs is also applicable here: "These hymns and coritos reveal the erotic nature of the Christian community. These grassroots Christian artists desire, want, and long for intimacy with Christ."[9] And like other choruses this song appears in many settings.

RHETORIC FROM THE MARGINS

Other stories of Latino/a spirituality come from the alternative spiritual tradition of *espiritismo*, known in English as spiritism. Spiritism typically refers to various types of beliefs and practices that assert the reality of a spiritual world in which the spirits of individual persons exist beyond death and can be communicated with through spiritual mediums or *espiritistas*, or some other agency. The many forms of spiritism often combine influences from Europeans, Native Americans, and Africans. One expression of spiritism that gained popularity in Latin America and is still influential among Latin Americans and Latinos has its origins in the nineteenth century as a result of the teachings of Allan Kardec (H. L. Rivail, 1804–69), including his strong belief in reincarnation.

Although heavily influenced by Kardec's teachings from Europe, *espiritismo* draws equally from traditions rooted in Africa and the indigenous Taíno Caribbean. Mario Dos Santos describes the eclectic nature of *espiritismo* (what he calls Caribbean Spiritualism and *Espiritismo Cruzado*): "Its practice varies greatly between individuals and groups. In all cases, Espiritismo has absorbed various practices from other religious and spiritual practices endemic to Latin America and the Caribbean, such as Roman Catholicism, Curanderismo (traditional, Latin American folk healing), Santería, Palo, and Vodou."[10]

As Spiritism developed in the Caribbean, distinct varieties emerged in Cuba, the Dominican Republic, and Puerto Rico. In the United States Latino/as practice a version known as *Santerismo*, which is a combination of Santería and spiritism. As the communities of adherents interact with each other, they may adopt elements from another expression. The complexity is compounded as different types of *espiritismo* fuse with African-based traditions. Margarite Fernández Olmos and Lizabeth Paravisini-Gebert identify "Scientific," or "Table," *Espiritismo*, *Espiritismo de Cordón*, and *Espiritismo Cruzado* as three different types of Cuban spiritism.[11]

Like other spiritual traditions *espiritismo* in all its varieties has regular formal services for its practitioners. In his primer of spiritism, dos Ventos provides a prayer commonly used to close a spiritual meeting:

> We give thanks to the good Spirits
> Who have come to communicate with us,
> And implore them to help us put into practice
> The instructions they have given, and also,
> That on leaving this ambient, they may help us
> To feel strengthened for the practice of goodness
> And love towards our fellow beings.
> We also desire that Your teachings help all those
> Spirits who are suffering, ignorant or corrupt,
> Who have participated in our meeting
> And for whom we implore God's mercy.[12]

This prayer demonstrates a clear belief in a reality inhabited by multiple spiritual entities. It reflects the belief that human beings interact with these spirits in ways that can produce healing and guidance in life.

The influence of the different types of spiritism in Latino/a communities is such that even those who are not regular adherents may seek consultations and assistance from time to time. Jesse Hoffung-Garskof gives an example of how this type of rhetoric not sanctioned by ecclesiastical authorities takes place in Dominican transnational settings:

> Many residents of Santo Domingo (including some in the middle class) frequently turn to spiritual explanations for both collective and individual improvement or decline. These explanations rely on African Dominican spirituality as well as popular Catholicism like Doña Francisca's. Anthropologists describe the popular concept of *desenvolvimiento* in Santo Domingo, an idea of unfolding, or spiritual health that guides communal and personal fortunes. It is possible to manage this *desenvolvimiento* by addressing and appeasing spirits through the mediation of local priestesses, or servidoras. The aspirations that shape Dominicans' migration to cities and to foreign lands may well be related to the secular idea of *progreso*. But they seem also frequently to rely on this notion of *desenvolvimiento*. Some people in the barrios leave their passports on the altars of local *servidoras,* asking saints or *guedes* (African Dominican deities) for help in getting visas. Some international migrants later return to cemeteries in Santo Domingo to thank both spiritual practitioners and spirits for their triumphs abroad. Even those who will not participate in rituals that they consider "witchcraft" often organize *horas santas*, or Catholic prayer circles, to ask for the intercession of saints or the Virgin on matters of migration, health, or economic fortune.[13]

Perhaps one of the most unusual examples of everyday sacred rhetoric is associated with a saint known as Santísima Muerte, Most Holy Death (and also known as Santa Muerte Blanca, Saint White Death). Most scholars trace this spiritual trend from some devotion to Mexico, but it has spread far beyond the borderlands and the U.S. Southwest. Among the unofficial and unsanctioned saints, Santa Muerte appears to be gaining popularity in Mexico and the United States. Illustrating the geographic breadth of the following of Santa Muerte, the *Minneapolis Star Tribune* newspaper reported the assessment of a St. Paul parish priest who has to deal with this movement in his congregation. "She is evil," said the Rev. Kevin Kenney, pastor of Our Lady of Guadalupe Catholic Church in St. Paul, who has found Santa Muerte candles left on the prayer altars of his church. "People don't realize that they have to sell their soul."[14] Father Kenney's opinion reflects the official Roman Catholic judgment regarding Santa Muerte, an opinion shared by many Protestant clergy as well. Nevertheless, the followers of Santa Muerte seem to be growing—if the sales of a candle are any indication.

It appears that the most common way this saint is accessed is through the purchase of votive candles. In Lancaster, Pennsylvania, I acquired a Santísima Muerte prayer candle manufactured in Mexico and sold at a *botánica* run by Dominicans. In its basic shape it resembles others readily available, a clear glass cylinder about eight inches tall and two inches in diameter, with white candle wax inside. On the front side is a gruesome image of Holy Death, a skeleton wearing a robe and hood, holding in its left hand a skull, with the printed words "Santísima Muerte" over the figure and "Holy Death" beneath. Other representations of Holy Death are similar, except that her hands may hold scales or a scythe, and in place of the skull, a globe. Holy Death is popular among members of the narcotic cartels in Mexico and drug dealers in the United States, and also among sex workers.[15] Whatever their context may be, many Latino/as who call upon Santísima Muerte believe that they live in a dangerous world and are in need of protection. Some pray to Santa Muerte for protection from harm, for heath, and to prevent sickness. Like other such prayer candles, the opposite side displays a prayer in English and Spanish:

Oración a la Santísima Muerte

Jesuscristo Vencedor, que en la Cruz fuiste vencido, vence a . . . que este vencido conmigo en el nombre del Señor. Si eres animal feoz, manso como la flor del romero, tienes que venir; pan comiste, de el me diste: agua también bebiste y de el también me dijiste por la palabra mas fuerte que me dijiste quiero que me traigas a. . . . Que este humillado, renido a mis planta, y ven por que yo te llamo, yo te domino; tranquilidad no a de tener hasta que venga a mi lado. Así como atraviese mi pensamiento en mitad de tu Corazón para que olvide al mujer o el hombere que tenga y yo le llamo.

Prayer to Holy Death

Oh Conquering Jesus Christ, that in the Cross were defeated, like you would tame a ferocious animal, tame the soul of (name). Tame as a lamb and tame as a rosemary flower he shall come to kneel before me and obey my every command. Holy Death, I plea of your immortal powers that God has given you towards mortals, place us in a Celestial Sphere where we'll enjoy days without nights for all eternity. In the name of the Father, the Son and the Holy Spirit, I plea for your protection. Grant all our wishes until the last day, hour, and moment that your Divine Majesty orders us to appear before you. Amen.

Given that these two prayers are next to each other on the votive candle it might seem that the English is simply a translation of the Spanish, but that is not the case. Although some of the content is repeated, there is a sense in which the prayers are complementary of each other, rather than one being a strict translation of the other. Devotees of Holy Death employ other prayers as well, some for each day of the week, others combined with a novena, and in some cases with ritual actions to accompany the words to ensure that the petitioner receives what is asked.

EVERYDAY SAYINGS

Another form of popular sacred rhetoric is that of the *consejo* (counsel) that comes from the Mexican American context and is often transmitted as coming from an *abuela* (grandmother). Scholar of religion Luis León relates a common saying, "My son, there are three things that pertain to our religion, the Lord, Our Lady of Guadalupe, and the Church. You can trust in the first two, but not the third."[16] Nonetheless, there are still many aspects of official church rhetoric that people trust and make part of their everyday experience.

Emphasizing sayings, proverbs, and practices that come from the experience of *lo cotidiano* does not mean endorsing an excessive focus on the present, a type of presentism. Everyone's experience of the everyday has a history that has contributed to each individual's today. Before I was born, my father led the family migration from a rural area of southern Puerto Rico to become a migrant agricultural worker in southern New Jersey and eventually ended up working in an iron foundry in an industrial city in southern Connecticut. In the early 1950s, like tens of thousands of others, my father left his beloved Boriquen to be a contract agricultural worker picking vegetables for a giant agribusiness in the fields southeast of Philadelphia.[17] Although the work was extremely demanding, he found satisfaction in the south Jersey farm labor since he himself was from *el campo* and had quite a bit of *jíbaro* in him. Shortly thereafter my mother joined him with their two children, my eldest siblings Zenayda and Mingo. In the years that followed six more of us were born into the family, all but guaranteeing that we would be members of multiple worlds.

Along the way our parents determined that it was in our best interest to speak primarily English so that we would do better in school and get ahead in the world. In our home we lived the bilingual bicultural reality of Spanglish even before the term "Spanglish" was in vogue: our parents would often address us in Spanish and we would reply in English. But there were a few phrases we kids always said in Spanish, taught to us by our parents. Whenever our father or mother would leave or come home, as a greeting or as a good-bye, we would say, *Bendición*, asking for a blessing. And the most common reply was, *Dios te bendiga*, "God bless you." Sometimes a parental hand placed on our heads accompanied this blessing. And this exchange was not limited to our parents. We were expected to do this with our *abuelos* and *abuelas* (grandparents), with *tíos* and *tíos* (uncles and aunts), all their *comadres* and *compadres*, as well as all kinds of adults. (I often did not know the exact nature of these relationships, or even if we were blood relatives.) This concrete way of asking for and receiving blessings, expressed and reaffirmed in a rhetorical exchange, may be formulaic, or even overlooked, but it fully expresses the common Latino/a understanding of extended family and community. These and other *dichos* (sayings) are part of the very spirituality and religiosity of Hispanics.

Everyday life in many Latino/a contexts is filled with similar sayings. Other formulaic greetings include the oft said, *Si Dios quiere*, which can be translated as "God willing." A New Mexican proverb, *Cuando Dios no quiere, santo no puede*, or "When God does not want it, the saint is not able," or more idiomatically, "When God is not willing, the saint cannot perform the miracle."[18] Both *dichos* illustrate at the very least an understanding of God that assumes a type of providence at work in daily life.

A pervasive spirituality based on *lo cotidiano* can be discerned even in everyday language. Many of these ordinary expressions that people use without giving them a second thought also have sacred roots, for example, *¡Ave María! ¡Ave María Purísima! ¡Ay Dios mio! ¡Ay Virgen! Con la ayuda de Dios*, and *¡Santo Niño de Atocha!*

The pervasiveness of this type of language is illustrated by Latina Protestant theologian Loida Martell-Otero, who, reflecting on the assessment made by social scientists (and theologians for that matter), maintains that U.S. Hispanic Protestants are in some sense "cultural Catholics." Martell-Otero writes that "A good example of this was my maternal grandmother, a life-long American Baptist and Sunday school teacher. Her typical exclamatory phrases were 'Ave María Purísima' ('Hail Mary, most pure') and 'Ay Virgen.'"[19]

When we children left the house for school or play, my mother would urge us to behave ourselves and remind us in English, as had her father, that "God was always watching us." I am not certain if we actually heard the charge and warning. But it was only when I was an adult that the words of *abuelo* made an impact on me as they never had before. Like many other Puerto Ricans of their generation, my parents purchased a retirement home in Puerto Rico, and I went to visit them shortly after their relocation. One day my mother and I were talking in Spanish about her family, her parents, and growing up in Puerto Rico, and then my mother repeated one of my grandfather's favorite phrases, *Papa Dios está mirando* (Father God is watching). I soon learned that this phrase was common to the Island branches of the family; Papa Dios, Father God, was part of the family. The everyday language exhibited a taken-for-granted intimacy with the Divine. One of the consequences of these types of stories, *consejos*, and *dichos*, and the practice of *bendición* is that they cultivate an awareness that the supernatural realm is very much part of daily life.

STORIES AS NARRATIVE SPIRITUALITY

In reflecting on the distinctive characteristics of Hispanic Protestant popular religion. theologian Luis Pedraja explains that *testimonios* (testimonies) in the context of worship services "allow lay people to share their faith, struggles, and hopes" and, along with prayer meetings and Bible studies, this expression of "language becomes a vehicle for empowerment in popular religion within these congregations."[20] While I agree with Pedraja's assessment, I think that it is applicable to a population much broader than

Hispanic Protestants. If testimony is understood as another name for a person's story of her or his encounter with what is considered sacred or holy, then Latinas and Latinos from many diverse traditions have stories to tell. These expressions of Latino/a sacred rhetoric may take the form of *testimonio*, story, song, or poem.[21]

Dominican American Yarehk Hernandez shares a bit of his own religious and spiritual story and journey to what he describes as "being" Muslim. Hernandez begins his story thus: "I came to Islam on the streets of New York via Rastafarian weed smoking sessions in Bed Stuy; Kabbalah study groups in City College hallway floors; Hare Krishna vegetarian temple feasts on hungry Sunday afternoons; failed attempts at Tantric Buddhist meditation in posh downtown lofts; and building with the gods in Washington Square Park."[22]

Hernandez relates that his story is not a typical conversion account of one who accepts Islam. That may be the case, however; even the opening of his story has much in common with other Latinas and Latinos who explore many paths in search of an authentic spirituality. Hernandez continued his search, eventually drawn to Sufism and befriended by Muslims at City College's Muslim Students' Association. "The first time I took *shahada*, it was like I was stealing the secret keys to the kingdom or taking some cookies from the jar."[23] But his Muslim faith was challenged as he lived through the aftermath of September 11, 2001, in New York City. Nonetheless Hernandez speaks of how this retrenchment was an opportunity to discover Islam again in a way that he found liberative. As part of his story flowing from his experience Hernandez asserts:

> If my Creator is the creator of all that exists, then He/She/It made me and helped me become the man that I am, which is a Muslim Dominican American. He/She/It then went on to make you, you and you, too. It's pretty gosh darn amazing considering that many in this creation are so prone to procrastination, like me. And if Allah makes Muslims and we don't, then He/She/It also makes Hindus, Buddhists, Jews, Christians, Jains, Daoists, and Wiccans. We can share our faith with others through our words and deeds. But it is ultimately up to that piece of Allah's breath inside them to move closer to whatever path motivates them toward a better them. The same is true for us. We follow the way that makes us move our feet.[24]

Moving the feet of many is part of what the rap/hip-hop group Orisha does through its music. The testimony of Orisha is also a profound example of the fusion of spirituality, sacred rhetoric, and popular culture, as seen in the song "Represent." Reflecting the group's popularity in the United Sates, Latin America, and Europe, "Represent" is a multicultural song employing Spanish, English, French, Yoruba, and Spanglish that also provides an example of sacred rhetoric across the generations.[25] In lyrics that have layers of meaning, the recurring word is "represent"; besides its usual meaning, its use in this hip-hop context means "to be accounted for."[26]

The band members, Yotuel Romero, Ruzzo Medina, Roldán González, and Flaco Nuñez (Flaco-Pro) represent the total mix (*mezcla*) that is Cuba: they represent the *orishas*, their generation, Cubans in diaspora, and a generation cognizant of their roots in Cuba and in Africa. The songs seeks to represent from the heart (*de corazón*) the history of the roots and music of Cuba, which in their view means the *orisha*, as they repeatedly sing *Cuba, Orishas son de la Habana* (Cuba, *Orishas* are from Havana). Neither the ancestors nor the saints are to be forgotten since they are valuable to Cuban identity. The testimony in song goes on to say that the music, the sun of Cuba can be found throughout the world, making Paris forget its gray sky, showing up in Chicago, Panama, and Tokyo. Then, in a dramatic shift that probably goes unnoticed by some listeners but is perfectly clear to those in the know, the group Orisha invokes some of the Afro-Cuban *orisha* by name: Olofin, Eleggua, Chango, Obatala, Yemaya, and Ochun.[27] The last refrain of the song summarizes its aim:

Que mi canto suba	That my song may rise
Pa' la gente de mi Cuba	for the people of my Cuba
Mis ancestros	My ancestors
Todos mis muertos	All my dead
Todo eso represento	All this I represent
Cuba.[28]	Cuba.

The rhetoric of this song clearly draws on Afro-Cuban practices and beliefs, but it is also transnational as it explores issues of identity, faithfulness, and cultural presence through the medium of hip-hop, which originated in the urban African American and Latino/a communities of the United States. Those non-Spanish-speaking fans who do not understand the words and are just grooving on the music and the beat may be unaware that the group is evoking *orisha* as they seek to represent their Cuban roots.

SACRED RHETORIC, MATERIAL CULTURE, AND LATINO/A SPIRITUALITY

Latino/a sacred rhetoric and discourse can also be explored through a consideration of material culture. The concept of material culture can be understood in several ways, either in reference to the physical artifacts left behind by people and cultures, or as objects within their own cultural context. In this latter sense a focus on the material aspects of culture includes the examination of objects, images, and combined artifacts used in everyday life. Such a focus on the material goes beyond seeing items solely as folklore, folk crafts, or decorative art.

One such example of an object that blends Hispanic sacred rhetoric and religious and spiritual practices is the very common funeral card. The following, while from Puerto Rico, is typical of funeral or memorial cards that appear throughout the United States in Latino/a communities. Usually the memorial cards measure about two by three inches and are printed double-sided with a religious image on one side and a prayer or a passage of scripture on the reverse. Common choices (in both English and Spanish) include Psalm 23, the Hail Mary, or a prayer to the Virgin of Guadalupe. This cards fold open like a mini-pamphlet. The front shows a color picture of a crucified Christ, with eyes open and looking heavenward, head tilted right with the words "Jesus Nazarenus, Rex Judaeorum" (Jesus of Nazareth, King of the Jews, all in capital letters) with rays of light emanating from above. On the left inside is a slightly edited quotation from the Gospel of John, laid out in this fashion:

Jesús dijo:
"Yo soy la Resurreción y la Vida. El que cree en mí, aunque esté muerto, vivirá; y el que haya creído en mí, no morirá para siempre."
San Juan 11:25, 26

Jesus said:
"I am the resurrection and the life. Those who believe in me, even though they die, will live, and everyone who lives and believes in me will never die."
St. John 11:25, 26

The right inside of the prayer card contains a specific reference to the deceased:

En memoria de
[Name of deceased]
[Date of death]

Una lágrima se evapora, una flor sobre mi tumba se marchita, mas una oración por mi alma la recoge Dios. No lloréis amados míos. Voy a unirme con Dios y los espero en el cielo. Yo muero, pero mi amor no muere, yo os amaré en el cielo como los he amado en la tierra. A todos los que me habéis querido os pido que rogueis por mi, ques es la mayor prueba de cariño.

In memory of
[Name of deceased]
[Date of death]

A tear evaporates, a flower on my tomb wilts, but God receives my soul's prayer. Do not cry my beloved ones. I'm going to unite with God, and I wait for you in heaven. I die, but my love does not die, and I will love you in heaven as I have loved you on earth. To everyone who loved me I ask that you pray for me, which is the greatest proof of affection.

[Name and address of funeral home]

The back of the prayer card displays another color picture of Jesus as the good shepherd, looking straight on. It is curious, of course, that the picture is a northern European image of Jesus with blondish hair, fair skin, wearing a red robe with a broach clasp, holding a lamb in arms, with a shepherd's staff in his right hand.

David Morgan speaks of what he calls the sacred gaze, by which he means "the particular configuration of ideas, attitudes, and customs that informs a religious act of seeing as it occurs within a given cultural and historical setting."[29] In many cases the funeral cards might have a picture of the deceased as well. The card itself provides the visual cue of how to behave and what attitude to embrace during the days of the wake and funeral. Moreover, the memorial card becomes an aid for the days, weeks, months, and in some cases years ahead as people remember the deceased.

Some people keep the funeral card on their home altar or on the bedroom dresser. For those who observe the Day of the Dead, the memorial card with the picture of the deceased may be part of those annual altars.

RHETORIC AND RELIGIOSITY

The rhetoric of *santo* is one way of entry into cultural values, religious beliefs, sensibilities, behaviors, and practices, and consideration of the variety of expressions of sacred rhetoric of the diverse Latino/a communities is a profitable way to understand their religiosity. Sociologist Daphne Wiggins defines religiosity "as an individual's beliefs and behaviors in relation to/on behalf of the supernatural, as well as the consequences of these aspects upon that individual."[30] Wiggins's definition seems applicable to communities as well. The religiosity displayed in Hispanic sacred rhetoric provides glimpses into spiritual worldviews that are larger than the words, sayings, discourses, and practices of which they are a part. And for Latino/a communities, which are often described as on the margins of the dominant society and experience life in cultural, social, economic, and religious borderlands, careful attention to sacred rhetoric can identify the voices and religiosity of those on the margins of the margins.

This brief consideration of different expressions of Latino/a sacred rhetoric identifies abundant areas for further examination. Because Latino/a spirituality is expressed not only through words, but also through actions, there is an abundance of resources with which to explore further the nexus between rhetoric, practice, beliefs, and sacred texts as they are related to daily piety, sources of spiritual sustenance, different types of faith, and identity within the varieties of Latino/a spirituality.

SIX

Sacred Places and Spaces

WHAT IS A SACRED SPACE?

Like many Latina women, Raquel often would say that while she had many difficulties in life, she was also very blessed. She married young while in Puerto Rico and later moved with her growing family to the northeastern United States. Like millions of migrants before her who took the brave and traumatic step and left their homes, Raquel hoped for a better life for her children and for herself. As they settled into new and strange lives, money always was tight although both she and her husband worked long hours. More children came into the family. and increasingly her life was focused on raising her children and providing for her family. As time passed, the husband-father became by his choice a kind of adjunct member of the *familia* with a whole other life and interests on the outside. He popped in now and then for a meal and a change of clothes, sometimes giving money to pay bills. But for all intents and purposes, most of the time Raquel was a single parent without the title.

Somehow a house was purchased in a better neighborhood of the city for them to live, but many difficulties remained. Along the way two of the older boys fell victims to drug abuse, and the risks of urban life for the younger ones always were very real. Nevertheless Raquel managed to get through it all. She related that one of the ways she dealt with the daily struggles and disappointments of life was by going down to the basement, which she counted as one of her blessings. There in the basement by the washing machine in her private spot she would cry out to God, pray, spit out her frustrations and anger, asking for help, wisdom, and strength to persevere when abandoned by husband, sisters, and brothers, to plead for little miracles to pay the bills, to deliver those hooked on drugs, to protect others as they went to school and out into the world beyond, to petition for the happiness of all, and to give thanks when it came. Although Raquel lived only a few blocks away from a local Catholic shrine, it was the basement that was her day-to-day sustaining sacred space where she had regular encounters with the holy.

This chapter examines the connection between devotional practices and spiritualities and the experience of sacred space in the everyday lives of Latinas and Latinos. In his study of the Fang and Zulu peoples of Africa, anthropologist James Fernandez found that any consideration of sacred spaces will show "men and women achieving emergent qualitative states in which both inchoate men and women and inchoate space itself are given shape, character, and meaning."[1] Fernandez asserts that both people and places in a certain sense are only partially formed. It is the interaction between people and physical spaces that yields places considered to be sacred or holy.

In examining the different expressions of Latino/a spirituality, to what extent does space have an impact on people and the people have an impact on the space? In the case of Raquel's special place, a mundane basement was re-shaped into a sacred space for her that had a direct impact on her spirituality and her daily encounter with *la lucha* (the struggle) for life, with cascading effects on her family and on everyone with whom she interacted. But in a symbiotic way it also was the constantly developing spirituality she brought downstairs with her that transformed the basement space, which in turn transformed her.

Exactly what is meant by sacred space? Answering that question is best achieved through asking a related one, namely, for whom is a space sacred? Answering the second question in a specific contextual way helps avoid the conclusion that the concept of sacred space is meaningless because it can mean anything.[2] It is this emphasis on persons as agents who define their own sacred space and determine why that space is holy for them that provides a means for understanding sacred space; it is also a crucial part of any focus on lived religions.[3] It is through such everyday religious and spiritual agency of choosing and creating social space as holy that the vitality of religion in modern social life is demonstrated.[4]

In a similar vein Louis Nelson and his colleagues suggest three interpretive rubrics for understanding the human construction of sacred space: "(1) places become inscribed as sacred through belief and practice, (2) sacred places are inextricably linked to sociopolitical identities, and

(3) sacred meanings are not stable."[5] The consideration here of Latino/a sacred spaces employs these analytical tools of inscription, identity, and instability to understand holy places in these contextualized expressions of lived religion.

Many people will define a building with a dedicated purpose, such as a cathedral, mosque, church sanctuary, temple, synagogue, kingdom hall, or a New England meeting house, as their sacred space, whereas for others buildings are not required to have an experience of the holy. Some people experience the holy in a special place in nature, in the mountains of New Hampshire, along the seashore as the waves roll in, or in the unique beauty of the high desert of northern New Mexico. But there are also people who find both dedicated buildings and locations in nature equally holy. Belden Lane suggests a foundational axiom for the study of sacred place when he asserts, "Above all else, sacred place is 'storied place.' Particular locales come to be recognized as sacred because of the stories told about them."[6] Raquel's story relates how a basement became a sacred place for her.

These storied sacred places can be private or public. Wherever and whatever they might be for Latino/as, they are sacred spots where people relate the experience of an intense sense of the presence of God, or the divine, or some higher power, or some other sense of what is holy to them. These spaces may be places of quiet contemplation, of prayer or meditation, or places where persons withdraw to recharge. The places called sacred might be locations where there is a feeling of safety and protection. Sometimes these holy places may be the sites of great awe, or they may be places that challenge, and yet people are still drawn to them. They may be places of corporate worship or places of corporate silence as all wait for the inspiration of the Spirit.[7] And sometimes the same site can generate all these reactions simultaneously.

Leaders of churches, synagogues, mosques, and temples may define sacred space, but groups and individuals without any formal authority also name sacred space. Sometimes popular religion asserts itself and the people recognize certain spots as holy before any authority bestows such a designation. As anthropologist Margaret Rodman asserts, "Places are not inert containers. They are politicized, culturally relative, historically specific, local and multiple constructions."[8] Places that are identified as sacred spaces can have multiple concurrent meanings for various individuals and groups. In order to understand the sacredness of a particular place it is necessary to focus on the lived religion and spirituality in that specific setting.

Within the diverse forms of Latino/a spirituality, "place" or location as social sacred spaces plays a prominent sustaining and creative role that touches other areas of life. These sacred spaces may be permanent places of repeated and regular use, or they may be spontaneous locations of the sacred. They may be fixed places or they might be moveable as individuals seek to bring their religion and spirituality with them wherever they go. Sacred places may be communal, where rituals and traditions of long standing are fervently reenacted, but new understandings and actions can also occur.[9] And in accord with the rubric of instability already mentioned, the meaning and understanding of particular sacred spaces may change as contexts change. It is possible that as communities engage sacred space over time, new meanings may replace older ones or multiple levels of meaning may accrue and in some sense operate concurrently. Again, the insight of James Fernandez on African sacred space is helpful; he says that "the qualities that emerge in sacred places are not all contained implicitly in the place, but are brought to it by performance, the acting out of images. Emergent qualities arise in the interaction of images men [sic] bring to scenes or sites with the sites themselves."[10] It is through examination of the performance (in the broadest sense) of Latino/a spiritualities that a sense of Latino/a sacred space will become clearer.

In some cases Latino/a sacred spaces may take on a transnational dimension. A prime example of this phenomenon in shrines and churches is the previously mentioned Cristo Negro (Black Christ) of Esquipulas appearing in Guatemala; San Antonio, Texas; and Chimayó, New Mexico; intense devotion is manifested at each location. Through the beliefs, experiences, and practices of devotees the Black Christ is inscribed at each place and in a specific way so that a connection between the place and the devotion has shaped sociopolitical as well as religious/spiritual identity. This is especially true when some sort of ritual is included.[11]

The extent of the devotion to the Virgin of Guadalupe is another transnational example of the construction of communal sacred places. Localized shrines of devotion to Guadalupe can appear in places as diverse as an Episcopal church in north Philadelphia, St. Patrick's Cathedral in New York City, a small mission church in the Diocese of Miami, a major shrine outside Chicago, a backyard holy place in south Phoenix, or on unnumbered home altars.[12] Other examples include the Shrine of the Virgin of Charity Cobre in Miami, Florida, or the celebration by Peruvians of the Lord of Miracles (el Señor de Milagros de Nazarenas) in Chicago, Dallas, Denver, Hartford, Miami, Milwaukee, and New York.[13]

As demonstrated in the cases of dedication to the Virgin of Guadalupe from Mexico, the Virgin de Caridad de Cobre of Cuba, the Dominican Republic's Our Lady of Altagracia, and the el Señor de Milagros from Peru, migration does not cut off devotions that have their roots in Latin America. Commenting on the transnational dimension of religious conviction, Manuel A. Vásquez and Marie F. Marquardt state:

> In the face of globalization, the nation-state can no longer contain religion within its boundaries. Released from the disciplinary power of the modern secular nation-state, religion is free to enter the globalizing, regionalizing, and localizing dynamics described here to generate new identities and territories. . . . Cities [and suburbs] become places where those displaced by globalization—be it Latino immigrants in the United States or peasants migrating to growing metropolises in Latin America—try to make sense of their baffling world by mapping and remapping sacred landscapes through religious practices like making pilgrimages, holding festivals, and constructing altars, shrines, and temples.[14]

In many cases the challenges of life in the United States reinforce beliefs and practices, but also contribute to the remapping of sacred landscapes. While it can be said that some sacred places are still rooted in their localities of origin, in another sense they have gone global as their adherents interact, giving shape and new meaning to their devotions in new locales. In this process the character of their spirituality is reshaped as they simultaneously craft new identities as Latinas and Latinos in the United States. Such profound multifaceted transformations already have had substantial effect on religion in U.S. American life.[15]

FIXED SPACES

"Fixed places" usually refer to synagogues, church buildings, mosques, temples, and other readily recognized religious gathering places. Such sacred buildings are places practitioners gather for worship, meditation, and encouragement. Permanent sacred places are sites for instruction and devotion where people may be nourished in community. Such structures are also repositories of sacred objects and texts. However, fixed sacred spaces are not confined to officially sanctioned edifices. Within the varieties of Latino/a spirituality, sacred places include special places in homes as well as seemingly impromptu shrines. One prominent example of transnational sacred space is found in different manifestations in the United States of widespread devotion to the Virgin of Guadalupe.

Virgin of Guadalupe at St. Patrick's Cathedral

One very prominent example of transnational fixed sacred space is found in the widespread devotion to the Virgin of Guadalupe in New York City. For a number of years on December 12, the feast day of Our Lady of Guadalupe, New York's St. Patrick's Cathedral becomes the pilgrimage destination of thousands of Mexican Americans and Mexicans, many of whom are immigrants, both documented and undocumented, and part of the global movements of peoples. Described by some as "America's parish church," St. Patrick's Cathedral was named for Ireland's patron saint and constructed in part with the financial gifts of nineteenth-century immigrants. Now in the early twenty-first century St. Patrick's is the annual sacred gathering site for new waves of immigrants and citizens as they join together in devotion and worship to honor the Virgin of Guadalupe, the patroness of the Americas.

Near the East 50th Street entrance on the cathedral's south side just to the right of the main sanctuary is found the Altar of the Sacred Heart where the image of the Virgin of Guadalupe is located, drawing more visitors than to any other area of the cathedral. The actions and practices of the devotees who visit this sacred place are similar to what occurs in Mexico: adherents pray, process, perhaps leave an offering of flowers, and kiss an image of the Virgin. However, in actions that reflect their context in New York, many also carry signs calling for immigration amnesty or declaring that no human being is illegal.

Anthropologist Ayshia Gálvez sees that for many undocumented Mexicans in New York, their devotion to Guadalupe, including the yearly pilgrimage to her shrine at St. Patrick's Cathedral, is not solely an expression of their religiosity and spirituality but also a source of power and an avenue for social and political engagement as they advocate for human rights, dignity, and immigration reform.[16] Gálvez relates how every December since 2002 there has been an organized binational torch relay run (La Antorcha Guadalupana) from the Basilica of Guadalupe to St. Patrick's Cathedral. "The runners wear shirts that read 'Messengers of a people divided by the border' and advocate immigration reform at the same time that they pay homage to their patroness."[17] The relay run starts in Mexico City, continues through the Mixteca region of Mexico, through Houston, San Antonio, and Dallas, through Louisiana, Mississippi, Alabama, and up the eastern seaboard through North Carolina and Philadelphia eventually arriving in New York City. The devotion shown in this relay run connects sacred place to sacred place and for a short period of time anoints its route as a sacred highway in what Gálvez describes as "space sacralized by movement."[18]

Both the fixed sacred spaces of the Basilica of Our Lady of Guadalupe in Mexico City and St. Patrick's Cathedral in New York City interact with other fixed sacred stops (such as San Fernando Cathedral in San Antonio) along the entire transit of the torch run, creating a transnational sacred pathway as the participants encounter the holy. Gálvez's assessment is that "the sober belief that the Virgin is to be found wherever those who believe in her may be is not only a vestige of pre-Reformation popular Catholicism, it is a continuation of a five-centuries tradition and an artifact of globalization."[19]

The Second Tepeyac in Illinois

The transnational aspect of Guadalupan sacred places is not solely the devotion of migrant Mexicans and Mexican Americans, it is also at work in the devotions of people of other national origins. Historian and cultural anthropologist Elaine A. Peña examined such manifestations in pilgrimages that take place to the shrine outside of Chicago called the Second Tepeyac of North America, a copy of the shrine at Tepeyac in Mexico. While, as expected, Mexicans and Mexican Americans participate in the devotions, Peña notes the transnational dimension as well: "On a crisp fall day in a northwest suburb of Chicago, Mexican, Salvadoran, Guatemalan, and Honduran Guadalupanas/os gathered in the gymnasium-cum-sanctuary at the Second Tepeyac of North America—a sanctioned replica of the hill in Tepeyac in Mexico City."[20]

Regardless of the weather, tens of thousands of people participate in the annual December festival in honor of the Virgin of Guadalupe held in Des Plaines, Illinois.[21] Yearly, hundreds of devotees walk in sacred procession over twenty miles, a journey that can take well over six hours, from parishes in Chicago and the communities of Cicero, Rolling Meadows, and Northbrook to the shrine in the northwest suburbs. These pilgrimages are additional examples of the spatial sacralization of the routes taken. With the shrine located on the grounds of Maryville Academy, it is estimated that between three thousand and thirty-five hundred people attend mass there every weekend.

The shrine itself is outdoors, with an enclosed replica of the *tilma* (cloak) that has Guadalupe's image and statues of Juan Diego kneeling before the Virgin of Guadalupe; it is situated on a manufactured knoll meant to evoke Tepeyac. Highlighting similarities between devotional practices at the original shrine and its Illinois replica, Peña interprets how "praying, chanting, and embodying the sixteenth-century master narrative sustains the cult of the Virgin of Guadalupe. Devotional performances allow geographically disparate Guadalupans spaces to live in concert across borders. Even then those practices produce results that are numerous and varied."[22] While both spaces are inscribed with deep meaning and draw upon shared Guadalupan devotion, the sociopolitical and religious identities of the spaces and devotees, different in each context, testify to the changeability of meanings.

At Second Tepeyac and paralleling what occurs in New York City, Peña contends that for undocumented devotees, the sacred space of Second Tepeyac serves as a shrine and pilgrimage destination but also as a safe haven and a site for political articulation. The leadership of Second Tepeyac provides naturalization and citizenship workshops and organizes trips to Chicago and Springfield, the state capital, to support immigration reform. Peña describes how a pan-Latino/a identity is nurtured in this context.

The Second Tepeyac provides an atmosphere in which communities are encouraged to celebrate their distinct heritages and homelands. Devotees, many of whom learn about and circulate religious practices along migration circuits, acknowledge each other's nationalist affiliations, but their religious principles often exceed secular identifications, even when national symbols such as flags formed part of their devotional spaces. Further, they appeal explicitly to the sacred when expressing collective pro-immigrant subjectivities.[23]

El Santuario de Chimayó

Not far from Taos, New Mexico, in the high desert within sight of the Sangre de Cristo Mountains, each year during the Christian Holy Week thousands of people make a pilgrimage to northern New Mexico to visit El Santuario de Chimayó and the Santo Niño Chapel, both fixed sacred spaces. Pilgrims make the journey for a variety of reasons. Many are motivated by a deep desire to connect with the passion of Christ; they believe that sacrifice and suffering are essential parts of the Christian life. Some go to the Santuario in the hope of healing from illness and unhappiness through the sacrifice of pilgrimage and by obtaining some of the healing dirt from the special spot in the sacristy.[24] Some call the chapel of Santo Niño de Atocha at Chimayó the most important shrine to Santo Niño in the United States, which partially explains the pilgrimages. The chapel is just a short walk from the Santuario.

Pilgrims drive or ride to the vicinity; others carrying crosses and glow sticks walk from ten to a hundred miles to this sacred space. Persons of all types, women and men, young and old, Hispanos and Native Americans from the pueblos in New Mexico and beyond make the trek. Spanish and English, Tiwa, Tewa, and Keres can be heard spoken by the pilgrims as they make their journey, giving audible testimony to the diversity of people drawn to El Santuario. Along the way pilgrims are making the journey in cars and trucks and on motorcycles.

Niño Fidencio

Pilgrimage takes place in other pathways of spirituality among Latino/as. Thousands from the United States and Mexico make pilgrimages each year, especially on March 19, the Feast Day of St. Joseph, and during four days in October, to the small community of Espinazo, Nuevo León, Mexico, where there is the *tumba* (tomb) of José de Jesús Fidencio Constantino Síntora, better known to his followers as Niño Fidencio (d. 1938). Devotees of the Niño Fidencio, in groups known as missions, participate in the Fidencio fiestas held twice yearly in March and October.[25] Niño Fidencio was a famous Mexican *curandero* (healer) and the fountainhead of a transnational spiritual movement and widely practiced healing tradition that continues into the present.[26] Held to be a folk saint, Niño Fidencio was believed to have *el don* (the gift) of healing, reputedly curing people of all kinds of maladies, including tuberculosis and leprosy, and delivering babies as well. Since his death the Fidencista adherents also believe that Niño Fidencio still speaks to them through mediums.

Groups of pilgrims—not just from border communities but also from Houston and Los Angeles, Florida, Illinois, Idaho, and Ohio—visit with the spirit of Niño Fidencio at Cerro de la Campana in Espinazo, one of the most prominent pilgrimage destinations in Mexico. The pilgrim groups are led by a spirit medium called a *materia* or *cajón* who is dressed in white like Niño Fidencio; they travel to show reverence, renew their faith, and have their healing powers rejuvenated at the place they hold sacred, the location of Niño's ministry. Carrying standards, banners, flowers, and incense, the pilgrim groups are led in procession to Niño Fidencio's tomb, singing holy songs, or *alabanzas*, and they receive a blessing from El Niño channeled through a medium. Antonio Zavaleta and Alberto Salinas Jr. describe how for the devotees of Niño Fidencio who travel to this sacred place, "the world changes all around them, but not so much here where history, culture, ritual, and memory merge and the spiritual life looms over the material world."[27] In a sense when adherents assemble at the sacred space they enter a state of suspension away from the routine, in order to be energized and return to daily life.

HOME ALTARS

When I was growing up as a Puerto Rican Catholic in Connecticut, in our home and those of Hispanic friends whose homes I visited, at least one spot in the apartment or house was always reserved for a gathering of pictures, candles, rosaries, and statues of saints. At certain times of the year it seemed as if the candles multiplied. Only later did I realize that these special places were home altars and shrines.

Theologian Michelle A. Gonzalez notes the leadership role of women in creating and maintaining home altars: "For Latinas, home altars mark the domestic space as sacred and demonstrate the importance of the sacred in Latina everyday life. They serve as a site of prayer, reflection, and remembrance."[28] Typical objects that might be found include a crucifix, Virgin

Mary, St. Anthony, St. Jude, St. Martin, family photographs, especially of deceased members of the family, a rosary or two, perhaps candles, palm fronds tied into a cross from some previous Palm Sunday. Depending on ethnicity, national original, and family traditions, home altars may take on a particular emphasis. For example, Guadalupe may be part of an altar found in Mexican American homes, whereas the Virgin of Charity of Cobre may be part of a Cuban American altar. Some home altars may be international with images of the patron saints from many nations, and a person or a family may have a particular devotion to a saint such as St. Martin of Porres.

In her study of transnational Dominican communities in Miraflores and Boston, Peggy Levitt notes the common belief that

> God is present, in whatever form, wherever the believer is. Certain home-based, informal folk practices, traditionally at the core of Mirafloreño religious life, transfer easily to Boston. It is as simple to create an altar, practice devotions or light candles to a particular saint, make *promesas*, or say the rosary in Boston as it is in Miraflores.[29]

The tradition and practice of small altars and devotional spaces in the home is widespread among Latinas and Latinos of all types throughout the United States. Some observers see in the home altars an expression of intimacy with the sacred. Laura E. Pérez asserts that "as a form of domestic religious practice outside the domain of dominant religiosities, the altar has been a site for the socially and culturally 'alter,' or other, to express, preserve, and transmit cultural and gender-based religious and political differences."[30]

These home altars appear in all kinds of Latino/a religious and spiritual contexts, not solely in Catholic homes. Altars in the home figure prominently in the beliefs and practices of various adherents of African-diaspora traditions: "Like most people who attend ceremonies of *orisha* worship, I was drawn at once to the altars. The decorated altar (also called throne or shrine) houses, sanctifies, and calls attention to the honored Orisha or Orishas."[31]

Laura Chester describes the components of a Rosicrucian altar that Loreto Mendez and Earl Niichel maintain in their home in Arizona: an enclosed temple place with a font for holy water and a skylight above a triangular altar that allows the movement of the light throughout the day;

a statue of the Virgin Mary with a crystal angel at her feet; and an image of the Infant of Prague, representing the Divine Child that resides in each person at a higher spot. Mexican American Mendez was raised a Catholic but now is devoted to Rosicrucianism as she explores mystical teachings and how they can help in daily life. Maintaining this home sacred space is part of their larger religious life as they participate in the metaphysical community of the Church of the Cosmic Christ with an Italian kabalistic minister. Loreto Mendez shared her reason for desiring a home chapel: "I wanted a place where I could feel safe, a sanctuary from the outside world."[32]

Home altars are not restricted to Catholics or Latinas and Latinos practicing alternative traditions. Some Hispanic Protestants *evangélico/as* who very intentionally moved away from the material expressions of traditional home altars, nevertheless still experience an impulse to have some dedicated sacred space in the home. Justo González notes that this impulse is addressed through the medium of *"el altar familiar—*a time and place set aside for Bible study and prayer—and designed to remind everyone of the larger family to which each belongs and to strengthen that larger family."[33] Some Latino/a Protestant churches provide specific suggestions on how to foster and sustain a family altar, with regular family time (typically of fifteen or twenty minutes) for Bible reading and prayer; they also suggest that such time be scheduled for just before children go to bed.

SACRED SPACES ON THE ROAD

Sacred spaces in Latino/a contexts are understood not only as religious buildings, shrines, and home altars, they can also be understood in the sacralized moves people make. Pilgrimage, referred to above, focuses on fixed sacred space. Pilgrimage also takes place in everyday expressions in public areas, which may be passed unnoticed each day by the uninformed, but are true sacred places for a few. In their study of pilgrimage Simon Coleman and John Elsner report, "A pilgrimage is not just a journey: it also involves the confrontation of travelers with rituals, holy objects and sacred architecture. . . . Moreover, pilgrimage is as much about returning home with the souvenirs and narratives of the pilgrim's adventure."[34] Once again it is the story that the pilgrim carries with him or her to the pilgrimage site, as well as the one they take away with them, that enables the significance of such sacred places and gives concrete physical expression to religious belief and practice. Pilgrimage represents a demonstration of the abiding pull of sacred places.

One such sacred story of a pilgrimage is related by anthropologist Paula Elizabeth Holmes-Rodman. In 1997 she joined a group of *guadalupana* pilgrims (devotees of the Virgin of Guadalupe) who made a one hundred-mile trek to the Santuario de Chimayó. A crucifix, which was their *guia* (literally "guide"), was carried at the front of the group of pilgrims while they walked toward Chimayó. Holmes-Rodman recounts the faith and dedication of the pilgrims she traveled with and how they welcomed her into their group and encouraged her to persevere. Holmes-Rodman also tells how at the end of their walk, "The last mile, all the pilgrims sing this song over and over, rounds of which I still hear in my head":

Vienen con alegría, Señor,	They come with joy, Lord.
Cantando vienen con alegría, Señor,	Singing they come with joy, Lord.
Los que caminan por la vida, Señor,	Those walking the path of life, Lord,
Sembrando tu paz y amor.	Spreading your peace and love.[35]

Pilgrimages and processions can provide renewal of faith, joy, and strength. Moreover, pilgrimages and processions can be reshaped in ways that express devotion and spirituality but also bring about transformation. One such example is given by Karen Mary Davalos, who describes what occurred with the practice of the Via Crucis (Way of the Cross) in Chicago. On Christmas Eve 1976 and New Year's Day 1977 the Latino/a neighborhood of Pilsen suffered two housing fires in quick succession that resulted in the loss of lives of members of the Latino/a community. Many community residents felt that the loss of life was the result of continuing poor housing conditions and the neglect of city officials in enforcing building codes as well as providing inadequate services to Pilsen.

In this context, St. Vitus Church parishioners "organized Pilsen's first Via Crucis the following Good Friday to bring attention to their current situation. By turning to this Catholic devotion, they communicated multiple messages to Pilsen and the city of Chicago, including a return to cultural heritage and faith, an act of solidarity, collective remembrance of the people who died in the fires, and a moment of consciousness-raising about conditions in Pilsen."[36]

Latina participants in the Via Crucis associated their everyday situation with the roles they played as the suffering women of Jerusalem and Mary, and they used the transitory sacralization of space to express a theological basis for action in Pilsen. Davalos states that the Pilsen Latinas

> were specific in naming the conditions of their neighborhood—*racismo e injusticia*—that forced them to keep a careful eye on their children. Many women told me that the Via Crucis gave them strength, knowing that Mary and her contemporaries also felt helpless and could not stop Christ's pain. "The Via Crucis is something we live in the barrio," a coordinator told a reporter. "The Virgin Mary cried for her son and now the mothers cry for their sons who use drugs and are in gangs. It's real."[37]

A Mexican American, born in Mexico into a Catholic family, and who describes herself as a very devout Catholic when she was a child, experienced a different type of pilgrimage. As an adult this Latina found herself on a pathway that sent her on a pilgrimage to study with the Dalai Lama in Asia. Telling her own story she says:

> I took refuge in the Tibetan Buddhist tradition with His Holiness the Dalai Lama when I least expected it. And although I have traveled and studied in Asia, I still don't like to call myself a Buddhist because I often find that I don't match whatever definition the other person has in mind! For many years, my practice was extremely personal and solitary; it is exciting to see my path becoming more expansive and inclusive. When I have to use categories, I describe myself as a person of multiple heritage, of both European and indigenous descent. I grew up in an "interspace" of cultures and languages, North and South, old world and new. As Latinos, we find ourselves in this "blessed predicament" of having to integrate a complex history into our sense of identity. I've had to look at myself through the eyes of both the colonizer and the colonized. It is an intense burden; only in retrospect do I feel it as a gift. Eastern philosophy, meditation, and the Buddhist exploration of the ultimate nature of reality have helped me to integrate seemingly irreconcilable universes.[38]

This pilgrimage to a geographic location was external, but it was also internal. Her journey to an external sacred place also gave her insight about an internal sacred space in which she could integrate universes.

There are other ways sacred spaces are found on the road besides pilgrimages and processions. There is an abundant and growing number of roadside shrines, memorials, and monuments that can be found across the United States. Typically called *descanos* (resting places) by Latino/as, they may mark the spot where a loved one lost her or his life in a traffic accident. The physical aspect of these sacred spots may be a small cross, flowers, or perhaps a stuffed animal at a certain spot along the side of a road.[39] In some parts of the country the shrine may include an image of a saint, or even votive candles. Alberto Barrera describes how in Texas "families build a *bóveda*, or small replica of a tomb, at the site, complete with a small glass door in front. Candles are lighted inside this small structure in much the same way others bring fresh flowers."[40]

Family members devote themselves to creating and maintaining these roadside shrines. Documenting this Latino/a custom, Sylvia Anne Grider suggests that the spread of this practice among non-Hispanics may be influenced by the growing dispersion of people from Mexico and Central America throughout the United States. Grider also suggests that the practice of creating *descansos* may have evolved from the custom of carrying the casket to the gravesite and marking where the pallbearers periodically took a rest. "At least in New Mexico and other parts of the Hispanic Southwest, this custom evolved into placing crosses near the site of death. It also came to include marking and decorating the grave of the deceased, especially for Días de los Muertos, or the Days of the Dead."[41]

Another very common expression of sacred space on the road is how motor vehicles are sacralized as expressions of piety and spirituality. The first car of my father's that I recall as a child was a long and big vehicle (of course I was much smaller back then) with tail fins and whitewall tires, and it seemed to be made of solid steel. Rides in my father's car were rare things for us kids, but one thing I remember from sitting in the back seat was looking forward at the dashboard where fixed in place by a magnet was a small, ivory-colored statue of a saint about four inches tall. I think it was either St. Jude or St. Christopher, but sadly I never thought of asking my father or mother who he was. The saint was not alone; there was more.

I remember the review mirror above the dashboard, from which hung rosary beads and at least one holy medal on a thin chain. And often present was a simple cross, made from folded palm fronds received from church on Palm Sunday. This was my father's mobile altar as he went through his daily routines.

Dashboard saints are not simply relics of the past or my dusty memory. A quick online search indicates multiple opportunities for a person to acquire her or his own motor vehicle saint. One website offers the Virgin de Regla statuette, inviting the purchaser to "dress up your car and conjure up some good luck with this lovely Virgin of Regla dashboard saint. Standing 4½ inches tall with a magnet in the base, this plastic representation of the patron saint of Cuba will be a stylish addition to your car."[42] And sacralizing motor vehicles is not limited to the dashboard. Shortly after I moved to Dallas as an adult I pulled into the parking lot of a supermarket and was struck by something I repeatedly saw during my time in Texas. A pickup truck driven by a young Latino was parked nearby, and on the back window of the cab was an elaborate painting of the Virgin of Guadalupe. This type of automotive sacred imagery can be seen all across the country.

PLACES FOR MOURNING

Typically in the United States there are four places connected with mourning in response to death: "(1) funeral homes, (2) houses of worship, (3) cemeteries, and (4) homes."[43] While in various European American contexts there is an emphasis on containing grief, more typically in Latino/a milieus there is a pattern of expressive mourning that connects each of these four settings. Historically, for Latino/as public mourning in response to death is accepted and important for the family and the community. People gather to pray for the soul of the departed, to honor his or her memory, and to show respect to the grieving family.

While churches, temples, and other formal religious structures are readily recognized as sacred spaces and funeral services are fairly standard, increasingly practices from countries of origin are replicated in the United States, which has resulted in an increase of in-home funeral services, with the home being reshaped as a different type of sacred space. Funeral homes are adjusting their practices and facilitating overnight viewings and family feasts in mortuaries. Often all four settings are part of the sacred spaces utilized in Latino/a mourning.

The cemetery as sacred space is one of the settings that has been significantly impacted by the Latino/a presence. Cemeteries often make people uneasy, as they are reminders of decay, pain, and loss, and the ultimate end of all flesh in the final journey of life. Moreover, in the United States we live in a dominant culture where one of the impulses is to distance and sanitize death. In addition, popular culture often portrays cemeteries as haunted places. In such a cultural environment cemeteries are a prominent reminder of what many people want to forget.

Paradoxically, some Hispanics consider cemeteries to be sacred space, public places that serve as gathering sites to remember and honor their deceased. Such gatherings become social occasions for religious and spiritual remembrance and activities and a catalyst for the transmission of family narratives. In the ethnic immigrations from eastern and southern Europe of the nineteenth and early twentieth centuries, people arrived along with their burial ceremonies, practices, and rites. Through their self-help organizations and associations some of these groups created their own cemeteries.

Similarly, recent immigrants from Latin America have brought their traditional burial traditions and rituals with them. Recent expansion of the Mexican Día de los Muertos (Day of the Dead) from the indigenous and *mestizo* practices of central and southern Mexico to rituals that are now recognized in U.S. popular culture testify to the power of this set of rituals for reclaiming sacred space connected to identity.[44] Today Day of the Dead commemorations are held in cemeteries throughout the United States, where families claim the cemetery as a sacred space to remember and celebrate their deceased family members and discover resources for continuing their own lives.

SUMMARY

Within the diverse forms of Hispanic/Latino spirituality, sacred spaces include fixed spaces of formal sanctuaries and temples, transitory and temporary spaces that are made holy for a period of time such as the moveable sacred places that are pilgrimages, as well as other sacred places for the presence of *santo*, including homes, roadside shrines, and memorials. Aspects of ethnic, religious, and spiritual belonging can be identified through an examination of how sacred space is defined and interacted with in Latino/a contexts. In this creation and re-creation of sacred space there is a type of sacred geography at work. Victor Turner describes this experience as a type of liminal and transformative space of both transition and potentiality.[45] Latino/a sacred space is the threshold between the struggles of everyday life and the sources of sustenance, fulfillment, and meaning that empower people to persevere in those places and settings that are not holy.

An examination of the varieties of Latino/a spirituality, particularly through the way places are made sacred through fixed structures, festivals, altars, and shrines, provides a window not only into those beliefs and practices, but also into the contemporary globalization of religions and cultures. Drawing on the work of Henri Lefebvre, Peña states that "belief needs a receptacle; ideology desires a vehicle. Sites of practice—Tepeyac, the Second Tepeyac, pilgrimage routes, the corner of Rogers and Honore on Chicago's Far North Side—are repositories for the sacred. Adherents' devotional performances, the Virgin's iconography, and the coded symbols that adorn shrines are conduits."[46] Peña's comments can be expanded to other expressions of Latino/a spirituality, far beyond those examined in Mexico and Illinois. Everyday beliefs and practices of Latino/a peoples need to be expressed and deposited to be drawn upon in the future, and the sacred spaces they create enable them to do so.

SEVEN

Exploring Spanglish Spirituality

In a public lecture on Latino/a spirituality I was honored by a very kind and generous introduction, which is fairly typical when a person is invited to speak at another educational institution.[1] After the dean highlighted my academic and scholarly accomplishments as part of the introduction, I think that I may have confounded my audience by beginning with the following:

Gracias for your kind palabras.

Muchísmas gracias for the invitation para hablar aquí con ustedes.

Many thanks to you students y la facultad, and a todos who came today.

Looking at your faces I can see that a majority of you may have similar questions,

"What is he saying?" "What's happening here?"

"Has something pushed Aponte over the edge?" "Did he crack?"

Maybe I have cracked, but one thing for certain, I'm hablando Spanglish!

LIVING IN SPANGLISH

By starting that way I wanted the audience to get something of the feel of living in Spanglish. The word "Spanglish" may be vaguely familiar; perhaps the word is known from the title of a movie a few years back with Adam Sandler, Paz López, and Téa Leoni,[2] or from the performance of Latino stand-up comedian Bill Santiago.[3] But Spanglish is more than a movie or a performance. Spanglish is a moving target; it is hard to pin down, but easily recognized. The term was coined to describe a fluid, constantly changing colloquial combination or mixture of primarily English and Spanish.

Some say that the Puerto Rican journalist Salvador Tió (1911–89) coined the word "Spanglish"in 1952.[4] Another version of a term to describe this phenomenon is Espanglish, which of course is Spanish for Spanglish.

Whether known as Espanglish or Spanglish, at the very least it is a living manner of communication that constantly shifts vocabulary and grammar among peoples of Latin American descent in the United States. Spanglish can be understood as a linguistic border-crossing that happens everywhere and regularly. Theologian Carmen Nanko-Fernández observes, "For some, especially the younger generations, Spanglish offers a voice that holds in creative tension the multiple dimensions of hybrid identities."[5] This describes one of the benefits of Spanglish as it expresses the current multiple identities that U.S. Hispanics carry with them. Users of Spanglish linguistically cross social and cultural borders many times each day. For numerous Latino/as of all generations Spanglish is the vehicle of choice for those daily border crossings.

Many call Spanglish a "mishmash" of Spanish and English and frown upon it. For example, Arlene Dávila notes how on a cable network's Spanish-language talk show *Cristina,* instances of Spanglish are beeped out as if they were obscenities.[6] In some circles there appears to be little room for those who use Spanglish on a daily basis. In a racialized and class differentiated cultural context in the United States—where Latino/a identity is tied to the Spanish language and "shaped by the dominant language ideology that equates working-class Spanish speakers with poverty and academic failure, and defines their bilingual children as linguistically deficient and cognitively confused"[7]—the presence of Spanglish puts identity classifications into doubt. Nevertheless, despite disapproval by some, Spanglish has its apologists, including the sometimes controversial Mexican-born author and scholar of Latin American and Latino culture Ilan Stavans. Stavans says,

> Yes it's a hodgepodge. . . . But its creativity astonishes me. In many ways, I see in it the beauties and achievements of jazz, a musical style that sprung up among African Americans as a result of improvisation and lack of education. Eventually, though it became a major force in America, a state of mind breaking out of the ghetto into the middle class and beyond. Will Spanglish follow a similar route?[8]

If Stavan's analysis is accurate and his image appropriate, then Spanglish/ Espanglish like jazz is a confluence of several linguistic traditions with recognizable themes, but a great deal of ad libbing and spontaneity. Jazz-like Spanglish continues to incorporate new elements as its performers interpret what has been received for the new moment. Although disparaged by many, the state of mind, being, and action that is Spanglish is much more significant than its detractors realize.

One of the main reasons to consider this linguistic expression is that Spanglish/Espanglish is here and it is not going to disappear. We would be hard pressed to find any school, college, university, or even those places known for teaching arcane languages—such as a seminary or university divinity school—that teaches Spanglish. And yet unnumbered bilingual people use it every day in some form, whether they are Spanish-dominant, English-dominant, or something in between. Spanglish is everywhere and yet many people do not know what it is. Spanglish is found throughout the United States and yet can differ in every place it is heard. Commenting on Chicano/a varieties of Spanish in the U.S. Southwest, Rosaura Sánchez observes:

> I do not pretend to suggest that the characteristics of the Spanish varieties presented here are unique to Chicanos or the Southwest. The popular varieties of Argentina, Chile, Mexico, Peru, Venezuela, and other Spanish-speaking areas share many of the features of Chicano Spanish. In general terms, all popular varieties share certain tendencies and certain rules. But despite similarities each specific context is distinct, and the mode of expression is necessarily different. In that sense, the language of Chicanos is a product of the Chicano community. It is the verbalization of communal experience.[9]

Whatever manifestation of Spanglish one encounters, it emerges from the experience of particular groups of people. Spanglish is not the affectation of individuals or small clusters, but of diverse, living communities of Latino/as navigating their daily experience.

As contextual expressions of *lo cotidiano* (routine daily life), Spanglish is remarkably fluid as a language. Someone may speak Spanglish and then switch from English to Spanish, back to English, and create new words that mix both languages. This occurs in everyday speech but is also a common phenomenon in rock, rap music, hip-hop culture, and reggaeton.[10] None of these contextually coined words appear in the *Oxford English Dictionary* or the *Diccionario de la Lengua Española* of the Real Academia Española. However, the absence of lexical endorsement does not prevent the words from being used.

While some people do think of Spanglish as a language, others consider it to be vulgar, undignified slang and a corruption that should be stamped out at every opportunity. And while I can appreciate the arguments and motivations of linguistic purists (both for Spanish and English), I judge their efforts to be in vain. In our lifetimes we are witnesses to the emergence of a new language, a grassroots manifestation of ways that people linguistically negotiate their worlds in the midst of the daily *lucha* (struggle) for life.

Because Spanglish is such a part of everyday speech for so many Latino/as, there are many illustrations that can be readily identified.[11] For example, in Dallas, signs reading *"washerterías."* can be seen throughout certain neighborhoods. Spanish does have a perfectly good word for laundromat in *lavandería*, but in lots of places in north Texas if you want to wash your clothes you must look for a *washertería*. There are many examples of Spanglish in everyday language and popular music in newly created verb forms such as

bipear: to page someone using a beeper

frizar: to freeze

frontear: a word used in reggaeton derived from the hip-hop term "frontin," meaning putting up a façade or "false front," usually with the sense of making false claims that cannot be backed up

jangeando: hanging out

parkear: to park a car

printear: to print

lonche: lunch

lonchando: having lunch.

Language researchers have demonstrated that Spanish-English code-switching that helps produce Spanglish is not simply random linguistic confusion.[12] Spanish verbal patterns seem to dominate Spanglish, but the language uses English words as substitutes for existing Spanish words or creates new verbs using English but following Spanish verb forms.[13]

Certainly, in the constant and imaginative linguistic movement of Spanglish there is endless borrowing.[14] This linguistic fusion reflects a larger contextual cultural creativity and synthesis that defies narrow definitions and fixed boundaries. Sometimes the Spanglish phenomenon finds a local expression with names such as Caló, Pachuco, or Pocho in the Southwest, "Tex-Mex" in Texas, New Mexican Spanish, or "Cubonics" in south Florida.

These forms of speech are characterized not only by the mixtures of English and Spanish, but also by idiosyncratic phrases and expressions.[15] For example, forms of Caribbean Spanish (Cuban, Dominican, Puerto Rican) also contain elements from African and Taíno languages, which then interact with American English to produce localized versions of Spanglish. Rather than perceiving that they are communicating in a sloppy or deficient manner, some of these linguistic performers take pride in their ability to move between languages in a type of trilingual fashion.

As already noted by the film of the same name, Spanglish seeps into mainstream popular culture as well as into the routines of comedians Sara Contreras, George López, John Leguizamo, Marilyn Martinez, Monique Marvez, Paul Rodríguez, Gabriel Iglesias, and Sandra Valls. In *How the García Girls Lost Their Accent*, Dominican American novelist and poet Julia Álvarez has one of her characters say, "In my *campo* we say a person has an *antojo* when they are taken by *un santo* who wants something."[16] Spanish also infuses the Pulitzer Prize–winning novel *The Brief Wonderful Life of Oscar Wao* by Dominican American Junot Díaz, giving the whole work a bilingual and Spanglish feel.[17] In music the fluidity of the languages that merge in Spanglish can be heard in the gritty lyrics of the Grammy Award–winning group Molotov in their song "Frijolero," which is a racially charged exchange between two characters. This recurring *calque* of the racist term "beaner" in reference to a Mexican, rendered in Spanish as *frijolero*, figures prominently in the defiant refrain of the song, "*No me llames beaner*" ("Don't call me a beaner).[18]

Spanglish is an everyday reality in the United States. In many places it is the improvisational language of the *calle*, the street. Spanglish rejects tidiness and does not always follow accepted rules, traditions, and conventions. Sometimes Spanglish seems risky and risqué. Sometimes Spanglish evokes humor and at other times a heartbreaking pathos. All of this does not mean that Spanglish is inferior or illegitimate to either Spanish or English, although it is certainly different. Without a doubt, there is a sense in which Spanglish revels in its difference.

A few people have made attempts to formally represent Spanglish, but that effort is still in its early stages.[19] Spanglish remains mostly a phenomenon of the moment, sometimes with a new expression that emerges out of a particular immediate context where communication is key or as people seek to express meaning or significance, or simply interact in culturally relevant ways.[20] Whether it is called a code-switching slang, insider language, Chicano, Pachuco, Tex-Mex, Tejano, Caló, Nuyorican, Boricua, Quisqueya, street slang, or by some other name, Spanglish often receives the disapproval of both professional linguists as well as other authorities.[21]

If Spanglish is not the language of all of the *pueblo*, it certainly provides needed verbal communication for some people. In a cultural context of fear, anxiety, and misunderstanding, where people argue about the use of Ebonics, others demand English-only laws, and some states pass oppressive immigration laws that encourage the racial profiling and persecution of Hispanics, some expressions of Spanglish are deemed not only grammatically incorrect but even offensive or illegal. But Spanglish will not stop, nor will it not go away; in its many forms Spanglish is a linguistic mixing that will continue to grow.

SPANGLISH AS CULTURAL MIXING

Spanglish not only represents types of linguistic border crossings, it also signifies new cultural locations and borderlands that can appear anywhere, and not just along the international border between Mexico and the United States. As such, Spanglish becomes a cultural mixing that refers to a fluid, living culture. It connects and retains elements of the past while it allows for the creation of new features that can merge with what was received. When new forms appear, sometimes there is a give and take, and other times there are fights; sometimes there are losses, other times there are gains. Cultural mixing is an essential part of cultural identity, and people who employ Spanglish continually cross social and cultural borders in culturally sophisticated if unrecognized ways. In addition, Spanglish helps create and shape types of pan-ethnic Latino/a identities.

It should not be surprising that Spanglish culture evolves alongside Spanglish language. There are Latino/as who may not use any form of spoken Spanglish, but nevertheless participate in some aspect of the Spanglish cultures in the United States. Being Latina or Latino means having coexisting multiple identities that connect with several distinct, but concurrent notions of pan-Latino/a identity. These multiple *latinidades* are redefining what it means to be multicultural in the United States. Even in the mixing of Spanglish cultures some shared concerns dominate the rhythms of Hispanic/Latino life in the United States such as the experience and marking of life passages. Cultural mixing is at work around the issues and activities of family, marriage and partnership, responses to death, and notions of what is beyond death (as was noted in chapter 4). These shared cultural concerns manifest themselves in many ways. And from attending to these shared concerns emerge sources of strength, sustenance, community, rituals of life, wisdom, and balance in the search for life and meaning.

Like spoken Spanglish, this continuing search for life and meaning defies being neatly pigeonholed. Latino/a cultural synthesis and the creation of shared *latinidades* do not often welcome restrictive labeling. The fluidity of Spanglish cultural mixing may be described using the concepts of *mestizaje* and *mulatez*. *Mestizaje*, rooted in the racial concept of the mixture of European and Amerindian/indigenous peoples, has gained wider usage to refer to the cultural mixing of all peoples in the Americas, whereas *mulatez*, related to the word "mulatto" indicates the combination of African and European peoples in the Americas, highlighting elements of African culture and race in Latin America.[22] Both *mestizaje* and *mulatez* are used to describe the cultural mixing and multifaceted identities of Latinas and Latinos. While people view Spanglish negatively today, likewise *mestizaje* and *mulatez* were previously rejected as negative designations before being retooled. Regardless of how it is named, cultural mixing remains an important part of individual and group identities for Latino/as.

The continual connection and replenishment that comes from Latin America contributes to the creation of Spanglish cultures. In an observation that goes beyond the parameters of theology, Michelle Gonzalez helpfully notes that "a more fluid understanding of Latino/a and Latin American theologies can be constructed, one that takes seriously the distinctiveness of their present conditions yet recognizes their shared history."[23]

While it is appropriate to distinguish between Latin Americans and Latino/as, the reality is that the U.S. Latino/a community is daily being replenished by new arrivals that settle in the United States. International media and communication networks without historical precedent compound the influence of the steady stream of new migrants. The mixed, creative expressions of *latinidad* in the United States are far more than watered-down extensions of Latin America; indeed, they reinvigorate various manifestations of Latino/a and Spanglish cultures and identities.

Developing Spanglish cultures risk being disconnected from or even disowned by their cultural roots, whether tossed out or choosing to leave or both. Mixtures are too often considered in need of correction or elimination. A common expression of this from within Hispanic/Latino communities comes in a phrase such as "You aren't really a Latina [Dominican, Puerto Rican, Mexican]" or whatever idealized and essentialized ethnic category is not satisfied by the multicultural Spanglish person.

When she speaks of Latino/a cultural identities and location, theologian Loida Martell-Otero uses the potentially shocking metaphor of *sato/sata* (mixed breed, mutt, or mongrel).[24] Although she takes some risks when she employs a term generally perceived as derogatory, Martell-Otero describes *sato/as* or "mutts" as typically unwanted mongrels or mixed-breeds. Puerto Rican society, like many others, drives away the mixed feral undesirable *sato/a*. In a discussion focused on Christology, Martell-Otero draws on the image of *sato/a*:

> I believe that *sata* is an appropriate term because it is a specifically cultural term that aids in the articulation of a contextual Christology from a Puerto Rican perspective. I also believe that it connotes the existential conjunction of mestizaje and periphery. It expresses the experience of being peripheralized—stereotyped, rejected, and insulted by the hegemonic centers of society. It underscores the experience of being relegated to the bottom rung of society precisely as one who is perceived to be nonhuman, impure, and of no intrinsic value—*sobraja*.[25]

Martell-Otero turns the derogatory connotation of the word of *sata* on its head to access the existential reality of people on the margins. Whatever in the past contributed to one's current social location and identity, this is what he or she is, a person of cultural mixture and fusion who is relegated to the fringes or, in some cases, told to "go back to where you came from." People reject cultural mixing in the same way that they reject linguistic mixing. Members of the dominant group may always choose to avoid any form of cultural mixing, regarding it as a mongrelization that is to be stamped out when it does occur.

RECOGNIZING SPANGLISH SPIRITUALITY

The parallels made between Spanglish as a language and as a culture can also be made with spirituality. Not all of Latino/a spirituality is Spanglish, but some of it is. Just as the interaction between languages produces something new and linguistically messy, so the contact of traditions produces a variety of spiritual and religious options and fusions that may be deemed untidy by some. The collective Latino/a identity produces a Spanglish linguistic, cultural, religious, and spiritual reality that challenges the status quo. The fundamental challenge is that there is no one way to express and to practice Latino/a spirituality; there is no simple formula to follow.

Many varieties of people are placed under the rubric of Hispanic or Latino/a. The multicultural Latino/a reality includes diversity and commonality in social, political, cultural, religious, and spiritual ways. These dimensions remain an underexplored aspect of life in the United States.

There is a shared common sense of the reality of the spiritual with a collective *latinidad* but very different understandings of what the spiritual means in particular contexts. Hilda Gutiérrez Baldoquín shares her story of one Latina's testimony which is a reminder of the diversity that exists:

When I first became involved with Soto Zen 11 years ago, some of my family were concerned. I was raised as a Roman Catholic with a strong emphasis of spiritism and with deep awareness of Santería. My family, who are first-generation Afro-Cuban immigrants (to this day, most of the elders are still monolingual Spanish speakers), worried that I had fallen prey to some strange California cult.

I remember attempting to dispel these concerns during a long-distance telephone call with my tía Lola. I decided to talk to her about the Four Noble Truths and about this man named Gautama. "The first insight," I told Lola, "is that life is suffering." She quickly interrupted me and smugly replied, "Ay mija, entonces yo he sido budista toda mi vida, pues eso yo siempre lo he sabido, no me tienes que decir mas nada." ("Oh, my daughter, then I've been Buddhist all of my life for I have always known that! You don't have to tell me anything else.")[26]

Here there are issues of roots, language, inherited family traditions, the family's Catholicism, of interaction with Afro-Caribbean religious tradition, generations, multiple identities, religious and cultural bridges—all in the story of one Latina's path to Buddhism. This illustrates the diversity of spirituality among Latino/as. The aunt's response also demonstrates another characteristic of Latino spirituality, namely, a willingness to embrace what rings true no matter its source

The U.S. collective *latinidad*, which operates as a cultural Spanglish, includes persons like Cuban American Hilda Gutiérrez Baldoquín, raised Catholic, who practiced Santería and then became a Buddhist. It includes Mexican Americans who are fourth-generation Protestants, and Jews who trace their family back to Spain and Portugal. It includes Muslims who made their Shahaddah, and Pentecostals. Concepts of the religious or spiritual may possess very specific regional, ethnic, even national roots that have different manifestations in different social settings such as urban or rural. And varieties of Spanglish spirituality emerge in those diverse contexts where the participants and creators of Spanglish culture cross spiritual, religious, social, and cultural borders daily.

While affirming the diversity of the different groups considered under the terms "Hispanic" or "Latino/a," we can also point to a constantly shifting sense of a shared *latinidad*. Spanglish reality is part of the *latinidad* developed in the United States, which shows understandings of religion and spirituality that will not be contained within hermetically sealed borders, whether they be a wall that scars the land between the United States and Mexico; the persistence of national identity and pride; regional, ethnic, or linguistic differences, imposed ethnic and racialized identities; denominational affiliation; or even differences in religious and spiritual traditions. The many Latino/a cultures are in constant yet shifting contact and exchange with other cultures and ways of being religious and spiritual.

CHALLENGES AND PROMISES OF
SPANGLISH SPIRITUALITY

The existence of different forms of eclectic Spanglish spirituality has several ramifications for ministry, theology, and theological education. While cultures and cultural practices mix and create something new, sadly it is too easy to put the resulting new mix in a box that can easily be put aside on a shelf and we deal with it when and if we want to. Some establishment Christian denominations and churches respond to the growing Hispanic presence in the United States by refusing to recognize that something new is happening before our eyes. Little attempt is made to become acquainted with the linguistic, ethnic, historical, and religious diversity of the different peoples named Hispanic or Latino/a. When an ecclesiastical decision is made that "something" needs to be done, many ministry approaches to the Latino/a population are totally ignorant of both the many differences and the great diversity of peoples of Latin American descent but also the complex cultural blending that is constantly occurring. Typically very little consideration is given to the religious and spiritual diversity that exists among Latino/a peoples or to the roles and practices of popular religiosity. Such approaches are typified by two attitudes: "They are all the same," and "Once the immigrant church is like us then all shall be well." The expectation of some church leaders is that these types of uniformed "quick and cheap" approaches to Hispanic ministry will reverse declines in denominational membership and generate new income streams. In a context where Latino/a spirituality includes Catholics, Pentecostals, Baptists, Jews, Buddhists, Muslims, Jehovah's Witnesses, practitioners of Lucumí, and many other religious traditions, plus the possibility of all kinds of combinations and innovations, clearly a one-size-fits-all approach will not work.

Moreover, many denominational efforts focus exclusively on new immigrants but in a way that fails to address the transnational aspects of their reality and their cultural mixing in the context of the United States. Certainly the continuing flow of immigrants comprises one aspect of the Latino/a population, and therefore the church in the United States, as we live in a time of large transnational migrations.[27] But at this very point churches, denominations, and seminaries make a critical error as they conclude that all efforts should focus on the immigrant experience. Pastors and pastoral workers are recruited from Latin America, and without any type of acculturation to the United States they are dropped into U.S. Latino/a contexts and told to do ministry. This typically is expressed in a course of action that says, "Let's find someone who speaks Spanish, then that person can do the ministry to Hispanics for us." Educational institutions do something similar when they say "That person can teach our seminary courses to the Hispanics." Some denominations and local congregations contract out Hispanic ministry and theology as if hiring day laborers to harvest crops, roof houses, or care for lawns. Moreover, a well-intentioned focus solely on monolingual immigrant ministry falls into the trap of generational myopia. There are many who are bilingual and bicultural, and sometimes multicultural, who are bypassed, even marginalized in an immigrant-only ministry focus.

The simple recognition of the differences between first generation and 1.5 generations should lead to an understanding that a vast number of Hispanics are members of the second and third generations and beyond. As Carmen Nanko-Fernández notes, Spanglish can provide cultural space for the many aspects of "hybrid identities,"[28] so also a spirituality informed by many sources develops to produce hybrid spiritualities.

Some language purists and cultural elitists declare that Spanglish indicates a troubled and deficient youth culture. But culturally Spanglish can be found across the generations, and it is not confined solely to the vocabulary of youth. As a personal example, I am Puerto Rican, but not the same type of Puerto Rican as my parents. When my father died I traveled to Puerto Rico for the funeral. Upon my return to Pennsylvania one of my Anglo colleagues asked, "How was your trip home?" I paused to discern what he asked since I had not visited Connecticut, my home recently. I have roots in both places. My cultural hybrid reality was confronted by imposed assumptions that did not allow for my complex existential situation. But what happened to me in that instance happens all the time to Latinas and Latinos when uninformed assumptions are acted upon, sadly with more serious repercussions than in my story. This mixed cultural reality is part of living in Spanglish, which is one aspect of the context of religious and spiritual life of Latinas and Latinos.

The multiplicity of generations results in a multiplicity of languages: Spanish, English, different expressions of Spanish, and many forms of Spanglish/Espanglish. Attention to the issues of generations and languages highlights the reality of multiple origins for peoples grouped together under two or three umbrella terms in the United States. Identifying and engaging these provoke questions of cultures—received, created, and re-created.[29] As Anita de Luna wrote, "Spirituality is mediated through lived experience, and experience is contextualized in culture."[30]

In the same way that grammar books may fail to express adequately the lived everyday reality of spoken Spanglish, so also rigid stereotypes and uninformed denominational pronouncements may ineffectually describe the everyday spiritual realities of Latinas and Latinos. But as we pay attention to varieties of Latino/a spirituality, including the jazz-like expressions of Spanglish cultures and spirituality, we are again reminded of the importance of the reality of *religiosidad popular*, popular religion, religious faith and practice. Theologian Luis Pedraja notes, "Popular religion is the concrete expression of the religious experiences of a community. However in most cases, popular religion takes the shape of cultural expressions that are not limited simply to accepted Christian practices."[31] And the assessment that Michelle Gonzalez gives about the Roman Catholic Church and the Cuban community is applicable to other traditions as well. "The Catholic Church must reckon with the fact that there are churched Catholics in the Cuban/Cuban American communities (and other Latino/a communities) who dabble in non-Christian practices, practices that may seem to them entirely consonant with their Catholic faith, even though they know them to be rejected by the official church."[32] This challenges establishment religion because cultural expressions and practices may include understandings of lived theology and spirituality that are considered beyond the boundaries of church doctrine. Just as speaking Spanglish is part of *lo cotidiano*, understanding the cultural mixing of Spanglish spirituality can lead to a better understanding of the interactions between boundaries, identities, and everyday spirituality.[33]

All kinds of groups in many social locations across the history of Christianity have held beliefs and practices that had little connection with official theology and more often were connected to popular culture. For example, historian David Hall writes about the New England Puritan colonists and says that "the mentality of the supernatural in seventeenth-century New England encompassed themes and motifs that owed very little to formal theology or to Puritanism."[34]

Researchers Milagros Ricourt and Ruby Danta in their study of Latina pan-ethnicity helpfully identified four existential characteristics of Latina pan-ethnicity at organizational and institutional levels and in daily life: (1) experiential pan-ethnicity; (2) categorical pan-ethnicity; (3) institutional pan-ethnicity; and (4) ideological pan-ethnicity. As demonstrated through this book all four are operative when considering a shared Hispanic spirituality.[35] By whatever name, Hispanic, Latino/a, Hispano, Latinamericano, a pan-ethnic identity is not a Platonic ideal out there somewhere for which people strive, but rather a contextual reality that is created and re-created in specific contexts. There are diverse forms of linguistic Spanglish, cultural Spanglish, and religious and spiritual Spanglish. The shared expressions—direct and indirect, intentional and fortuitous—of popular religion among Hispanic faith communities is one of the factors in developing shared pan-ethnic senses of what it means to be Hispanic/Latino. While there are multiple expressions of shared pan-ethnic spirituality, that does not automatically result in universal religious and spiritual harmony among Latino/as. In some cases there are ecumenical discussions and cooperation around specific projects and occasionally interreligious conversations and activities, but at the same time there are many Latino/as, especially at grassroots level, who eye Hispanics of other religious and spiritual traditions and convictions with suspicion. But ironically even with contention Latino/as still draw upon common characteristics in their spiritual practice.

The everyday varieties of Spanglish spirituality encompass critical reflection and the nimble coping skills for everyday life.[36] Insights from Spanglish spirituality challenge people to reexamine, for example: (1) concepts of Christian community; (2) the different ways that faith is formed; (3) the varied spiritual life journeys; (4) alternative expressions of congregational life; (5) creativity in ministry; (6) retooling theologies; (7) innovation in theological education. Religious and spiritual traditions play significant roles in the struggle against hegemonic domination. Otto Maduro speaks of the relationship between religion and the empowerment of Latino/as, particularly as one takes seriously the self-perspectives of Latino/a religious communities:

> Religion could be—besides and, at times, despite other functions—a possible medium, among others, for the articulation and proactive stimulation of a people's empowerment, that is, for the actualization

of their capacity to transform their social environment in consonance with their own interests. This might be particularly true in the case of U.S. Hispanics, for whom all too often our religious traditions and institutions occupy a central place in our worldview, one of our scarce sources for self-identity as well as for the ethical assessment of our typically alien environment.[37]

From this perspective religion, and more broadly self-identified spiritual traditions and practices, can be seen as central to Latino/Hispanic worldviews and activity in the world as self-initiated agents of transformation and empowerment. This occurs in the context of an alternative public space on the margins/borderlands of the dominant society, which oppresses, alienates, and determines that some will be pushed to the "fringes."

Spanglish spirituality and other types of contemporary cultural and religious blending demand an expansion of the understanding of the many forms of Latina and Latino spirituality and contribute to a greater understanding of the nature of human spirituality. In the varieties of Latino/a and especially in Spanglish spirituality many types of spiritual, religious, and theological fusions reflect a larger contextual cultural creativity and synthesis. But this insight also reminds us that all peoples experience linguistic, cultural, religious, and spiritual fluidity. For those engaged in Christian ministry and theology, in order to respond to the challenge of the many types of Spanglish spirituality, there is a need to acknowledge that it impacts the shared faith and life together that Christians are called to embody. The reality of Spanglish spirituality is an opportunity for all of us to look at all of our contexts and callings in new ways. The varieties of Latino/a spirituality are the articulation in words and actions of individual and communal experience of navigating and making sense of the world.

If the truth be told my broders y hermanas, Spanglish spirituality no es only about ellos y ellas, it is not just about them. Spanglish spirituality is about todos nosotros también, is about all of us. Spanglish spirituality is important for all of us.

Appendix

TABLE OF ASSOCIATIONS BETWEEN
SELECTED AFRO-CUBAN ORISHAS/ORICHAS
AND CATHOLIC SAINTS

Oricha	Chief Characteristics	Associated Saint/Santo
Obatalá	Chief among the *orishas*, ruler of white cloth, creator of humanity, god of justice, peace, and purity, one of the Siete Potencias Africanas (Seven African Powers).	Our Lady of Mercy
Elegguá, Eshu, Elegbara	A warrior deity, the guardian of the crossroads and the overseer of pathways, often considered mischievous and a trickster, one of the Siete Potencias Africana	St. Anthony of Padua (or the Child Jesus in St. Anthony's arms), the Holy Child of Atocha, St. Martin of Porres
Oggún	The warrior god of iron, warfare, and hunting; associated with employment, one of the Siete Potencias Africanas	St. Peter, St. James the Greater (Santiago de Compostela), Archangel Michael
Ochosi	A warrior *orisha* associated with hunting and justice, one of the Siete Potencias Africanas.	St. Norbert
Orula, Orúnla, Orúnmila, Ifá	Orula is the god of wisdom and destiny, the patron of *babalawos* and divinization, and is one of the Siete Potencias Africanas.	St. Francis of Assisi
Changó	Changó often is the *orisha* of fire, lightning, and thunder. He is associated with war, virility, and employment, and is one of the Siete Potencias Africana	St. Barbara
Babalú Ayé	The *orisha* associated with illness and disease. Often seen as the one who is the source of both the causes and cures of sickness.	St. Lazarus
Yemayá	A river goddess in Africa, in the Americas Yemayá is connected to the power of the ocean and is associated with motherhood, womanhood, fertility, and is one of the Siete Potencias Africanas	Our Lady of Regla
Oshún, Ochún	A river deity, the goddess of love and beauty who exercises control over the erotic sphere of life and is associated with financial prosperity and women's mysteries, one of the Siete Potencias Africanas	Our Lady of Charity of Cobre
Oyá	Associated with the all wind, as well as lightning, and ceremony, and is identified with the cemetery and the dead. Oyá is called upon for protection against death	Our Lady of La Candelaria, St. Therese of Lisieux

149

Notes

Introduction

1. Although often thought to be found in the U.S. Constitution, the direct antecedent for the common phrase "wall of separation," is found in Thomas Jefferson's 1802 correspondence with the Danbury Baptist Association as Jefferson quoted the First Amendment to the Constitution: "I contemplate with sovereign reverence that act of the whole American people which declared that their legislature should 'make no law respecting an establishment of religion, or prohibiting the free exercise thereof' thus building a wall of separation between Church and State."

2. See President George W. Bush, "President's Remarks at National Day of Prayer and Remembrance," September 14, 2001, The White House, Office of the Press Secretary.

3. See President Barack H. Obama, "Remarks by the President at a Memorial Service for the Victims of the Shooting in Tucson, Arizona, McKale Memorial Center, University of Arizona, Tucson, Arizona," January 12, 2011, The White House, Office of the Press Secretary.

4. Leigh Eric Schmidt, *Restless Souls: The Making of American Spirituality* (New York: HarperCollins, 2005), 23.

5. Robert Wuthnow, *After the Baby Boomers: How Twenty- and Thirty-Somethings Are Shaping the Future of American Religion* (Princeton, N.J.: Princeton University Press, 2007), 112.

6. Studies on the growing religious diversity, pluralism, and the impact on religious and spiritual attitudes and actions in the United States include Thomas Banchoff, ed., *Democracy and the New Religious Pluralism* (New York: Oxford University Press, 2007); Courtney Bender, *The New Metaphysicals: Spirituality and the American Religious Imagination* (New York: Columbia University Press, 2010); Diana L. Eck, *A New Religious America: How a "Christian Country" Has Now Become the World's Most Religiously Diverse Nation* (San Francisco: Harper San Francisco, 2001); Paul Froese and Christopher Bader, *America's Four Gods: What We Say about God and What That Says about Us* (New York: Oxford University Press, 2010); John B. Cobb, Jr., Bruce G. Epperly, and Paul S. Nancarrow, *The Call of the Spirit: Process Spirituality in a Relational World* (Claremont, Calif.: P&F Press, 2005); William R. Hutchison, *Religious Pluralism in America: The Contentious History of a Founding Ideal* (New Haven: Yale University Press, 2003); Thomas A. Tweed and Stephen Prothero, eds., *Asian Religions in America: A Documentary History* (New York: Oxford University Press, 1999); Robert D. Putnam and David

E. Campbell, *American Grace: How Religion Divides and Unites Us* (New York: Simon & Schuster, 2010).

7. Joe McDermott, "Range of Worship Widens in the Valley," *The Allentown Morning Call*, Allentown, Pa. December 22, 2003, A1, A2.

8. Ironically, the contemporary descendants of European immigrants did not view each other in such harmonized ways and were considered strange and unusual by those who arrived before them. Cynthia Campbell comments on this: "Religious diversity in the United States is not new news. In fact, it is as old as the country itself and was a significant issue in its founding. While we don't often think of it, the colonies of North America were made up of diverse religious groups who considered one another to be 'other religions' rather than divergent streams of Christianity" (Cynthia M. Campbell, *A Multiple of Blessings: A Christian Approach to Diversity* [Louisville: Westminster John Knox, 2007], 1).

9. Thomas Banchoff, ed., *Religious Pluralism, Globalization, and World Politics* (New York: Oxford University Press, 2008).

10. Jon C. Dalton, David Eberhardt, Jillian Bracken, and Keith Echols, "Inward Journeys: Forms and Patterns of College Student Spirituality," *Journal of College and Character* 7 (2006): 8–10.

11. Examples of the new atheism include Richard Dawkins, *The God Delusion* (New York: Houghton Mifflin, 2008); Daniel C. Dennett, *Breaking the Spell: Religion as a Natural Phenomenon* (New York: Penguin, 2006); Sam Harris, *The End of Faith: Religion, Terror, and the Future of Reason* (New York: W. W. Norton, 2004); Christopher Hitchens, *God Is Not Great: How Religion Poisons Everything* (New York: Twelve Books, 2007); Victor J. Stenger, *God: The Failed Hypothesis—How Science Shows That God Does Not Exist* (Amherst, N.Y.: Prometheus Books, 2007).

12. Prothero makes a case that there exists a type of religious illiteracy and that there is a need for greater religious (and I would add spiritual) knowledge in the interest of the common good. He asserts, "Americans' knowledge of religion runs as shallow as Americans' commitment to religion runs deep" (Stephen Prothero, *Religious Literacy: What Every American Needs to Know—and Doesn't* [New York: Harper Collins, 2007], 34).

13. For example, Han F. de Wit, *The Spiritual Path: An Introduction to the Psychology of the Spiritual Traditions*, trans. Henry Jansen and Lucia Hofland-Jansen (Pittsburgh: Duquesne University Press, 1999); Bruce G. Epperly, *The Center Is Everywhere: Celtic Spirituality in the Postmodern World* (Cleveland, Tenn.: Parson's Porch Books, 2011). For another survey of the spiritual search in the United States, see David G. Meyers, *The American Paradox: Spiritual Hunger in an Age of Plenty* (New Haven: Yale University Press, 2000).

14. Reid B. Locklin, *Spiritual but Not Religious? An Oar Stroke Closer to the Farther Shore* (Collegeville, Minn.: Liturgical Press, 2005), 2–4; Robert C. Fuller,

Spiritual but Not Religious: Understanding Unchurched America (New York: Oxford University Press, 2001); Schmidt, *Restless Soul.*

15. For one overview account on the diversity of spiritual and religious beliefs in the United States, see Phillip L. Berman, *The Search for Meaning: Americans Talk about What They Believe and Why* (New York: Ballantine Books, 1990). On the spread of Wiccan spirituality, see, for example, Jason J. Barry, "Wicca: It's Not Broomsticks and Black Hats," *Meriden (Conn.) Record-Journal,* July 23, 2003, 9. One example of a soulful approach in business advocating a connection between work and spirit is Lee G. Bolman and Terrence E. Deal, *Leading with Soul: An Uncommon Journey of Spirit,* rev. ed. (San Francisco: Jossey-Bass, 2001).

16. Meyers, *The American Paradox,* 258–59.

17. Ibid., 260.

18. Ibid., xi.

19. Bruce David Forbers and Jeffrey H. Mahan, eds., *Religion and Popular Culture in America,* rev. ed. (Berkeley and Los Angeles: University of California Press, 2005).

20. In what has become a classic definition Hunter describes culture wars as "political and social hostility rooted in different systems of moral understanding." See James Davison Hunter, *Culture Wars: The Struggle to Define America* (New York: Basic Books, 1991), 42. Although just a few years ago some declared the culture wars passé, the fervor of culture war rhetoric used by the proponents of the populist movement self-described as the Tea Party dispels that type of wishful thinking. Moreover, some observers see the concept of culture wars as more nuanced and complicated. See, for example, Irene Taviss Thomson, *Culture Wars and Enduring American Dilemmas* (Ann Arbor: University of Michigan Press, 2010). See also Stephen L. Carter, *The Culture of Disbelief: How American Law and Politics Trivialize Religious Devotion* (New York: Anchor Books, 1993); Eldon J. Eisenach, *The Next Religious Establishment: National Identity and Political Theology in Post-Protestant America* (Lanham, Md.: Rowan & Littlefield Publishers, 2000).

21. See Arthur J. Schlesinger, Jr., *The Disuniting of America: Reflections on a Multicultural Society,* rev. ed. (New York: W. W. Norton, 1998); Samuel P. Huntington, *Who Are We? America's National Identity and the Challenges It Faces* (New York: Simon & Schuster, 2004).

22. Philip Jenkins, "A New Spirituality: Hispanic Americans Are Influencing Religious Trends in the United States," *Ethnic News* (Winter 2003).

23. U.S. Census Bureau, *The Hispanic Population, 2010, 2010 Census Brief,* May 2011; U.S. Census Bureau, 1970, 1980, 1990, and 2000 Decennial Censuses; Population Projections, July 1, 2010, to July 1, 2050.

24. U.S. Census Bureau, Public Information Office, "Young, Diverse, Urban: Hispanic Population Reaches All-Time High of 38.8 Million, New Census Bureau Estimates Show," June 19, 2003.

25. For further discussion on the terms "Hispanic" and "Latino/a" and the relationship to Latin American identity, see Miguel A. De La Torre and Edwin David Aponte, *Introducing Latino/a Theologies* (Maryknoll, N.Y.: Orbis Books, 2001), 9–28.

26. See Jorge J. E. Gracia, *Hispanic/Latino Identity: A Philosophical Perspective* (Oxford, U.K. and Malden, Mass.: Blackwell Publishers, 2000), 1–26. Part of the difficulties with pan-ethnic identifications indeed is the great diversity, even with some shared roots of the peoples under consideration. As Segovia points out, the Hispanic/Latino heterogeneity highlights the deficiencies in the still dominant vision of a racial/ethnic "melting-pot" in the United States. Pan-ethnic descriptions should be nuanced enough to allow for the self-understandings of Hispanic/Latino groups. See Fernando F. Segovia, "In the World but Not of It: Exile as Locus for a Theology of the Diaspora," in *Hispanic/Latino Theology: Challenge and Promise*, ed. Ada María Isasi-Díaz and Fernando F. Segovia (Minneapolis: Fortress Press, 1996), 195–97.

27. For example, Jenkins moves from a discussion about Latin American churches to a discussion of Hispanic theology as if they exist as a seamless whole without any apparent awareness of the very real historical, social, and theological community contexts involved. See Philip Jenkins, *The Next Christendom: The Coming of Global Christianity* (New York: Oxford University Press, 2002), 116–18.

28. Benjamín Valentín, ed., *New Horizons in Hispanic/Latino(a) Theology* (Cleveland: Pilgrim Press, 2003), 2.

29. One notable exception to this prevalent trend is Timothy Matovina, *Guadalupe and Her Faithful: Latino Catholics in San Antonio, from Colonial Origins to the Present* (Baltimore: Johns Hopkins University Press, 2005).

30. Private correspondence.

31. Elizabeth Conde Frazier, "Hispanic Protestant Spirituality," in *Teología en Conjunto: A Collaborative Hispanic Protestant Theology*, ed., José David Rodríguez and Loida I. Martell-Otero (Louisville: Westminster John Knox, 1997), 128.

32. See Will Herberg, *Protestant, Catholic, Jew: An Essay in American Religious Sociology* (Garden City, N.Y.: Doubleday & Co., 1955). Kevin M. Schultz discusses the role and influence of this three-fold paradigm in *Tri-Faith America: How Catholics and Jews Held Postwar America to Its Protestant Promise* (New York: Oxford University Press, 2011). Wuthnow notes that at the same time the three-fold model was advanced, "grassroots ethnocentrism still pervaded much of the population, and even the Holocaust had been regarded with surprising indifference in many quarters. When public opinion surveys began asking questions about religious attitudes in the 1950s and early 1960s, a sizable percentage of American Protestants and Catholics expressed misgivings about interacting with Jews. Increasing, though, Americans came to regard Judaism in the manner that Herberg's title suggested: as a legitimate third option alongside Protestantism and

Catholicism" (Robert Wuthnow, *America and the Challenges of Religious Diversity* [Princeton, N.J.: Princeton University Press, 2005], 31).

33. After I embarked on this research path I was encouraged in this approach by my re-acquaintance with Anthony B. Pinn's *Varieties of African American Religious Experience* (Minneapolis: Fortress Press, 1998).

34. R. Laurence Moore, *Religious Outsiders and the Making of Americans* (New York: Oxford University Press, 1986), 207–8.

35. Often when I mention "cultural history" I am asked to explain my understanding of the discipline. Curiously, the exact nature of cultural history is part of ongoing discussions within the field. Categorizations of subfields in history do not have universal agreement. Perhaps central to this discussion is what is meant by "cultural." Citing the changing character of culture there are some who view cultural history as evolutionary. See Joseph Fracchia, "Does Culture Evolve?" *History and Theory* 99, 38, no. 4 (December 1999): 52–79. Despite the debate, cultural history does exist as a discipline with its own history (e.g., *Kulturgeschichte* and "the new cultural history"). Moreover, as Peter Burke observes, "Cultural history is not a monopoly of historians. It is multidisciplinary as well as interdisciplinary" (*What Is Cultural History?* 2nd ed. [Malden, Mass.: Polity Press, 2008], 135). Michael Kammen states a consensus among many historians of American culture who hold that "cultural history deals with human values, customs, practices and their meaning understood in concrete historical contexts" (*In the Pastlane: Historical Perspectives on American Culture* [New York: Oxford University Press, 1997], x). As I understand it, cultural history includes the seven characteristics that Knight identifies: (1) a concern for subaltern history; (2) an affirmation of the agency of subalterns; (3) political engagement in some manner by subalterns; (4) related to the previous point, this is "history with the politics put back in" (144); (5) "The new cultural history is concerned with the mentalities, signifiers, representations, imaginings, discourses, and manners and morality" (144); (6) consideration of textual evidence, especially provenance and deconstruction in light of popular culture; and finally (7) interdisciplinary interests and methodologies. See Alan Knight, "Subalterns, Signifiers, and Statistics: Perspectives on Mexican Historiography" *Latin American Research Review* 37, no. 2 (2002): 140–48.

36. An extremely helpful discussion on the value and role of personal voice in cultural studies as part of a "hermeneutics of otherness and engagement" is found in Fernando F. Segovia, *Decolonizing Biblical Studies: A View from the Margins* (Maryknoll, N.Y.: Orbis Books, 2000), 145–56.

37. David Maldonado Jr. expounds on an aspect of this conventional wisdom, which assumes that all "Hispanics are Catholic." See his essay "Hispanic Protestant Conversions" in *Hispanic Christian Thought at the Dawn of the 21st Century: Apuntes in Honor of Justo L. González*, ed. Alvin Padilla, Roberto Goizueta, and Eldin Villafañe (Nashville: Abingdon Press, 2005), 214–25.

1. *Santo* and Spirituality

1. "Philadelphia Attracts Record Number of Tourists," *www.msnbc.msn.com /id/43006440/ns/travel.destination_travel/t/philadelphia-attracts-record-number-tourists/*.

2. For one description of life in the Philadelphia "Bad Lands," see the fictionalized account by Steve López, *Third and Indiana: A Novel* (New York: Penguin Books, 1994). For a more recent, of the Bad Lands, see Steve Volk's "Top 10 Drug Corners" *Philadelphia Weekly*, May 7, 2007.

3. Daniel A. Rodríguez succinctly states the difference between evangelical and *evangélico:* "among Latin Americans and Spanish-dominant Latinos in the United States, *evangélico* is a term that is usually synonymous with the broader term 'Protestant.' Experts observe that since *evangelical* defines a specific religious movement in the United States, its meaning is much more limited than the traditional *evangélico* in Spanish" (*A Future for the Latino Church: Models for Multilingual, Multigenerational Hispanic Congregations* [Downers Grove, Ill.: InterVarsity Press, 2011], 28).

4. Loida I. Martell-Otero, "Creating a Sacred Space: An *Iglesia Evangélica* Response to Global Homelessness," *Dialog: A Journal of Theology* 49, no. 1 (2010): 10.

5. Timothy Matovina, *Guadalupe and Her Faithful: Latino Catholics in San Antonio, from Colonial Origins to the Present* (Baltimore: Johns Hopkins University Press, 2005), 15; Juan-Lorenzo Hinojosa, "Culture, Spirituality, and the United States," in *Frontiers of Hispanic Theology in the United States*, ed. Allan Figueroa Deck (Maryknoll, N.Y.: Orbis Books, 1992), 154. See also Raúl A. Ramos, *Beyond the Alamo: Forging Mexican Ethnicity in San Antonio, 1821–1861* (Chapel Hill: University of North Carolina Press, 2008), 233.

6. For an outstanding study on the initial conquest, evangelization, and colonization of the Americas, see Luis N. Rivera-Pagán, *Evangelización y Violencia: La Conquista de América* (San Juan, P.R.: Editorial CEMÍ, 1990), which appears in English as Luis N. Rivera, *A Violent Evangelism: The Political and Religious Conquest of the Americas* (Louisville: Westminster John Knox Press, 1992). For the role of Mexico in the Spanish empire, see Stanley J. Stein and Barbara H. Stein, *Apogee of Empire: Spain and New Spain in the Age of Charles III, 1759–1789* (Baltimore: Johns Hopkins University Press, 2003). On the growth of the Anglo presence in Texas, see Gary Clayton Anderson, *The Conquest of Texas: Ethnic Cleansing in the Promised Land, 1820–1875* (Norman: University of Oklahoma Press, 2005).

7. Virgilio Elizondo and Timothy M. Matovina. *San Fernando Cathedral: Soul of the City* (Maryknoll, N.Y.: Orbis Books, 1998).

8. Roberto S. Goizueta, *Caminemos con Jesús: A Theology of Accompaniment* (Maryknoll, N.Y.: Orbis Books, 1995), 34.

9. For more on the Virgin of Guadalupe as an object of devotion in lived religion and religious symbol, see Jeanette Rodríguez, *Our Lady of Guadalupe:*

Faith and Empowerment among Mexican-American Women (Austin: University of Texas Press, 1994), 143–58; Andrés G. Guerrero, *A Chicano Theology* (Maryknoll, N.Y.: Orbis Books, 1987), 96–117; Timothy Matovina, *Guadalupe and Her Faithful: Latino Catholics in San Antonio, from Colonial Origins to the Present* (Baltimore: Johns Hopkins University Press, 2005); Edwin E. Sylvest, Jr., curator, *Nuestra Señora de Guadalupe: Mother of God, Mother of the Americas* (Dallas: Bridwell Library, Southern Methodist University, 1992), 14–18.

10. For more on the Guatemalan pilgrimage, see Cal Kendall, "The Power of Pilgrimage: The Black Christ of Esquipulas," in *Pilgrimage in Latin America*, ed. N. Ross Crumrine and Alan Morinis (Westport, Conn.: Greenwood Press, 1991), 139–56.

11. Virgilio P. Elizondo, "Conversations with God," in Elizondo and Matovina, *San Fernando Cathedral*, 54.

12. Martha Egan, *Milagros: Votive Offerings from the Americas* (Santa Fe: Museum of New Mexico Press, 1991), 14.

13. Almost from the start of the Spanish conquests in the Americas indigenous peoples were enslaved and resettled on grants of land given by the Crown. Describing the *encomienda* system in the area that became the U.S. Southwest historian David Webber wrote: "One legal means of exploitation involved the collection of tribute, which the Crown determined that all subject natives owed. In New Mexico, the Crown transferred its right to collect tribute to a few privileged citizens or *encomenderos*—trustees who held a specified number of natives in trust or in *encomienda*" (David J. Weber, *The Spanish Frontier in North America* [New Haven, Conn.: Yale University Press, 1992], 124). The major overt battles against the Spanish colonizing and evangelization efforts were the Pueblo Revolts of 1680 and 1696. See David J. Weber, ed., *What Caused the Pueblo Revolt of 1680?* (New York: Bedford/St. Martin's Press, 1999); J. Manuel Espinosa, ed., *The Pueblo Indian Revolt of 1696 and the Franciscan Missions in New Mexico: Letters of the Missionaries and Related Documents* (Norman: University of Oklahoma Press, 1988).

14. Andrew L. Knaut, *The Pueblo Revolt of 1680: Conquest and Resistance in Seventeenth-Century New Mexico* (Norman: University of Oklahoma Press, 1995), 122.

15. Ramón A. Gutierrez, *When Jesus Came, the Corn Mothers Went Away: Marriage, Sexuality, and Power in New Mexico, 1500–1846* (Stanford, Calif.: Stanford University Press, 1991), 78; John L. Kessell, *Pueblos, Spaniards, and the Kingdom of New Mexico* (Norman: University of Oklahoma Press, 2010).

16. The full name of the *penitente* brotherhood is La Fraternidad Piadosa de Nuestro Padre Jesús Nazareno. See Alberto López Pulido, *The Sacred World of the Penitentes* (Washington, D.C.: Smithsonian, 2000), xiii–xiv, 10–16.

17. David M. Mellott, *I Was and I Am Dust: Penitente Practices as a Way of Knowing* (Collegeville, Minn.: Liturgical Press, 2009); Craig Varjabedian and Michael Wallis, *En Divina Luz: The Penitente Moradas of New Mexico*

(Albuquerque: University of New Mexico Press, 1994); David Wakely and Thomas A. Drain, *A Sense of Mission: Historic Churches of the Southwest* (San Francisco: Chronicle Books, 1994), 4.

18. Barbe Awalt and Paul Rhetts, *Our Saints among Us/Nuestros Santos entre Nosotros: 400 Years of New Mexican Devotional Art* (Albuqurque: LPD Press, 1998).

19. Thomas J. Steele, S.J., *Santos and Saints: The Religious Folk Art of Hispanic New Mexico* (Santa Fe: Ancient City Press, 1994), 2.

20. Marie Romero Cash, *Santos: A Coloring Book of New Mexican Saints* (Santa Fe: Sunstone Press, 2008), 7.

21. William Wroth, *Images of Penance, Images of Mercy: Southwestern Santos in the Late Nineteenth Century* (Norman: University of Oklahoma Press, 1991), 64.

22. Ricardo E. Alegría, "Transición del santo como objeto de culto a objeto de valor cultural," in *Los Santo de Puerto Rico: Estudio de la imaginería popular*, ed. Doreen M. Colón Camacho (San Juan, P.R.: Instituto de Cultura Puertorriqueña, 2003), 3–12; Samuel P. Harn Museum of Art, *Santos: Contemporary Devotional Folk Art in Puerto Rico* (Gainesville: Samuel P. Harn Museum of Art, University of Florida, 2003).

23. Elizabeth Kay, *Chimayo Valley Traditions* (Santa Fe: Ancient City Press, 1987), 47–49.

24. Juan Javier Pescador, *Crossing Borders with the Santo Niño de Atocha* (Albuquerque: University of New Mexico Press, 2009).

25. For another example, see David Parkyn, "Emerging Patterns of Catholic-Protestant Relations in Contemporary Guatemala," *SECOLAS ANNALS: Journal of the Southeastern Council on Latin American Studies* 30 (March 1999): 13–27.

26. Magarite Fernández Olmos and Lizabeth Paravisini-Gebert, *Creole Religions of the Caribbean: An Introduction from Vodou and Santería to Obeah and Espirtismo*, 2nd ed. (New York: New York University Press, 2011), 33–87; Joseph M. Murphy, *Working the Spirit: Ceremonies of the African Diaspora* (Boston: Beacon Press, 1994), 81; Christian López, *Lukumi: Santeria's Beliefs, Principles, and Direction in the Twenty-first Century* (Lincoln, Neb.: iUniverse, Inc., 2004), 1–2.

27. Ysamur Flores-Peña and Roberta J. Evanchuk, *Santería Garments and Altars: Speaking without a Voice* (Jackson: University Press of Mississippi, 1994); Arturo Lindsay, ed., *Santería Aesthetics in Contemporary Latin American Art* (Washington, D.C.: Smithsonian Institution Press, 1996).

28. Thomas A. Tweed, *Our Lady of Exile: Diasporic Religion at a Cuban Catholic Shrine in Miami* (New York: Oxford University Press, 1997), 48–49.

29. Murphy acknowledges and agrees with the shortcomings of the term *santería* but also notes that "it continues to be the term most often employed in scholarly literature; it has been accepted at least provisionally by members of the religion in Their public struggle for free exercise before federal courts; it distinguishes the Cuban developments of Yoruba religion from other Yoruba traditions;

the words *santero* and *santera* are in general usage without prejudice within the communities of worship; and I believe the parallelism of the Catholic tradition is important in the development of the religion in Cuba" (Murphy, *Working the Spirit*, 220, n. 1).

30. Miguel A. De La Torre, *Santería: The Beliefs and Rituals of a Growing Religion in America* (Grand Rapids: Eerdmans, 2004), xiii.

31. Nathaniel Samuel Murrell, *Afro-Caribbean Religions: An Introduction to Their Historical, Cultural, and Sacred Traditions* (Philadelphia: Temple University Press, 2010), 101.

32. Isabel Castellanos, "A River of Many Turns: The Polysemy of Ochún in Afro-Cuban Tradition," in *Òsun across the Waters: A Yoruba Goddess in Africa and the Americas*, ed. Joseph M. Murphy and Mei-Mei Sanford (Bloomington: Indiana University Press), 36.

33. See the Appendix for a table of associations between Afro-Cuban *orichas* and Catholic saints.

34. For more on the roles of *botánicas* in Latino/a communities, see Edwin David Aponte, "Metaphysical Blending in Latino/a Botánicas in Dallas," in *Rethinking Latino/a Religion and Identity*, ed. Miguel A. De La Torre and Gastón Espinosa (Cleveland: Pilgrim Press, 2006), 46–68.

35. This is the usual and literal translation of this phrase into English. However, Raul Canizares suggests that a more appropriate understanding is to take the phrase as referring to "the seven empowering orishas, those that give the santero or santera the generative strength to produce certain effects" (*Cuban Santeria: Walking with the Night* [Rochester, Vt.: Destiny Books, 1999], 49).

36. See Martin A. Cohen, *The Martyr: Luis de Carvajal, a Secret Jew in Sixteenth-Century Mexico* (Philadelphia: Jewish Publication Society of America, 1973; reprint, Albuquerque: University of New Mexico Press, 2001), 31–36.

37. For a more extensive discussion on terminology, see Stanley M. Hordes, *To the End of the Earth: A History of the Crypto-Jews of New Mexico* (New York: Columbia University Press, 2005), 5–7.

38. Cary Herz, *New Mexico's Crypto-Jews: Images and Memory* (Albuquerque: University of New Mexico Press, 2007); Gloria Golden, *Remnants of Crypto Jews among Hispanic Americans* (Mountain View, Calif.: Floricanto Press, 2004); Janet Liebman Jacobs, *Hidden Heritage: The Legacy of Crypto-Jews* (Berkeley and Los Angeles: University of California Press, 2002), 2; Emma Montoya, "New Mexico's Sephardim: Uncovering Jewish Roots," *La Herencia del Norte* (Winter 1996): 9–12; Richard Santos, "Chicanos of Jewish Descent in Texas," *Western States Jewish Historical Quarterly* 15, no. 4 (1983): 289–333.

39. Herz, *New Mexico's Crypto-Jews*, 91–95.

40. Jacobs, *Hidden Heritage*, 65; David Nidel, "Modern Descendants of Conversos in New Mexico," *Western States Jewish Historical Quarterly* 16, no. 3 (1984): 257.

41. Ibid., 66.

42. Andrea Greenbaum, ed., *Jews of South Florida* (Lebanon, N.H.: Brandeis University Press, 2005), 29.

43. Margalit Bejarno, *Cuba as America's Back Door: The Case of Jewish Immigration* (Jerusalem: Univeritaria Magnes Press and Hebrew University, 1993), 46.

44. Caroline Bettinger-López, *Cuban-Jewish Journeys: Searching for Identity, Home, and History in Miami* (Knoxville: University of Tennessee Press, 2000), 3–6.

45. María Cristina Garcia, *Havana USA: Cuban Exiles and Cuban Americans in South Florida, 1959–1994* (Berkeley and Los Angeles: University of California Press, 1996), 94.

2. *Santo:* Beyond the Usual Expections

1. From private correspondence with the author. Taíno/a is the name of an indigenous people of the Caribbean who populated Cuba, Hispaniola, and Puerto Rico. Scholars are divided about whether the Taíno were completely eradicated as a result of the Conquest, or if some descendants survive to the present day. At the very least there is an ongoing Taíno cultural influence. *Boricua* is an alternative name for a Puerto Rican, coming from the Taíno word for the island *Borikén* (usually appearing in Spanish as *Borinquen*). The Chichimeca are an indigenous Nahua people of Mexico. For more information on these people, see Antonio M. Stevens-Arroyo, *Cave of the Jagua: The Mythological World of the Taínos*, rev. ed. (Scranton, Pa.: University of Scranton Press, 2006); Yolanda Lastra, Joel Sherzer, and Dina Sherzer, *Adoring the Saints: Fiestas in Central Mexico* (Austin: University of Texas Press, 2009).

2. Hjamil A. Martínez-Vázquez, *Latino/a y Musulman: The Construction of Latino/a Identity among Latino/a Muslims in the United States* (Eugene, Ore.: Pickwick Publications, 2010), 2–3.

3. Patrick D. Bowen, "The Latino American Da'wah Organization and the 'Latina/o Muslim' Identity in the United States," *Journal of Race, Ethnicity, and Religion* 1, no. 11 (September 2010), 1, *http://raceandreligion.com/JRER/Volume_1_%282010%29.html.*

4. Martínez-Vázquez, *Latino/a y Musulman*, 15.

5. Patrick D. Bowen, "Early U.S. Latina/o-African American Muslim Connections: Paths to Conversion," *Muslim World* 100, no. 4 (2010): 390–413.

6. Martínez-Vázquez, *Latino/a y Musulman*, 16.

7. David W. Damrel, "Latina/o Muslim Americans," in *Encyclopedia of Muslim-American History*, ed. Edward E. Curtis IV (New York: Facts on File, 2010), 334–35.

8. Juan Galvan, "Who Are Latino Muslims?" *Islamic Horizons Magazine* 1429 (July/August 2008): 26–30.

9. Chris L. Jenkins, "Islam Luring More Latinos: Prayers Offer a More Intimate Link to God, Some Say," *Washington Post*, January 7, 2001, C1; Lisa Viscidi,

"Latino Muslims a Growing Presence in America," *Washington Report on Middle East Affairs* 22, no. 5 (June 2003): 56.

10. James W. Blair Jr., "Small Wave of Latinos Feel Draw of Islam," *Christian Science Monitor*, August 19, 1999, 17.

11. Martínez-Vázquez, *Latino/a y Musulman*, 48–66.

12. "Reversion Stories," *www.hispanicmuslims.com/stories/*.

13. In fact, during the Middle Ages there were periods when Muslims, Christians, and Jews lived harmoniously together in shared context. An accessible history about this can be found in María Rosa Menocal, *The Ornament of the World: How Muslims, Jews, and Christians Created a Culture of Tolerance in Medieval Spain* (Boston: Little, Brown, 2002).

14. For more on the *reconquista*, see Joseph F. O'Callaghan, *Reconquest and Crusade in Medieval Spain* (Philadelphia: University of Pennsylvania Press, 2003).

15. L. P. Harvey, *Muslims in Spain, 1500 to 1614* (Chicago: University of Chicago Press, 2005), 31–44.

16. Jane I. Smith, *Islam in America*, 2nd ed. (New York: Columbia University Press, 2009), 52. Additionally some enslaved African Muslims were brought to the Americas and contributed to the African diaspora population there. See Kambiz GhaneaBassiri, *A History of Islam in America: From the New World to the New World Order* (Cambridge: Cambridge University Press, 2010), 14; Sylviane A. Diouf, *Servants of Allah: African Muslims Enslaved in the Americas* (New York: New York University Press, 1998).

17. Kenny Yusuf Rodríguez, "My Acceptance Story: From the Book of Genesis to Surah Al-Fatihah," *The Latino Muslim Voice* (July–September 2002), *www.latinodawah.org/newsletter/july-sept2k2.html#5*.

18. Martínez-Vázquez, *Latino/a y Musulman*, 94.

19. For more on those communities in Latin America, see Abdeluahed Akmir, ed., *Los árabes en América Latina: Historia de una emigración* (Madrid: Siglo XXI de España Editores,2009); Diego G. Castellanos, *Islam en Bogotá: Presencia inicial y diversidad* (Bogotá: Universidad del Rosario, 2010); John Tofik Karam, *Another Arabesque: Syrian-Lebanese Ethnicity in Neoliberal Brazil* (Philadelphia: Temple University Press, 2007).

20. Tom Kisken, "Victory over Violence, Teen-age Hispanic Buddhist Travels from Oxnard to Los Angeles This Weekend in Praise of Peace," Ventura County Star, October 6, 2001, E1.

21. See online "Ikeda Youth Ensemble," *www.sgi-usa.org/memberresources/fncc/conferences/ 2011/iye.php*.

22. Teresa K. Weaver, "Book Buzz: Zen informs Latina novelist's work; Latina novelist blends cultures," *Atlanta Journal-Constitution*, November 22, 2002, 1E.

23. For example, Thich Nhat Hanh, *The Miracle of Mindfulness: An Introduction to the Practice of Meditation* (Boston: Beacon Press, 1976); *Peace Is Every Step:*

The Path of Mindfulness in Everyday Life (New York: Bantam, 1991); *Happiness: Essential Mindfulness Practices* (Berkeley: Parallax Press, 2009).

24. Sandra Recommends," *www.sandracisneros.com/recommended.php.*

25. Transcript of Interview, *PBS News Hour with Jim Lehrer*, October 15, 2002, *www.pbs.org/newshour/conversation/july-dec02/cisneros_10-15.html.*

26. Jorge Chino, "The Buddalupist: The Spiritual Life of Sandra Cisneros," *El Andar: A Latino Magazine for the New Millennium* (Winter 1999), *www.elandar. com/back/winter99/stories/story_cisneros.html.*

27. Jenine Arteaga, "Latina Buddhist," February 8, 2011, in *Gozamos: A Spotlight on Chicago Community and Culture, http://gozamos.com/2011/02/latina-buddhist/.*

28. Ibid.

29. Cabezón's works include José Ignacio Cabezón, ed., *Tibetan Ritual* (New York: Oxford University Press, 2010).

30. José Ignacio Cabezón, "Jesus Christ through Buddhist Eyes," *Buddhist-Christian Studies* 19 (1999): 51.

31. For example, see the Dalai Lama, *Answers: Discussions with Western Buddhists*, ed. José Ignacio Cabezón (Ithaca, N.Y.: Snow Lion Publications, 2001).

32. José Ignacio Cabezón, "Identity and the Work of the Scholar of Religion," in *Identity and the Politics of Scholarship in the Study of Religion*, ed. José Ignacio Cabezón and Sheila Greeve Davaney (New York: Routledge, 2004), 53.

33. Gastón Espinosa, "Latino Clergy and Churches in Faith-Based Political and Social Action in the United States," in *Latino Religions and Civic Activism in the United States*, ed. Gastón Espinosa, Virgilio Elizondo, Jesse Miranda (New York: Oxford University Press, 2005), 281, 303.

34. Juhem Navarro-Rivera, Barry A. Kosmin, and Ariela Keysar, *U.S. Latino Religious Identification 1990–2008: Growth, Diversity and Transformation* (Hartford, Conn.: Institute for the Study of Secularism in Society and Culture), 20.

35. See Allison Pond, "A Portrait of Mormons in the U.S.," July 24, 2009, Pew Forum on Religion and Public Life, *http://pewresearch.org/pubs/1292/ mormon- religion-demographics-beliefs-practices-politics.*

36. Jan Shipps, *Sojourner in the Promised Land; Forty Years among the Mormons* (Urbana and Chicago: University of Illinois Press, 2000), 300.

37. "Hi, I'm Marcelo," Official Web site of The Church of Jesus Christ of Latter-day Saints, *http://mormon.org/me/61Q3/.* Author's translation.

38. Mara Knaub, "Yuma Sees Rise in Hispanic Jehovah Witnesses," *Yuma Sun*, June 18, 2011, *www.yourwestvalley.com/topstory/article_669bb4aa-9937-11e0-9294-001cc4c002e0.html*

39. Hans-Diether Riemer, "Jehovah Witnesses," in *The Encyclopedia of Christianity: J–O*, vol. 3, ed. Erwin Fahlbusch, et al., trans. Geoffrey W. Bromiley (Grand Rapids: Eerdmans, 2003), 13–14.

40. Gastón Espinosa, "Latinizing American Christianity: Pluralism, Pentecostalism, and the Future of American Catholicism," *Conscience* 28 (Summer 2007): 30.

41. Interview, January 3, 2002.

42. "Spiritual Talk with Carlos Santana," *JamBase*, November 8, 2007, *www.jambase.com/Articles/Story.aspx?StoryID=11942.*

43. "Carlos Santana Biography," *www.santana.com/carlos/default.aspx.*

44. John Storm Roberts, *The Latin Tinge: The Impact of Latin American Music on the United States* (New York: Oxford University Press, 1999), 184.

45. Carlos Santana, *Sacred Fire: Live in Mexico,* executive producers Jeanne Mattiussi and Peter Nydrle, director Peter Nydrle. The Island Def Jam Music Group, 1993, DVD. Author's translation.

46. Santana, *Sacred Fire.* Author's translation.

47. Private correspondence with author, January 6, 2002.

48. Sandra M. Schneiders, "Approaches to the Study of Christian Spirituality," in *The Blackwell Companion to Christian Spirituality,* ed. Arthur Holder (Malden, Mass.: Blackwell, 2011), 16.

49. Michael Downey, *Understanding Christian Spirituality* (Mahwah, N.J.: Paulist Press, 1997), 14.

50. Michael Downey, *Altogether Gift: A Trinitarian Spirituality* (Maryknoll, N.Y.: Orbis Books, 2000), 61.

51. Wade Clark Roof, *A Generation of Seekers: The Spiritual Journeys of the Baby Boom Generation* (San Francisco: HarperSanFrancisco, 1993), 76–77.

52. Robert A. Orsi, *Between Heaven and Earth: The Religious Worlds People Make and the Scholars Who Study Them* (Princeton, N.J.: Princeton University Press, 2005), 187–88.

53. Peter R. Holmes, "Spirituality: Some Disciplinary Perspectives," in *A Sociology of Spirituality,* ed. Kieran Flanagan and Peter C. Jupp (Burlington, Vt.: Ashgate Publishing Company, 2007), 24–25.

54. Robert Wuthnow, *After Heaven: Spirituality in America since the 1950s* (Berkeley: University of California Press, 1998), 11.

55. Flora Wilson Bridges, *Resurrection Song: African-American Spirituality* (Maryknoll, N.Y.: Orbis Books, 2001), 3.

56. Ronald Rolheiser, *The Holy Longing: The Search for a Christian Spirituality* (New York: Doubleday, 1999), 7.

57. See Evan B. Howard on the nature of Christian spirituality, *The Brazos Introduction to Christian Spirituality* (Grand Rapids: Brazos Press, 2008), 16.

58. Roberto S. Goizueta, *Caminemos con Jesús: Toward a Hispanic/Latino Theology of Accompaniment* (Maryknoll, N.Y.: Orbis Books, 1995), 19.

59. Charles H. Lippy, *Being Religious, American Style: A History of Popular Religiosity in the United States* (Westport, Conn.: Praeger, 1994), 10.

60. Harold J. Recinos, "Popular Religion, Political Identity, and Life Story Testimony in an Hispanic Community," in *The Tie That Binds: African American and Hispanic American/Latino/a Theologies in Dialogue*, ed. Anthony B. Pinn and Benjamín Valentín (New York: Continuum, 2001), 116.

61. Orlando O. Espín, "Traditioning: Culture, Daily Life and Popular Religion, and Their Impact on Christian Tradition," in *Futuring Our Past: Explorations in the Theology of Tradition*, ed. Orlando O. Espín and Gary Macy (Maryknoll, N.Y.: Orbis Books, 2006), 6.

3. Latino/a Peoples and the "Holy"

1. Steven Vertovec, *Transnationalism* (New York: Routledge, 2009), 4–13.

2. Jorge Duany, *Blurred Borders: Transnational Migration between the Hispanic Caribbean and the United States* (Chapel Hill: University of North Carolina Press, 2011), 20–21.

3. Philip J. Williams, Manuel A. Vásquez, and Timothy J. Steigena, "Introduction: Understanding Transnationalism, Collective Mobilization, and Lived Religion in New Immigrant Destinations," in *A Place to Be: Brazilian, Guatemalan, and Mexican Immigrants in Florida's New Destinations*, ed. Philip J. Williams, Timothy J. Steigena, and Manuel A. Vásquez (New Brunswick, N.J.: Rutgers University Press, 2009), 5.

4. Manuel A. Vásquez and Marie F. Marquardt, *Globalizing the Sacred: Religion across the Americas* (New Brunswick, N.J.: Rutgers University Press, 2003), 3.

5. Robert Courtney Smith, *Mexican New York: Transnational Lives of New Immigrants* (Berkeley and Los Angeles: University of California Press, 2006), 6–9.

6. Daniel A. Rodríguez, *A Future for the Latino Church: Models for Multilingual, Multigenerational Hispanic Congregations* (Downers Grove, Ill.: InterVarsity Press, 2011), 17.

7. On the Atlantic world, see Thomas Benjamin, *The Atlantic World: Europeans, Africans, Indians and Their Shared History, 1400–1900* (Cambridge: Cambridge University Press, 2009); Jack P. Greene and Philip D. Morgan, eds., *Atlantic History: A Critical Appraisal* (New York: Oxford University Press, 2009); Kathryn Joy McKnight and Leo J. Garofalo, eds., *Afro-Latino Voices: Narratives from the Early Ibero-Atlantic World, 1550–1812* (Indianapolis: Hackett Publishing, 2009); Richard L. Kagan and Philip D. Morgan, eds., *Atlantic Diasporas: Jews, Conversos, and Crypto-Jews in the Age of Mercantilism* (Baltimore: Johns Hopkins University Press, 2009); J. Lorand Matory, *Black Atlantic Religion: Tradition, Transnationalism, and Matriarchy in Afro-Brazilian Candomblé* (Princeton, N.J.: Princeton University Press, 2005).

8. Timothy J. Henderson, *A Glorious Defeat: Mexico and Its War with the United States* (New York: Hill and Wang, 2007), 177.

9. Laura E. Gómez, *Manifest Destinies: The Making of the Mexican American Race* (New York: New York University Press, 2007), 18, 64.

10. Zaragosa Vargas, *Proletarians of the North: A History of Mexican Industrial Workers in Detroit and the Midwest, 1917–1933* (Berkeley and Los Angeles: University of California Press, 1993); Dennis Nodín Valdés, *Al Norte: Agricultural Workers in the Great Lakes Region, 1917–1970* (Austin: University of Texas Press, 1991).

11. Francisco E. Balderrama and Raymond Rodríguez, *Decade of Betrayal: Mexican Repatriation in the 1930s*, rev. ed. (Albuquerque: University of New Mexico Press, 2006). For a memoir of this period, see Albino R. Pineda, *Among the Repatriated: Autobiography of a Mexican American* (Bloomington, Ind.: Xlibris, 2008).

12. Deborah Cohen, *Braceros: Migrant Citizens and Transnational Subjects in the Postwar United States and Mexico* (Chapel Hill: University of North Carolina Press, 2011), 22–26. See also Kitty Calavita, *Inside the State: The Bracero Program, Immigration, and the I.N.S.*, rev. ed. (New Orleans: Quid Pro Books, 2010); Ronald L. Mize, *Consuming Mexican Labor: From the Bracero Program to NAFTA* (North York, Ontario: University of Toronto Press, 2011), 3–10.

13. See Louis A. Pérez Jr., *The War of 1898: the United States and Cuba in History and Historiography* (Chapel Hill: University of North Carolina Press, 1998).

14. Carmen Teresa Whalen, *From Puerto Rico to Philadelphia: Puerto Rican Workers and Postwar Economies* (Philadelphia: Temple University Press, 2001); Jorge Duany, "A Transnational Colonial Migration: Puerto Rico's Farm Labor Program," *New West Indian Guide* 84, nos. 3–4 (2010): 232–35; Susan S. Baker, *Understanding Mainland Puerto Rican Poverty* (Philadelphia: Temple University Press, 2002), 32–50.

15. Virginia Sánchez Korrol, *From Colonia to Community: The History of Puerto Ricans in New York City*, rev. ed. (Berkeley and Los Angeles: University of California Press, 1994); Carmen Teresa Whalen and Víctor Vásquez-Hernández, ed., *The Puerto Rican Diaspora: Historical Perspectives* (Philadelphia: Temple University Press, 2005); Gina M. Pérez, *The Near Northwest Side Story: Migration, Displacement, and Puerto Rican Families* (Berkeley and Los Angeles: University of California Press, 2004).

16. Jesse Hoffnung-Garskof, *A Tale of Two Cities: Santo Domingo and New York after 1950* (Princeton, N.J.: Princeton University Press, 2008).

17. Bruce J. Calder, *The Impact of Intervention: The Dominican Republic during the U.S. Occupation of 1916–1924* (Austin: University of Texas Press, 1984).

18. See José Itzigsohn, *Encountering American Faultlines: Race, Class, and Dominican Experience in Providence* (New York: Russell Sage Foundation, 2009), 145–49; Peggy Levitt, *Transnational Villagers* (Berkeley and Los Angeles: University of California Press, 2001); Hoffung-Garskof, *A Tale of Two Cities*.

19. Jorge Duany, "Dominican Migration to Puerto Rico: A Transnational Perspective," *Central Journal* 17, no. 1 (2005): 242–69; Ginetta E. B. Candelario,

Black behind the Ears: Dominican Racial Identity from Museums to Beauty Shops (Durham, N.C.: Duke University Press, 2007), 157.

20. Thomas W. Walker, *Nicaragua: Living in the Shadow of the Eagle*, 4th ed. (Boulder, Colo.: Westview Press, 2003); María Cristina García, *Seeking Refuge: Central American Migration to Mexico, the United States, and Canada* (Berkeley and Los Angeles: University of California Press, 2006), 1; Stephen Schlesinger and Stephen Kinzer, *Bitter Fruit: The Story of the American Coup in Guatemala*, rev. ed. (Cambridge, Mass.: David Rockefeller Center for Latin American Studies, 2005); Nick Cullather, *Secret History: The CIA's Classified Account of Its Operations in Guatemala, 1952–1954*, 2nd ed. (Stanford, Calif.: Stanford University Press, 2006).

21. Mark Hugo López and Daniel Dockterman, *U.S. Hispanic Country-of-Origin Counts for Nation, Top 30 Metropolitan Areas* (Washington, D.C.: Pew Hispanic Center, 2011), 2. For example, Beth Baker-Cristales, *Salvadoran Migration to Southern California: Redefining El Hermano Lejano* (Gainesville: University Press of Florida, 2004); Patricia Foxen, *In Search of Providence: Transnational Mayan Identities* (Nashville: Vanderbilt University Press, 2007); James Loucky and Marilyn M. Moor, eds., *The Maya Diaspora: Guatemalan Roots, New American Lives* (Philadelphia: Temple University Press, 2000); Cecilia Menjívar, *Fragmented Ties: Salvadoran Immigrant Networks in America* (Berkeley and Los Angeles: University of California Press, 2000).

22. Jorge Durand, "The Peruvian Diaspora: Portrait of a Migratory Process," *Latin American Perspectives* 37, no. 5 (September 2010): 12–28; Ann Miles, From *Cuenca to Queens: An Anthropological Story of Transnational Migration* (Austin: University of Texas Press, 2004).

23. Timothy J. Henderson, *Beyond Borders: A History of Mexican Migration to the United States* (Malden, Mass.: Blackwell, 2011), 1–2.

24. Juan Flores, *The Diaspora Strikes Back: Caribeño Tales of Learning and Turning* (New York: Routledge, 2009), 49.

25. Aviva Ben-Ur, *Sephardic Jews in America: A Diasporic History* (New York: New York University Press, 2009), 50.

26. Ibid., 179–80. For a prominent example of a crypto-Jew in colonial New Spain, see Martin Aaron Cohen, *The Martyr: Luis de Carvajal, A Secret Jew in Sixteenth-Century Mexico* (Albuquerque: University of New Mexico Press, 2001). Stanley M. Hordes present a case for the cultural survival of Jewish identity and practice in his *To the End of the Earth: A History of the Crypto-Jews of New Mexico* (New York: Columbia University Press, 2005).

27. Pew Hispanic Center, "Statistical Portrait of Hispanics in the United States, 2009" (Washington, D.C.: Pew Hispanic Center, February 17, 2011), Table 2; Shrin Hakimzadeh and D'Vera Cohn, "English Usage among Hispanics in the United States" (Washington, D.C.: Pew Hispanic Center, 2007).

28. María Rosario Jackson, "Profile of an Afro-Latina: Black, Mexican, Both," in *The Afro-Latin@ Reader: History and Culture in the United States*, ed. Miriam Jiménez and Juan Flores (Durham, N.C.: Duke University Press, 2010), 434.

29. Manuel A. Vásquez, "Central and South American Religious Communities," in *Religion and American Cultures: An Encyclopedia of Traditions, Diversity, and Popular Expressions*, ed. Gary Laderman and Luis León (Santa Barbara: ABC-CLIO, 2003), 185.

30. John Charles Chasteen, *Born in Blood and Fire: A Concise History of Latin America*, 2nd ed. (New York: W. W. Norton, 2006), 157. See also Luiz Alberto Moniz Bandiera, "¿América Latina o Sudamérica? at Claín.com, *http://edant.clarin.com/diario/2005/05/16/opinion/o-01901.htm*.

31. Walter D. Mignolo, *The Idea of Latin America* (Malden, Mass., and Oxford: Wiley-Blackwell, 2005), x–xii; 77–80. Addressing the challenges of Eurocentrism in moral theology and ethics, Miguel A. De La Torre observes that "Eurocentric thought, unconscious of how the discipline of religion has been racialized, claims to exemplify a color-blind excellence in scholarship for all humanity. By its very nature, Eurocentric ethical theory maintains that universal moral norms can be achieved independent of place, time, or people group" (*Latina/o Social Ethics: Moving beyond Eurocentric Moral Thinking* [Waco, Tex.: Baylor University Press, 2010], x).

32. Edna Nashon, ed., *From the Ghetto to the Melting Pot: Israel Zangwill's Jewish Plays* (Detroit: Wayne State University Press, 2006).

33. The provisional nature of "whiteness" as a racial designation and identity can be seen historically by tracing how some contemporary ethnic groups, such as Armenian, Irish, Italian, Polish, and Jewish, were held to be outside the white category. See Karen Brodkin, *How Jews Became White Folks: And What That Says about Race in America* (New Brunswick, N.J.: Rutgers University Press, 1998); David R. Roediger, *Working toward Whiteness: How America's Immigrants Became White, the Strange Journey from Ellis Island to the Suburbs* (New York: Basic Books, 2005); Noel Ignatiev, *How the Irish Became White* (New York; Routledge, 1995).

34. Michelle A. Gonzalez, *Afro-Cuban Theology: Religion, Race, Culture, and Identity* (Gainesville: University Press of Florida, 2011), 146.

35. Michel Foucault, "Society Must Be Defended": Lectures at the Collège de France, 1975–1976, quoted in J. Kameron Carter, *Race: A Theological Account* (New York: Oxford University Press, 2008), 39.

36. Jill M. Bystydzienski, *Intercultural Couples: Crossing Boundaries, Negotiating Difference* (New York: New York University Press, 2011); Renee C. Romano, *Race Mixing: Black-White Marriage in Postwar America* (Cambridge, Mass.: Harvard University Press, 2003).

37. A standard approach on this topic is Michael Novak, *Unmeltable Ethnics: Politics and Culture in American Life* (Edison, N.J.: Transaction Publishers, 1995). For a personal memoir on this subject told by a Mexican American who grew up

in a Methodist orphanage in Los Angeles, see Robert Sanabria, *Stewing in the Melting Pot: The Memoir of a Real American* (Sterling, Va.: Capital Books, 2001).

38. Candelario, *Black behind the Ears*, 170.

39. Lynn Stephen, *Transborder Lives: Indigenous Oaxacans in Mexico, California, and Oregon* (Durham, N.C.: Duke University Press, 2007), 229.

40. Michael Omi and Howard Winant, *Racial Formation in the United States: From the 1960s to the 1990s*, 2nd ed. (New York: Routledge, 1986), 54.

41. Howard Winant, *The New Politics of Race: Globalism, Difference, Justice* (Minneapolis: University of Minnesota Press, 2004), x.

42. Omi and Winant, *Racial Formation in the United States*, 62.

43. The contingent nature of racial identity is tied to what Foucault called the configurations of identity/difference relationships, discourses, and knowledge, which are part of larger contexts. See Michel Foucault, *The Archaeology of Knowledge and the Discourse on Language* (New York: Pantheon, 1969, 1972), 32–33.

44. Benjamín Valentín, *Mapping Public Theology: Beyond Culture, Identity, and Difference* (Harrisburg, Pa.: Trinity Press International, 2002), 9; Arlene Dávila, *Latinos, Inc.: The Marketing and Making of a People* (Berkeley and Los Angeles: University of California Press, 2001), 41.

45. Hector Avalos, *Strangers in Our Own Land: Religion in U.S. Latina/o Literature* (Nashville: Abingdon Press, 2005), 182.

46. Gonzalez, *Afro-Cuban Theology*, 32.

47. Juana María Rodríguez, *Queer Latinidad: Identity Practices, Discursive Spaces* (New York: New York University Press, 2003), 9–10.

48. Marta Caminero-Santangelo, *On Latinidad: U.S. Latino Literature and the Construction of Ethnicity* (Gainsville: University Press of Florida, 2007), 215. See also Suzanne Bost, *Mulattas and Mestizas: Representing Mixed Identities in the Americas* (Athens: University of Georgia Press, 2003).

49. Henry Goldschmidt, *Race and Religion among the Chosen Peoples of Crown Heights* (New Brunswick, N.J.: Rutgers University Press, 2006), 235.

50. Robert Atkinson, "Toward a Fluid Latino Identity," in *Latino Voices in New England*, ed. David Carey Jr. and Robert Atkinson (Albany: State University of New York Press, 2009), 207.

51. Michelle A. Gonzalez, *Embracing Latina Spirituality: A Woman's Perspective* (Cincinnati: St. Anthony Messenger Press, 2009), xiii.

52. Dwight N. Hopkins, *Being Human: Race, Culture, and Religion* (Minneapolis: Fortress Press, 2005), 78.

53. For an excellent examination on the conceptual challenges of *mestizaje* in light of the heterogeneity of Latino/a populations, see Néstor Medina, *Mestizaje: (Re)Mapping Race, Culture, and Faith in Latina/o Catholicism* (Maryknoll, N.Y.: Orbis Books, 2009).

4. Rituals in the Passage of Life

1. Sonia G. Austrian, "Introduction," in *Developmental Theories through the Life Cycle*, ed. Sonia G. Austrian (New York: Columbia University Press, 2008), 2. Austrian also claims that while there are different models of the life cycle most address certain shared aspects of human needs at different development stages: "(1) survival of the infant; (2) separation and individuation; (3) capacity for relatedness; (4) gender identification; (5) capacity for intimacy; and (6) adaptation to sociocultural demands" (5–6).

2. An example of this is Peggy Levitt's study of the transnational community forged by Dominicans in Miraflores in the Dominican Republic and in the Jamaica Plain neighborhood of Boston. See *The Transnational Villagers* (Berkeley and Los Angeles: University of California Press, 2001), 74.

3. I was helped with this small but not minor distinction through an essay by Hilda Ryumon Gutiérrez Baldoquín, a Soto Zen priest and founder of the San Francisco Zen Center People of Color Sitting Group and cofounder of the Buddhist Meditation Group for the LGBTQ community at The Center in San Francisco. She wrote, "When I began to practice the teachings of the Buddha—I purposely don't say, 'when I began to practice Buddhism,' because Gautama Buddha did not teach Buddhism, he taught the Dharma." See her essay "Don't Waste Time," in *Dharma, Color, and Culture: New Voices in Western Buddhism*, ed. Hilda Gutiérrez Baldoquín (Berkeley: Parallax Press, 2004), 179.

4. Jeanette Rodríguez, "Mestiza Spirituality: Community, Ritual, and Justice," *Theological Studies* 65 (2004): 334.

5. Roy A. Rappaport, *Ritual and Religion in the Making of Humanity* (Cambridge and New York: Cambridge University Press, 1999), 30.

6. Tom F. Driver, *The Magic of Ritual: Our Need for Liberating Rites that Transform Our Lives and Communities* (Boulder, Colo.: Westview Press, 1998), 16.

7. Catherine M. Bell, *Ritual: Perspectives and Dimensions* (New York: Oxford University Press, 1997), 94.

8. Ibid., 95.

9. James W. Fowler, *Stages of Faith: The Psychology of Human Development and the Quest for Meaning* (New York: Harper Collins, 1981), 117–211.

10. Nancy Pineda-Madrid, "Traditioning: The Formation of Community, the Transmission of Faith," in *Futuring Our Past: Explorations in the Theology of Tradition*, ed. Orlando O. Espín and Gary Macy (Maryknoll, N.Y.: Orbis Books, 2006), 210.

11. Arlene M. Sánchez Walsh, *Latino Pentecostal Identity: Evangelical Faith, Self, and Society* (New York: Columbia University Press, 2003), 75.

12. Brandon Bayne, "From Saint to Seeker: Teresa Urrea's Search for a Place of Her Own," *Church History* 75 (2006): 611–31; James S. Griffith, *Folk Saints of the Borderlands: Victims, Bandits, and Healers* (Tucson: Río Nuevo Publishers, 2003); Frank Graziano, *Cultures of Devotion: Folk Saints of Spanish America* (New York:

Oxford University Press, 2007), 210; Rafaela G. Castro, *Chicano Folklore: A Guide to the Folktales, Traditions, Rituals, and Religious Practices of Mexican Americans* (New York: Oxford University Press, 2001), 133; Robert T. Trotter II and Juan Antonio Chavira, *Curanderismo: Mexican American Folk Healing,* 2nd ed. (Athens: University of Georgia Press, 1997), 78; Paul J. Vanderwood, *Juan Soldado: Rapist, Murderer, Martyr, Saint* (Durham, N.C.: Duke University Press, 2004), 211–20; Cymene Howe, Susanna Zaraysky, and Lois Ann Lorentzen, "Devotional Crossings: Transgender Sex Workers, Santísima Muerte, and Spiritual Solidarity in Guadalajara and San Francisco," in *Religion on the Corner of Bliss and Nirvana: Politics, Identity, and Faith in New Migrant Communities,* ed. Lois Ann Lorentzen, Joaquin Jay Gonzales III, Kevin M. Chun, and Hein Duc Do (Durham, N.C.: Duke University Press, 2009), 26–32.

13. Josefina M. Contreras, Kathryn A. Kerns, and Angela M. Neal-Barnett, *Latino Children and Families in the United States: Current Research and Future Directions* (Westport, Conn.: Praeger, 2002), 17.

14. Loida I. Martell-Otero, "Creating a Sacred Space: An Iglesia Evangélica Response to Global Homelessness," *Dialog: A Journal of Theology* 49, no.1 (2010): 15.

15. Daniel Ramírez, "A Historian's Response," *Pneuma* 30 (2008): 245–54.

16. See Arlene Sánchez Walsh, "The Mexican American Religious Experience," in *Introduction to the U.S. Latina and Latino Religious Experience,* ed. Hector Avalos (Boston: Brill Academic Publishers, 2004), 32–33, 38–39.

17. James Empereur and Eduardo Fernández, *La Vida Sacra: Contemporary Hispanic Sacramental Theology* (Lanham, Md.: Rowan & Littlefield, 2006), 69.

18. Eugenio Matibag, "The Dominican American Religious Experience," in *Introduction to the U.S. Latina and Latino Religious Experience,* ed. Hector Avalos (Boston: Brill Academic Publishers, 2004), 103.

19. Mark R. Francis and Arturo J. Pérez-Rodríguez, *Primero Dios: Hispanic Liturgical Resources* (Chicago: Liturgy Training Publications, 1997), 27.

20. A tradition with roots in Puerto Rico is *echar agua* (lit. "to throw water"), a type of unofficial baptism that appears to be connected to the practice of emergency baptism but has developed into something distinct. While not officially approved in normal circumstances, in some cases it is done within a family even when baptism will take place at a later time. Water is poured on the baby and the same words are uttered, "Me lo entregaste moro, y te lo devuelvo cristiano." See Ana María Díaz-Stevens and Anthony M. Stevens-Arroyo, *Recognizing the Latino Resurgence in U.S. Religion: The Emmaus Paradigm* (Boulder, Colo.: Westview Press, 1998), 69, 72; Francis and Pérez-Rodríguez, *Primero Dios,* 20.

21. The *aqiqah* is an optional Muslim birth rite since there is a hadith that states that each child is born a Muslim. The *aqiqah* involves an animal sacrifice (goat or sheep). See John L. Esposito, ed., *The Oxford Dictionary of Islam* (New York: Oxford University Press, 2003) 22; 44.

22. Shinoa Matos, "My Daughter's Aqiqah," *Latino Muslim Voice*, January–March 2010, *www.latinodawah.org/newsletter/jan-mar2k10.html#2*. Reflecting the multicultural and international nature of Islam Imam Muhmmd Shamsi Ali of New York City's largest mosque, the Islamic Cultural Center, originally is from Indonesia.

23. *Quiero mis Quince*, *www.tr3s.com/*, MTV Networks, 2011; *Quinceañera*, DVD, directed by Richard Glatzer and Wash Westmoreland (Culver City, Calif.: Sony Pictures, 2006).

24. Empereur and Fernández, *La Vida Sacra*, 115.

25. Timothy M. Matovina, "Marriage Celebrations in Mexican-American Communities," in *Mestizo Worship: A Pastoral Approach to Liturgical Ministry*, ed. Virgilio P. Elizondo and Timothy M. Matovina (Collegeville, Minn.: Liturgical Press, 1998), 94.

26. Michelle A. Gonzalez, *Embracing Latina Spirituality: A Woman's Perspective* (Cincinnati: St. Anthony's Messenger Press, 2009), 50.

27. Ada María Isasi-Díaz, *En la Lucha/In the Struggle: Elaborating a Mujerista Theology*, rev. ed. (Minneapolis: Fortress Press, 2004), 37.

28. Orlando O. Espín, *Grace and Humanness: Theological Reflections because of Culture* (Maryknoll, N.Y.: Orbis Books, 2007), 63.

29. "The Dilemma of a Marriage for a Muslim Convert Girl," *Muslim Latinidad: Latina, Muslim y Viviendo la Vida*, June 26, 2011, *http://fliflablah.wordpress.com/*.

30. New Life Covenant Church website, *http://mynewlife.org/*.

31. Cesareo Gabaraín Azurmendi, words and music, "Tú Has Venido a la Orilla," trans. Gertrude C. Suppe, George Lockwood, and Raquel Gutiérrez-Achon, in *The United Methodist Hymnal* (Nashville: United Methodist Publishing House, 1989). This song is testimony to the transnational and transdenominational aspects of Latino/a spirituality. Originally entitled "Pescador de hombres" (Fisher of Men") it was composed by Gabaraín (1936–91), a Roman Catholic priest in Spain. His songs gained international popularity, have been translated into many languages, and are used in diverse settings.

32. Yolanda Broyles-González, "Indianizing Catholicism: Chicana/India/Mexican Indigenous Spiritual Practices in Our Image," in *Chicana Traditions: Continuity and Changes*, ed. Norma E. Cantú and Olga Nájera-Ramírez (Urbana: University of Illinois Press, 2002), 118.

33. Ibid., 120.

34. Ibid., 122. For an account of a different context where the encounter of Protestant Christianity and Native American culture and beliefs yielded parallel results, see David J. Silverman, *Faith and Boundaries: Colonists, Christianity, and Community among the Wampanoag Indians of Martha's Vineyard, 1600–1871* (Cambridge and New York: Cambridge University Press, 2005).

35. Broyles-González, "Indianizing Catholicism," 118.

36. Thomas G. Long, *Accompany Them with Singing: The Christian Funeral* (Louisville: Westminster John Knox, 2009), 4.

37. Lara Medina, "Days of the Dead (Días de los Muertos)," in *Religion and American Cultures: An Encyclopedia of Traditions, Diversity, and Popular Expressions*, ed. Gary Laderman and Luis León (Santa Barbara: ABC-CLIO, 2003), 380.

38. Regina M. Marchi, *Day of the Dead in USA: The Migration and Transformation of a Cultural Phenomenon* (New Brunswick, N.J.: Rutgers University Press, 2009), 10–14. See also Luis D. León, *La Llorona's Children: Religion, Life, and Death in the U.S.-Mexican Borderlands* (Berkeley and Los Angeles: University of California Press, 2004), 124.

39. In her research Marchi noted public records of celebrations of Day of the Dead in Omaha, Kansas City, Seattle, Cincinnati, Anchorage, Milwaukee, New Orleans, Atlanta, as well as in other locations in the United States. Moreover, Chicano-influenced Day of the Dead celebrations appeared in Canada, Europe, Australia, New Zealand, and Japan. All of these occurred in places outside the U.S. Southwest and Borderlands. See Marchi, *Day of the Dead in USA*, 140; 150, n. 5.

40. Hannah E. Gill, *The Latino Migration Experience in North Carolina: New Roots in the Old State* (Chapel Hill: University of North Carolina Press, 2010), 160.

41. See Marchi, *Day of the Dead in USA*, 140.

5.   Rhetoric and Traditions

1. See Susan Friend Harding, *The Book of Jerry Falwell: Fundamentalist Language and Politics* (Princeton, N.J.: Princeton University Press, 2000), 34–35.

2. Justo L. González, "Scripture, Tradition, Experience, and Imagination: A Redefinition," in *The Tie That Binds: African American and Hispanic American/Latino/a Theologies in Dialogue*, ed. Anthony B. Pinn and Benjamín Valentín (New York: Continuum, 2001), 69.

3. María Pilar Aquino, "Theological Method in U.S. Latino/a Theology," in *"From the Heart of Our People: Theological Reflections on Popular Catholicism,"* ed. Orlando O. Espín and Miguel H. Díaz (Maryknoll, N.Y.: Orbis Books, 1999), 39.

4. See Edwin David Aponte, "*Coritos* as Active Symbol in Latino Protestant Popular Religion," *Journal of Hispanic/Latino Theology* 2, no. 3 (1995) 57–66.

5. Sammy Alfaro, *Divine Compañero: Toward a Hispanic Pentecostal Christology* (Eugene, Ore.: Pickwick Publications, 2010), 138.

6. Daniel Ramírez, "Alabaré a mi Señor: Culture and Ideology in Latino Protestant Hymnody," in *Los Evangélicos: Portraits of Latino Protestantism in the United States*, ed. Juan F. Martínez and Lindy Scott (Eugene, Ore.: Wipf and Stock, 2009), 169.

7. Private correspondence with author.

8. Author's translation.

9. Carlos F. Cardoza-Orlandi, "Qué Lindo Es Mi Cristo: The Erotic Jesus/ Christ in the Caribbean, Latin American, and Latino/a Protestant Christian Music," in *Jesus in the Hispanic Community: Images of Christ from Theology to Popular Religion*, ed. Harold J. Recinos and Hugo Magallanes (Louisville: Westminster John Knox Press, 2009), 164.

10. Mario dos Ventos, *Sea El Santísimo: A Manual for Misa Espiritual and Mediumship Development*, rev. ed. (Raleigh, N.C.: Nzo Quimbanda Exu Ventania/ Lulu Publishing, 2008), 14.

11. Margarite Fernández Olmos and Lizabeth Paravisini-Gebert, *Creole Religions of the Caribbean: An Introduction from Vodou and Santería to Obeah and Espiritismo*, 2nd ed. (New York: New York University Press, 2011), 209–12.

12. dos Ventos, *Sea El Santísimo*, 119.

13. Jesse Hoffung-Garskof, *A Tale of Two Cities: Santo Domingo and New York after 1950* (Princeton, N.J.: Princeton University Press, 2008), 49.

14. Herón Márquez Estrada, "Saint of Death Casts Pall," *Minneapolis Star Tribune*, *www.startribune.com/lifestyle/wellness/121131814.html*.

15. Cymene Howe, Susana Zaraysky, and Lois Ann Lorentzen, "Devotional Crossings: Transgender Sex Workers, Santísima Muerte, and Spiritual Solidarity in Guadalajara and San Francisco," in *Religion at the Corner of Bliss and Nirvana: Politics, Identity, and Faith in New Migrant Communities*, ed. Lois Ann Lorentzen, Joaquin Jay Gonzalez III, Kevin M. Chun, Hien Duc Do (Durham, N.C.: Duke University Press, 2009), 3–38.

16. Luis D. León, *La Llorona's Children: Religion, Life, and Death in the U.S.-Mexican Borderlands* (Berkeley and Los Angeles: University of California Press, 2004), 93.

17. For one overview of this story, see Carmen Teresa Whalen, *From Puerto Rico to Philadelphia: Puerto Rican Workers and Postwar Economies* (Philadelphia: Temple University Press, 2001).

18. Barbe Awalt and Paul Rhetts, *Our Saints among Us/Nuestros Santos entre Nosotros: 400 Years of New Mexican Devotional Art* (Albuqurque: LPD Press, 1998), 6.

19. Loida I. Martell-Otero, "Lo Cotidiano: Finding God in the Spaces of the Everyday," *Witness* 83, no. 12, (December 2000).

20. Luis G. Pedraja, *Jesus Is My Uncle: Christology from a Hispanic Perspective* (Nashville: Abingdon Press, 1999), 21.

21. Anthropologist, theologian, pastor, and poet Harold J. Recinos combines insights from multiple areas. See his poetry in the following works: *Jesus Weeps: Global Encounters on Our Doorstep* (Nashville: Abingdon Press, 1992); *Good News from the Barrio: Prophetic Witness for the Church* (Louisville: Westminster John Knox Press, 2006); Harold J. Recinos and Hugo Magallanes, eds., *Jesus in the Hispanic Community: Images of Christ from Theology to Popular Religion* (Louisville: Westminster John Knox Press, 2009).

22. Yarehk Hernandez. "To Sink or Swim," in *Progressive Muslim Identities: Personal Stories from the U.S. and Canada*, ed. Vanessa Karam, Olivia Samad, and Ani Zonneveld (West Hollywood, Calif.: Oracle Releasing, 2011), 85–86.

23. Ibid., 88.

24. Ibid., 91.

25. On the Spanglish dimension Juan Flores observes: "In terms of poetic language, Spanglish rap is embedded in the everyday speech practices of the larger community over the course of several generations. *"From Bomba to Hip-Hop: Puerto Rican Culture and Latino Identity* (New York: Columbia University Press, 2000), 138.

26. Alonzo Westbrook, *Hip Hoptionary* (New York: Random House, 2002), 115.

27. See the Appendix for a listing of *orishas*.

28. Orisha, "Represent," *A lo Cubano*, Universal Latino, 2000, compact disc.

29. David Morgan, *The Sacred Gaze: Religious Visual Culture in Theory and Practice* (Berkeley and Los Angeles: University of California Press, 2005), 3.

30. Daphne C. Wiggins, *Righteous Content: Black Women's Perspectives of Church and Faith* (New York: New York University Press, 2005), 3.

6. Sacred Places and Spaces

1. James F. Fernandez, "Emergence and Convergence in Some African Sacred Places," in *The Anthropology of Space and Place: Locating Culture*, ed. Setha M. Low and Denise Lawrence-Zúñiga (Malden, Mass.: Blackwell, 2003), 201.

2. See Peter Williams, "Sacred Space in North America," *Journal of the American Academy of Religion* 70 (September 2002): 593–609.

3. See David D. Hall, ed., *Lived Religion in America: Toward a History of Practice* (Princeton, N.J.: Princeton University Press, 1997).

4. Nancy T. Ammerman, "Studying Everyday Religion: Challenges for the Future," in *Everyday Religion: Observing Modern Religious Lives*, ed. Nancy T. Ammerman (New York: Oxford University Press, 2007), 234.

5. Louis P. Nelson, "Introduction," in *American Sanctuary: Understanding Sacred Spaces*, ed. Louis P. Nelson (Bloomington: Indiana University Press, 2006), 5–6.

6. Belden C. Lane, *Landscapes of the Sacred: Geography and Narrative in American Spirituality*, rev. ed. (Baltimore: Johns Hopkins University Press, 2001), 15.

7. While people may use the same word, that does not necessarily imply a shared meaning. For an extremely helpful examination between Western Christian understandings of the Holy Sprit and Eastern concepts of *chi*, see Grace Ji-Sun Kim, *The Holy Spirit, Chi, and the Other: A Model of Global and Intercultural Pneumatology* (New York: Palgrave Macmillan, 2011). For an exploration of spirit,

soul, and sacred from one perspective in business leadership, see Lee G. Bolman and Terrence E. Deal, *Leading with Soul: An Uncommon Journey of Spirit*, 3rd ed. (San Francisco: Jossey-Bass, 2011).

8. Margaret C. Rodman, "Empowering Place: Multilocality and Multivocality," in *The Anthropology of Space and Place: Locating Culture*, ed. Setha M. Low and Denise Lawrence-Zúñiga (Malden, Mass.: Blackwell, 2003), 205.

9. See Henri Lefebvre, *The Production of Space*, trans. Donald Nicholson-Smith (Malden, Mass.: Blackwell, 1991), 73.

10. Fernandez, "Emergence and Convergence in Some African Sacred Places," 201.

11. See the discussion on liminality and *communitas* in Victor Turner, *The Ritual Process: Structure and Anti-Structure* (Chicago: Aldine, 1969), 94–130.

12. Noemí Báez, María de los Angeles Rey, and Terry Rey, "Faith in the Fields: Mexican Marianism in Miami–Dade County," in *Churches and Charity in the Immigrant City: Religion, Immigration, and Civic Engagement in Miami*, ed. Alex Stepick, Terry Rey, and Sarah J. Mahler (New Brunswick, N.J.: Rutgers University Press, 2009), 193–95; Elaine A. Peña, *Performing Piety: Making Sacred Space with the Virgin of Guadalupe* (Berkeley and Los Angeles: University of California Press, 2011); Kristy Nabhab-Warren, *The Virgin of El Barrio: Marian Apparitions, Catholic Evangelizing, and Mexican American Activism* (New York: New York University Press, 2005).

13. Thomas A. Tweed, *Our Lady of Exile: Diasporic Religion at a Cuban Catholic Shrine in Miami* (New York: Oxford University Press, 1997); "Lord of Miracles," in *Encyclopedia of Catholic Devotions and Practices*, ed. Ann Ball (Huntington, Ind.: Our Sunday Visitor Publishing, 2003), 326–27.

14. Manuel A. Vásquez and Marie F. Marquardt, *Globalizing the Sacred: Religion across the Americas* (New Brunswick, N.J.: Rutgers University Press, 2003), 45.

15. See, for example, the analysis in Timothy Matovina, *Latino Catholicism: Transformation in America's Largest Church* (Princeton, N.J.: Princeton University Press, 2011), 245–50.

16. See Ayshia Gálvez, *Guadalupe in New York: Devotion and the Struggle for Citizenship Rights among Mexican Immigrants* (New York: New York University Press, 2009), 141.

17. The full name of the relay race is Carrera Internacional del Antorcha Guadalupana. See ibid., 5, and 140–66.

18. Ibid., 105.

19. Ibid., 82.

20. Elaine A. Peña, *Performing Piety: Making Sacred Space with the Virgin of Guadalupe* (Berkeley and Los Angeles: University of California Press, 2011), 17.

21. Lisa Black, "Virgin of Guadalupe: More Than 100,000 Expected at Festival This Weekend," *Chicago Tribune*, December 12, 2009.

22. Peña, *Performing Piety*, 146.

23. Ibid., 19.

24. Elizabeth Kay, *Chimayo Valley Traditions* (Santa Fe: Ancient City Press, 1987), 67–69; Sam Howarth and Enrique R. Lamadrid, *Pilgrimage to Chimayó: Contemporary Portrait of a Living Tradition* (Albuquerque: Museum of New Mexico Press, 1999).

25. Frank Graziano, *Cultures of Devotion: Folk Saints of Spanish America* (New York: Oxford University Press, 2007), 210.

26. Antonio Zavaleta and Alberto Salinas Jr., *Curandero Conversations: El Niño Fidencio, Shamanism and Healing Traditions of the Borderlands* (Bloomington, Ind.: Author House, 2009), 12–14; Luis D. León, *La Llorona's Children: Religion, Life, and Death in the U.S.-Mexican Borderlands* (Berkeley and Los Angeles: University of California Press, 2004), 151–57.

27. Dore Gardner, *Niño Fidencio: A Heart Thrown Open* (Santa Fe: Museum of New Mexico Press, 1992), 9.

28. Michelle A. Gonzalez, *Embracing Latina Spirituality: A Woman's Perspective* (Cincinnati: St. Anthony Messenger Press, 2009), 65.

29. Peggy Levitt, *Transnational Villagers* (Berkeley and Los Angeles: University of California Press, 2001), 169.

30. Laura E. Pérez, *Chicana Art: The Politics of Spiritual and Aesthetic Altarities* (Durham, N.C.: Duke University Press, 2007), 91; Marie Romero Cash, *Living Shrines: Home Altars of New Mexico* (Santa Fe: Museum of New Mexico Press, 1998).

31. Roberta J. Evanchuk, "The Altars of Orisha Worship," in *Santería Garments and Altars: Speaking without a Voice*, ed. Ysamur Flores-Peña and Roberta J. Evanchuk (Jackson: University Press of Mississippi, 1994), 27.

32. Laura Chester, *Holy Personal: Looking for Small Private Places of Worship* (Bloomington: Indiana University Press, 2000), 58.

33. Justo L. González, "In Quest of a Protestant Hispanic Ecclesiology," in *Teología en Conjunto: A Collaborative Hispanic Protestant Theology*, ed. José David Rodríguez and Loida I. Martell-Otero (Louisville: Westminster John Knox Press, 1997), 93.

34. Simon Coleman and John Elsner, *Pilgrimage: Past and Present in the World Religions* (Cambridge, Mass.: Harvard University Press, 1995), 6.

35. Paula Elizabeth Holmes-Rodman, "Pilgrimage to Chimayo, New Mexico," in *Intersecting Journeys: The Anthropology of Pilgrimage and Tourism*, ed. Ellen Badone and Sharon R. Roseman (Urbana and Chicago: University of Illinois Press, 2004), 37.

36. Karen Mary Davolos, "'The Real Way of Praying': The Via Crucis, *Mexicano* Sacred Space, and the Architecture of Domination," in *Horizons of the Sacred: Mexican Traditions in U.S. Catholicism*, ed. Timothy Matovina and Gary Riebe-Estrella (Ithaca, N.Y.: Cornell University Press), 47.

37. Ibid., 50–51.

38. Teresa M. G. Navarro's story in Rosa Zubizarreta, comp., "El Latinismo y sus Bellos Colores: Voices of Latina and Latino Buddhists," Eastbay Meditation Center, *www.eastbaymeditation.org/index.php?short=index.php&s=64&o=2*.

39. Holly J. Everett, *Roadside Crosses in Contemporary Memorial Culture* (Denton: University of North Texas Press, 2002).

40. Alberto Barrera, "Mexican-American Roadside Crosses in Starr County," in *Hecho en Tejas: Texas-Mexican Folk Arts and Crafts*, ed. Joe S. Graham (Denton: University of North Texas Press, 1991), 280.

41. Sylvia Anne Grider, "Roadside Shrines," in *Religion and American Cultures: An Encyclopedia of Traditions, Diversity, and Popular Expressions*, ed. Gary Laderman and Luis León (Santa Barbara: ABC-CLIO, 2003), 387.

42. At "All Pop," *www.all-pop.com/goodluck_pages/GL0040_virginsderegla-dashboard.htm*.

43. Melvin Delgado, *Death at an Early Age and the Urban Scene: The Case for Memorial Murals and Community Healing* (Westport, Conn.: Praeger, 2003), 50.

44. Regina M. Marchi, *Day of the Dead in the USA: The Migration and Transformation of a Cultural Phenomenon* (New Brunswick, N.J.: Rutgers University Press, 2009), 137–38.

45. Victor Turner and Edith L. B. Turner, *Image and Pilgrimage in Christian Culture* (New York: Columbia University Press, 1978), 2–4.

46. Peña, *Performing Piety*, 150. On Peña's use of Henri Lefebvre, see *The Production of Space*, 44.

7.   Exploring Spanglish Spirituality

1. An earlier version of this chapter was delivered as the Archbishop Oscar Romero Lecture at Wesley Theological Seminary in Washington, D.C., March 9, 2010.

2. *Spanglish*, 2004. Directed by James L. Brooks, written by James L. Brooks. Columbia Pictures.

3. Bill Santiago. *Pardon My Spanglish: One Man's Guide to Speaking the Habla* (Philadelphia: Quirk Books, 2008).

4. Salvador Tió, *Teoría del espanglish: A fuego lento, cien columnas de humor y una cornisa* (Rio Pierdras: University of Puerto Rico, 1954), 60–65; John M. Lipski, *Varieties of Spanish in the United States* (Washington, D.C.: Georgetown University Press, 2008), 41.

5. Carmen Nanko-Fernandez, *Theologizing en Espanglish: Context, Community, and Ministry* (Maryknoll, N.Y.: Orbis Books, 2010), 65.

6. Arlene Dávila, *Latinos, Inc.: The Marketing and Making of a People* (Berkeley and Los Angeles: University of California Press, 2001), 168.

7. Ana Celia Zentella, "Dime con quién hablas, y te diré quién eres": Linguistic (In)security and Latina/o Unity," in *A Companion to Latina/o Studies*, ed. Juan Flores and Renato Rosaldo (Malden, Mass.: Blackwell, 2007), 25–26.

8. Ilan Stavans, *Spanglish: The Making of a New American Language* (New York: Rayo, 2003), 3.

9. Rosaura Sánchez, "Our Lingusitic and Social Context," in *Spanglish*, ed. Ilan Stavans (Westport, Conn.: Greenwood Press, 2008), 41.

10. Juan Flores, *From Bomba to Hip-Hop: Puerto Rican Culture and Latino Identity* (New York: Columbia University Press, 2000), 138; Deborah Pacini Hernández, "The Name Game: Locating Latinas/os, Latins, and Latin Americans in the U.S. Popular Music Lanscape," in *A Companion to Latina/o Studies*, ed. Juan Flores and Renato Rosaldo (Malden, Mass.: Blackwell, 2007), 49–52; Raquel Z. Rivera, Wayne Marshall, and Deborah Pacini Hernández, eds., *Reggaeton* (Durham, N.C.: Duke University Press, 2009).

11. For a dictionary of Spanglish, see Ilan Stavans, *Spanglish: The Making of a New American Language* (New York: Harper Collins, 2003), 65–250; see also Bill Cruz, *The Official Spanglish Dictionary* (New York: Simon & Schuster, 1998).

12. Ana Celia Zentella, *Growing up Bilingual: Puerto Rican Children in New York* (Malden, Mass.: Blackwell, 1997), 116, 122.

13. And of course when North Americans say "Spanish" typically they mean Castilian, one of the languages of Iberia. It was in the fifteenth century during the reign of the "Catholic monarchs" Fernando and Isabel (Ferdinand and Isabella) that the language of Castile began to be referred to as Spanish. See David A. Pharies, *A Brief History of the Spanish Language* (Chicago: University of Chicago Press, 2007), 143–44.

14. The linguistic concept of *calques* (itself a loan word from French) refers to the borrowing of one word or phrase from one language by another. A common and acceptable example of this is the Spanish *rascacielos* for the English word "skyscraper."

15. *Caló* typically is recognized as a youth culture dialect of Chicano Spanish frequently employed by some Chicanos, especially *batos (vatos) locos*, and homeboys. Some consider Caló solely as inappropriate slang rather than a legitimate dialect. For examples of Caló, see Harry Polkinhorn, Afredo Velasco, and Malcom Lambert, *El Libro de Calo: The Dictionary of Chicano Slang*, rev. ed. (Chicago: Floricanto Press, 2005); Rubén Cobos, ed., *A Dictionary of New Mexico and Southern Colorado Spanish* (Santa Fe: Museum of New Mexico Press, 2003).

16. Julia Álvarez, *How the García Girls Lost Their Accent* (Chapel Hill, NC: Algonquin Books, 1991), 8.

17. Junot Díaz, *The Brief Wondrous Life of Oscar Wao* (New York: Riverhead Books, 2007).

18. Molotov, "Frijolero," *Dance and Dense Denso*, Audio CD, Universal Latino, 2003.

19. Ed Morales, *Living in Spanglish: The Search for Latino Identity in America* (New York: St. Martin's Press, 2002); Stavans, *Spanglish*, 1–55.

20. See Clifford Geertz on the creation of "webs of significance" in "Thick Description: Toward an Interpretive Theory of Culture," in *The Interpretation of Cultures* (New York: Basic Books, 1973), 5.

21. For more on *caló*, see Manuel de Jesús Hernández-Gutiérrez and David William Foster, eds., *Literatura chicana, 1965–1995: An Anthology in Spanish, English, and Caló* (New York: Routledge, 1997); Laura L. Cummings, *Pachucas and Pachucos in Tucson: Situated Border Lives* (Tucson: University of Arizona Press, 2009).

22. See Néstor Medina, *Mestizaje: (Re)mapping Race, Culture, and Faith in Latina/o Catholicism* (Maryknoll, N.Y.: Orbis Books, 2009).

23. Michelle A. Gonzalez, *Afro-Cuban Theology: Religion, Race, Culture, and Identity* (Gainesville: University Press of Florida, 2011), 145.

24. Loida Martell-Otero, "Of Satos and Saints: Salvation from the Periphery," *Perspectivas: HTI Occasional Papers* 4 (Summer 2001), 8–9.

25. Loida Martell-Otero, "Encuentro con el Jesús Sato: An Evangélica Soterology," in *Jesus in the Hispanic Community: Images of Christ from Theology to Popular Religion*, ed. Harold J. Recinos and Hugo Magallanes. (Louisville: Westminster John Knox Press, 2009), 77.

26. Hilda Gutiérrez Baldoquín's story in Rosa Zubizarreta, "El Latinismo y sus Bellos Colores: Voices of Latina and Latino Buddhists," Eastbay Meditation Center, *www.eastbaymeditation.org/index.php?short=index.php&s=64&o=2*.

27. Manuel A. Vásquez and Marie F. Marquardt, *Globalizing the Sacred: Religion across the Americas* (New Bruswick, N.J.: Rutgers University Press, 2003).

28. Nanko-Fernández, *Theologizing en Espanglish*, 65.

29. For an analysis of a Latin American migration in another context, see Rafael Reyes-Ruiz, "Music and the (Re)creation of Latino Culture in Japan," *Journal of Latin American Cultural Studies* 14 (August 2005): 223–39.

30. Anita de Luna, *Faith Formation and Popular Religion: Lessons from the Tejano Experience* (Lanham, Md.: Rowman & Littlefield, 2002), 38.

31. Luis G. Pedraja, "Guideposts along the Journey: Mapping North American Hispanic Theology," in *Protestantes/Protestants: Hispanic Christianity within Mainline Traditions*, ed. David Maldonado, Jr. (Nashville: Abingdon Press, 1999), 133.

32. Gonzalez, *Afro-Cuban Theology*, 119.

33. This observation on the role of language was suggested by Carmen Nanko-Fernández: "The significance of language in the navigation of boundaries and in the negotiation of identities within and across generations merges as a legitimate and necessary locus for theological reflection" (*Theologizing en Espanglish*, 62).

34. David D. Hall, "A World of Wonders: The Mentality of the Supernatural in Seventeenth-Century New England," in *Religion and American Culture: A Reader*, ed. David D. Hall (New York: Routledge, 1995), 46.

35. Milagros Ricourt and Ruby Danta, *Hispanas de Queens: Latino Panethnicity in a New York City Neighborhood* (Ithaca, N.Y.: Cornell University Press, 2003), 10.

36. See Evelyn L. Parker's discussion on emancipatory hope and potent African American adolescent spirituality in *Trouble Don't Last Always: Emancipatory Hope among African American Adolescents* (Cleveland: Pilgrim Press, 2003), 22–24.

37. Otto Maduro, "Notes towards a Sociology of Latina/o Religious Empowerment," in *Hispanic/Latino Theology: Challenge and Promise*, ed. Ada María Isasi-Díaz and Fernando F. Segovia (Minneapolis: Fortress Press, 1996), 155.

Select Bibliography

Alfaro, Sammy. *Divine Compañero: Toward a Hispanic Pentecostal Christology*. Eugene, Ore.: Pickwick Publications, 2010.

Aponte, Edwin David. "*Coritos* as Active Symbol in Latino Protestant Popular Religion." *Journal of Hispanic/Latino Theology* 2, no. 3 (1995): 57–66.

————. "Metaphysical Blending in Latino/a Botánicas in Dallas." In *Rethinking Latino/a Religion and Identity*. Edited by Miguel A. De La Torre and Gastón Espinosa. Cleveland: Pilgrim Press, 2006.

Aquino, María Pilar. "Theological Method in U.S. Latino/a Theology." In *From the Heart of Our People: Theological Reflections on Popular Catholicism*. Edited by Orlando O. Espín and Miguel H. Díaz. Maryknoll, N.Y.: Orbis Books, 1999.

Avalos, Hector. *Strangers in Our Own Land: Religion in U.S. Latina/o Literature*. Nashville: Abingdon Press, 2005.

Awalt, Barbe, and Paul Rhetts. *Our Saints among Us/Nuestros Santos entre Nosotros: 400 Years of New Mexican Devotional Art*. Albuquerque, N.M.: LPD Press, 1998.

Báez, Noemí, María de los Angeles Rey, and Terry Rey. "Faith in the Fields: Mexican Marianism in Miami–Dade County." In *Churches and Charity in the Immigrant City: Religion, Immigration, and Civic Engagement in Miami*. Edited by Alex Stepick, Terry Rey, and Sarah J. Mahler. New Brunswick, N.J.: Rutgers University Press, 2009.

Bayne, Brandon. "From Saint to Seeker: Teresa Urrea's Search for a Place of Her Own." *Church History* 75 (2006): 611–31.

Bowen, Patrick D. "Early U.S. Latina/o-African American Muslim Connections: Paths to Conversion." *Muslim World* 100, no. 4 (2010): 390–413.

————. "The Latino American Da'wah Organization and the 'Latina/o Muslim' Identity in the United States." *Journal of Race, Ethnicity, and Religion* 1, no. 11 (September 2010): 1, http://raceandreligion.com/JRER/Volume_1_%282010%29.html.

Broyles-González, Yolanda. "Indianizing Catholicism: Chicana/India/Mexican Indigenous Spiritual Practices in Our Image." In *Chicana Traditions: Continuity and Changes*. Edited by Norma E. Cantú and Olga Nájera-Ramírez. Urbana and Chicago: University of Illinois Press, 2002), 118.

Cabezón, José Ignacio. "Jesus Christ through Buddhist Eyes." *Buddhist-Christian Studies* 19 (1999): 51–61.

Canizares, Raul. *Cuban Santeria: Walking with the Night*. Rochester, Vt.: Destiny Books, 1999.

Cardoza-Orlandi, Carlos F. "Qué lindo es mi Cristo: The Erotic Jesus/Christ in the Caribbean, Latin American, and Latino/a Protestant Chistian Music." In *Jesus in the Hispanic Community: Images of Christ from Theology to Popular Religion* Edited by Harold J. Recinos and Hugo Magallanes. Louisville: Westminster John Knox Press, 2009.

Conde Frazier, Elizabeth. "Hispanic Protestant Spirituality." In *Teología en Conjunto: A Collaborative Hispanic Protestant Theology*. Edited by José David Rodríguez and Loida I. Martell-Otero. Louisville: Westminster John Knox, 1997.

Damrel, David W. "Latina/o Muslim Americans." In *Encyclopedia of Muslim-American History.* Edited by Edward E. Curtis IV. New York: Facts On File, 2010.

Davolos, Karen Mary. "'The Real Way of Praying': The Via Crucis, *Mexicano* Sacred Space, and the Architecture of Domination." In *Horizons of the Sacred: Mexican Traditions in U.S. Catholicism.* Edited by Timothy Matovina and Gary Riebe-Estrella. Ithaca, N.Y.: Cornell University Press, 2002.

De La Torre, Miguel A., and Edwin David Aponte. *Introducing Latino/a Theologies.* Maryknoll, N.Y.: Orbis Books, 2001.

De La Torre, Miguel A. *Latina/o Social Ethics: Moving beyond Eurocentric Moral Thinking.* Waco, Tex.: Baylor University Press, 2010.

———. *Santería: The Beliefs and Rituals of a Growing Religion in America.* Grand Rapids: Eerdmans Publishing Company, 2004.

de Luna, Anita. *Faith Formation and Popular Religion: Lessons from the Tejano Experience.* Lanham, Md.: Rowman & Littlefield, 2002.

Díaz-Stevens, Ana María, and Anthony M. Stevens-Arroyo. *Recognizing the Latino Resurgence in U.S. Religion: The Emmaus Paradigm.* Boulder, Colo.: Westview Press, 1998.

dos Ventos, Mario. *Sea El Santisimo: A Manual for Misa Espiritual and Mediumship Development.* Rev. ed. Raleigh, N.C.: Nzo Quimbanda Exu Ventania/Lulu Publishing, 2008.

Egan, Martha. *Milagros: Votive Offerings from the Americas.* Santa Fe: Museum of New Mexico Press, 1991.

Elizondo, Virgilio, and Timothy M. Matovina. *San Fernando Cathedral: Soul of the City.* Maryknoll, N.Y.: Orbis Books, 1998.

Empereur, James and Eduardo Fernández, *La Vida Sacra: Contemporary Hispanic Sacramental Theology.* Lanham, Md.: Rowan & Littlefield, 2006.

Espín, Orlando O. *Grace and Humanness: Theological Reflections Because of Culture.* Maryknoll, N.Y.: Orbis Books, 2007.

———. "Traditioning: Culture, Daily Life and Popular Religion, and Their Impact on Christian Tradition." In *Futuring Our Past: Explorations in the Theology of Tradition.* Edited by Orlando O. Espín and Gary Macy. Maryknoll, N.Y.: Orbis Books, 2006.

Espinosa, Gastón. "Latinizing American Christianity: Pluralism, Pentecostalism and the Future of American Catholicism." *Conscience* 28 (Summer 2007): 30.

———. "Latino Clergy and Churches in Faith-Based Political and Social Action in the United States." In *Latino Religions and Civic Activism in the United States.* Edited by Gastón Espinosa, Virgilio Elizondo, and Jesse Miranda. New York: Oxford University Press, 2005.

Fernández Olmos, Margarite, and Lizabeth Paravisini-Gebert. *Creole Religions of the Caribbean: An Introduction from Vodou and Santería to Obeah and Espirtismo.* 2nd ed. New York: New York University Press, 2011.

Flores-Peña, Ysamur, and Roberta J. Evanchuk. *Santería Garments and Altars: Speaking without a Voice.* Jackson: University Press of Mississippi, 1994.

Francis, Mark R., and Arturo J. Pérez-Rodríguez. *Primero Dios: Hispanic Liturgical Resource.* Chicago: Archdiocese of Chicago: Liturgy Training Publications, 1997.

Galvan, Juan. "Who Are Latino Muslims?" *Islamic Horizons Magazine* 1429 (July/August 2008): 26–30.

Gálvez, Ayshia. *Guadalupe in New York: Devotion and the Struggle for Citizenship Rights among Mexican Immigrants.* New York: New York University Press, 2009.

Gardner, Dore. *Niño Fidencio: A Heart Thrown Open*. Santa Fe, N.M.: Museum of New Mexico Press, 1992.

Goizueta, Roberto S. *Caminemos con Jesús: A Theology of Accompaniment*. Maryknoll, N.Y.: Orbis Books, 1995.

Jacobs, Janet Liebman. *Hidden Heritage: The Legacy of Crypto-Jews*. Berkeley and Los Angeles: University of California Press, 2002.

González, Justo L. "In Quest of a Protestant Hispanic Ecclesiology." In *Teología en Conjunto: A Collaborative Hispanic Protestant Theology*. Edited by José David Rodríguez and Loida I. Martell-Otero. Louisville: Westminster John Knox Press, 1997.

————. "Scripture, Tradition, Experience, and Imagination: A Redefinition." In *The Tie That Binds: African American and Hispanic American/Latino/a Theologies in Dialogue*. Edited by Anthony B. Pinn and Benjamín Valentín. New York: Continuum, 2001.

Gonzalez, Michelle A. *Afro-Cuban Theology: Religion, Race, Culture, and Identity*. Gainesville: University Press of Florida, 2011.

————. *Embracing Latina Spirituality: A Woman's Perspective*. Cincinnati: St. Anthony Messenger Press, 2009.

Griffith, James S. *Folk Saints of the Borderlands: Victims, Bandits, and Healers*. Tucson, Ariz.: Rio Nuevo Publishers, 2003.

Gutiérrez Baldoquín, Hilda. "Don't Waste Time." In *Dharma, Color, and Culture: New Voices in Western Buddhism*. Edited by Hilda Gutiérrez Baldoquín. Berkeley, Calif.: Parallax Press, 2004.

Hernández, Yarehk. "To Sink or Swim." In *Progressive Muslim Identities: Personal Stories from the U.S. and Canada*. Edited by Vanessa Karam, Olivia Samad, and Ani Zonneveld. West Hollywood, Calif.: Oracle Releasing, 2011.

Hinojosa, Juan-Lorenzo. "Culture, Spirituality, and the United States." In *Frontiers of Hispanic Theology in the United States*. Edited by Allan Figueroa Deck. Maryknoll, N.Y.: Orbis Books, 1992.

Howarth, Sam, and Enrique R. Lamadrid. *Pilgrimage to Chimayó: Contemporary Portrait of a Living Tradition*. Albuquerque: Museum of New Mexico Press, 1999.

Howe, Cymene, Susana Zaraysky, and Lois Ann Lorentzen. "Devotional Crossings: Transgender Sex Workers, Santísima Muerte, and Spiritual Solidarity in Guadalajara and San Francisco." In *Religion at the Corner of Bliss and Nirvana: Politics, Identity, and Faith in New Migrant Communities*. Edited by Lois Ann Lorentzen, Joaquin Jay Gonzalez III, Kevin M. Chun, and Hien Duc Do. Durham, N.C.: Duke University Press, 2009.

Isasi-Díaz, Ada María. *En la Lucha / In the Struggle: Elaborating a Mujerista Theology*. Rev. ed. Minneapolis: Fortress Press, 2004.

Kay, Elizabeth. *Chimayo Valley Traditions*. Santa Fe, N.M.: Ancient City Press, 1987.

Lamadrid, Enrique. R. *Hermanitos Comanchitos: Indo-Hispano Rituals of Captivity and Redemption*. Albuquerque: University of New Mexico Press, 2003.

León, Luis D. *La Llorona's Children: Religion, Life, and Death in the U.S.–Mexican Borderlands*. Berkeley and Los Angeles: University of California Press, 2004.

Lindsay, Arturo, ed. *Santería Aesthetics in Contemporary Latin American Art*. Washington, D.C.: Smithsonian Institution Press, 1996.

López Pulido, Alberto. *The Sacred World of the Penitentes*. Washington, D.C.: Smithsonian Institution Press, 2000.

Maduro, Otto. "Notes towards a Sociology of Latina/o Religious Empowerment." In *Hispanic/Latino Theology: Challenge and Promise.* Edited by Ada María Isasi-Díaz and Fernando F. Segovia. Minneapolis: Fortress Press, 1996.

Maldonado, David, Jr. *Crossing Guadalupe Street: Growing Up Hispanic and Protestant.* Albuquerque: University of New Mexico Press, 2001.

————. "Hispanic Protestant Conversions." In *Hispanic Christian Thought at the Dawn of the 21st Century: Apuntes in Honor of Justo L. González.* Edited by Alvin Padilla, Roberto Goizueta, and Eldin Villafañe. Nashville: Abingdon Press, 2005.

Marchi, Regina M. *Day of the Dead in USA: The Migration and Transformation of a Cultural Phenomenon.* New Brunswick, N.J.: Rutgers University Press, 2009.

Martell-Otero, Loida I. "Creating a Sacred Space: An Iglesia Evangélica Response to Global Homelessness." *Dialog: A Journal of Theology* 49 (2010): 9–18.

————. "Lo Cotidiano: Finding God in the Spaces of the Everyday." *Witness* 83 (December 2000): 21–22.

————. "Encuentro con el Jesús Sato: An Evangélica Soteriology." In *Jesus in the Hispanic Community: Images of Christ from Theology to Popular Religion.* Edited by Harold J. Recinos and Hugo Magallanes. Louisville: Westminster John Knox Press, 2009.

————. "Of Satos and Saints: Salvation from the Periphery." *Perspectivas: HTI Occasional Papers* 4 (Summer 2001), 8–9.

Martínez-Vázquez, Hjamil A. *Latino/a y Musulman: The Construction of Latino/a Identity among Latino/a Muslims in the United States.* Eugene, Ore.: Pickwick Publications, 2010.

Martínez, Juan F., and Lindy Scott, eds. *Los Evangélicos: Portraits of Latino Protestantism in the United States.* Eugene, Ore.: Wipf and Stock, 2009.

Matibag, Eugenio. "The Dominican American Religious Experience." In *Introduction to the U.S. Latina and Latino Religious Experience.* Edited by Hector Avalos. Boston: Brill Academic Publishers, 2004.

Matovina, Timothy M. *Guadalupe and Her Faithful: Latino Catholics in San Antonio from Colonial Origins to the Present.* Baltimore: Johns Hopkins University Press, 2005.

————. *Latino Catholicism: Transformation in America's Largest Church.* Princeton, N.J.: Princeton University Press, 2012.

Medina, Lara. "Days of the Dead (Días de los Muertos)." In *Religion and American Cultures: An Encyclopedia of Traditions, Diversity, and Popular Expressions.* Edited by Gary Laderman and Luis León. Santa Barbara, Calif.: ABC-CLIO, 2003.

Medina, Néstor. *Mestizaje: (Re)Mapping Race, Culture, and Faith in Latina/o Catholicism.* Maryknoll, N.Y.: Orbis Books, 2009.

Mellott, David M. *I Was and I Am Dust: Penitente Practices as a Way of Knowing.* Collegeville, Minn.: Liturgical Press, 2009.

Murrell, Nathaniel Samuel. *Afro-Caribbean Religions: An Introduction to Their Historical, Cultural, and Sacred Traditions.* Philadelphia: Temple University Press, 2010.

Nabhab-Warren, Kristy. *The Virgin of El Barrio: Marian Apparitions, Catholic Evangelizing, and Mexican American Activism.* New York: New York University Press, 2005.

Nanko-Fernandez, Carmen. *Theologizing en Espanglish: Context, Community, and Ministry.* Maryknoll, N.Y.: Orbis Books, 2010.

Pedraja, Luis G. "Guideposts along the Journey: Mapping North American Hispanic Theology." In *Protestantes/Protestants: Hispanic Christianity within Mainline Traditions.* Edited by David Maldonado Jr. Nashville: Abingdon Press, 1999.

———. *Jesus Is My Uncle: Christology from a Hispanic Perspective*. Nashville: Abingdon Press, 1999.

Peña, Elaine A. *Performing Piety: Making Sacred Space with the Virgin of Guadalupe*. Berkeley and Los Angeles: University of California Press, 2011.

Pérez, Laura E. *Chicana Art: The Politics of Spiritual and Aesthetic Altarities*. Durham, N.C.: Duke University Press, 2007.

Pineda-Madrid, Nancy. "Traditioning: The Formation of Community, the Transmission of Faith." In *Futuring Our Past: Explorations in the Theology of Tradition*. Edited by Orlando O. Espín and Gary Macy. Maryknoll, N.Y.: Orbis Books, 2006.

Ramírez, Daniel. "Alabaré a mi Señor: Culture and Ideology in Latino Protestant Hymnody." In *Los Evangélicos: Portraits of Latino Protestantism in the United States*. Edited by Juan F. Martínez and Lindy Scott. Eugene, Ore.: Wipf and Stock, 2009.

———. "A Historian's Response." *Pneuma* 30 (2008); 245–54.

Recinos, Harold J. *Good News from the Barrio: Prophetic Witness for the Church*. Louisville: Westminster John Knox Press, 2006.

———. "Popular Religion, Political Identity, and Life Story Testimony in an Hispanic Community." In *The Tie That Binds: African American and Hispanic American/Latino/a Theologies in Dialogue*. Edited by Anthony B. Pinn and Benjamín Valentín. New York: Continuum, 2001.

Recinos, Harold J., and Hugo Magallanes, eds. *Jesus in the Hispanic Community: Images of Christ from Theology to Popular Religion*. Louisville: Westminster John Knox Press, 2009).

Rodríguez, Daniel A. *A Future for the Latino Church: Models for Multilingual, Multigenerational Hispanic Congregations*. Grove, Ill.: InterVarsity Press, 2011.

Rodríguez, Jeanette. "Mestiza Spirituality: Community, Ritual, and Justice." *Theological Studies* 65 (2004): 317–39.

———. *Our Lady of Guadalupe: Faith and Empowerment among Mexican-American Women*. Austin: University of Texas Press, 1994.

Rodríguez, Juana María. *Queer Latinidad: Identity Practices, Discursive Spaces*. New York: New York University Press, 2003.

Rodríguez, Kenny Yusuf. "My Acceptance Story: From the Book of Genesis to Surah Al-Fatihah." *The Latino Muslim Voice* (July–September 2002), *www.latinodawah.org/newsletter/july-sept2k2.html#5*.

Rodríguez, Rubén Rosario. *Racism and God-Talk: A Latino/a Perspective*. New York: New York University Press, 2008.

Sánchez Walsh, Arlene M. *Latino Pentecostal Identity: Evangelical Faith, Self, and Society*. New York: Columbia University Press, 2003.

———. "The Mexican American Religious Experience." In *Introduction to the U.S. Latina and Latino Religious Experience*. Edited by Hector Avalos. Boston: Brill Academic Publishers, 2004.

Segovia, Fernando F. *Decolonizing Biblical Studies: A View from the Margins*. Maryknoll, N.Y.: Orbis Books, 2000.

———. "In the World but Not of It: Exile as Locus for a Theology of the Diaspora." In *Hispanic/Latino Theology: Challenge and Promise*. Edited by Ada María Isasi-Díaz and Fernando F. Segovia. Minneapolis: Fortress Press, 1996.

Steele, Thomas J. *Santos and Saints: The Religious Folk Art of Hispanic New Mexico.* Santa Fe, N.M: Ancient City Press, 1994.

Stevens-Arroyo, Antonio M., and Ana María Díaz-Stevens, eds. *An Enduring Flame: Studies on Latino Popular Religiosity.* New York: Bildner Center for Western Hemisphere Studies, 1994.

Stevens-Arroyo, Antonio M., and Andres I. Pérez y Mena, eds. *Enigmatic Powers: Syncretism with African and Indigenous Peoples' Religions among Latinos.* New York: Bildner Center for Western Hemisphere Studies, 1995.

Stevens-Arroyo, Antonio M., and Gilbert R. Cadena, eds. *Old Mask, New Faces: Religion and Latino Identities.* New York: Bildner Center for Western Hemisphere Studies, 1995.

Sylvest, Jr., Edwin E., curator. *Nuestra Señora de Guadalupe: Mother of God, Mother of the Americas.* Dallas: Bridwell Library, Southern Methodist University, 1992.

Trotter, Robert T., II, and Juan Antonio Chavira. *Curanderismo: Mexican American Folk Healing.* 2nd ed. Athens: University of Georgia Press, 1997.

Valentín, Benjamín. *Mapping Public Theology: Beyond Culture, Identity, and Difference.* Harrisburg, Pa.: Trinity Press International, 2002.

Valentín, Benjamín, ed. *New Horizons in Hispanic/Latino(a) Theology.* Cleveland: Pilgrim Press, 2003.

Vásquez, Manuel A., and Marie F. Marquardt. *Globalizing the Sacred: Religion across the Americas.* New Brunswick, N.J.: Rutgers University Press, 2003.

Zavaleta, Antonio, and Alberto Salinas Jr., *Curandero Conversations: El Niño Fidencio, Shamanism and Healing Traditions of the Borderlands.* Bloomington, Ind.: Author House, 2009.

Zentella, Ana Celia. "Dime con quién hablas, y te diré quién eres": Linguistic (In)security and Latina/o Unity." In *A Companion to Latina/o Studies.* Edited by Juan Flores and Renato Rosaldo. Malden, Mass.: Blackwell, 2007.

Index